DEFEND AMERICA FIRST

Books by Garet Garrett:

Where the Money Grows, 1911
The Blue Wound, 1921
The Driver, 1922
The Cinder Buggy, 1923
Satan's Bushel, 1924
*Ouroboros, Or the Mechanical Extension
   of Mankind,* 1926
Harangue, 1927
The American Omen, 1928
Other People's Money, 1931 (pamphlet)
A Bubble that Broke the World, 1932
A Time is Born, 1944
A Wild Wheel, 1952
The People's Pottage, 1953, consisting of:
   "The Revolution Was" (1944)
   "Ex America" (1951)
   "Rise of Empire" (1952)
The American Story, 1955
Salvos Against the New Deal, 2001

Defend
America First

THE ANTIWAR EDITORIALS
OF THE SATURDAY EVENING POST,
1939-1942

BY GARET GARRETT

INTRODUCTION BY

BRUCE RAMSEY

CAXTON PRESS
2003

Library of Congress Cataloging-in-Publication Data

Garrett, Garet, 1878-1954.
Defend America first : the antiwar nationalist editorials of the
Saturday evening post, 1939-1942 / by Garet Garrett ; introduc-
tion by Bruce Ramsey.
      p. cm.
Includes bibliographical references and index.
  ISBN 0-87004-433-8
  1. World War, 1939-1945--United States. 2. Saturday evening
post. 3. Nationalism--United States--History--20th century. 4.
Neutrality--United States--History--20th century. 5.
Isolationism--United States--History--20th century. 6.
Editorials--United States--History--20th century. 7. United
States--Politics and government--1933-1945. 8. United States--
Foreign relations--1933-1945. I. aturday evening post. II. Title.
  D753.G27 2003
  940.53'73--dc21   2003000265

Printed in the United States of America
CAXTON PRESS
169307

CONTENTS

Introduction

By Bruce Ramsey

In autumn 2002, when George W. Bush asked Congress for permission to wage war against Iraq, there ensued a national debate. Americans asked, "When is it proper to attack a country that has not attacked us? If we sense a threat, need it be an obvious threat or can it be a presumed threat?"

What of a threat to another country? In the case of Israel, a special claim for America's protection was advanced because Israel was a democracy. Was that a valid claim? Is America bound to defend any democracy?

Other questions presented themselves. In October 2002, Congress granted the war power to President Bush, though he had said two months before that he had the power already. If the president had it already, there was a question of how he had acquired it, because the Constitution grants it to Congress.

None of these questions were new. People had asked them about the war in Vietnam, and before that, about World War II. When Daniel Ellsberg came to write his memoir of Vietnam, *Secrets,* he said that the weakness in the government that allowed America to be committed unthinkingly to Vietnam was "the concentration of power within the executive branch since World War II."

And that pointed to the man judged by modern academics to be the century's greatest president, Franklin D. Roosevelt.

Americans sentimentally remember Roosevelt's war as "The Good War" and the last officially declared by Congress. Americans forget the year and a half of executive war before December 7, 1941.

In 1940 and 1941 Americans debated many of today's

11

questions. Are we at war? For what shall Americans fight? Who shall decide? If the president decides, what does that tell us about the sort of government we have?

That debate ended at Pearl Harbor. Today the memories of World War II and Adolf Hitler are invoked to remind Americans of a settled conclusion—that their government must assert its power, early and often. But there were other arguments before Japan cut short the discussion.

This is a book of those arguments and the largely forgotten history behind them.

These essays were written in a different America. Sixty-five years ago this country was not presumed to be the protector and promoter of democracy everywhere. Americans had had a taste of that doctrine in World War I, and had recoiled from it. The Western Front had been a horror of rats, machine guns and poison gas. Billed as a war for democracy, the four years of slaughter had replaced monarchy with Bolshevism and unstable republics. The war had not ended well. The British and the French had ganged up on President Wilson and his plan to protect the rights of the little nations. A decade later, Britain and France stiffed the U.S. Treasury for billions in loans. These were the settled conclusions in the late 1930s: that war wrecks all political infatuations and that Europeans were not to be trusted.

President Washington had said, "Europe has a set of primary interests which to us have none, or a very remote relation. Hence she must be engaged in frequent controversies, the causes of which are essentially foreign to our concerns." Washington had counseled Americans to stay neutral and strong. That way, Americans could choose "peace or war, as our interest, guided by justice, shall counsel."

But as World War II began to take form among the European vapors, there came a different idea. This book presents arguments against that idea, and for the traditional theme stated by Washington.

The specific argument here is against going to war for Britain. Today, Britain is a poodle of the United States;

sixty years ago it was the British Empire. It acted on its own account, and Americans were not responsible for what it did. Britain had not asked permission of America when, in 1939, it had abandoned its appeasement policy and recklessly promised to defend Poland from the attentions of Hitler. By mid-1940 Britain faced Germany alone.

To convince the American mind to go to war for Britain, it would be enough today to argue that Britain needed it. Then it was not. Americans had to be persuaded that they needed Britain, that America's first line of defense was in Europe. Thus the main aid-to-Britain group called itself the Committee to Defend America by Aiding the Allies. This group, wrote historian Wayne S. Cole in *America First* (1953), was "something of an unofficial public relations organization for President Roosevelt's foreign policies."

On the anti-aid-to-Britain side was the America First Committee, formed in September 1940. "America First" was an old slogan and, until then, not a controversial one. Woodrow Wilson had used it. In my home town, Hearst's *Seattle Post-Intelligencer* used it on its masthead, between the wings of a stylized eagle. It was a simple statement of nationalism. But part of the art of politics is injecting new meanings into words.

The America Firsters were called isolationists. It was their opponents who called them that. They replied that they were not trying to isolate their country from the world, but only from war. New Dealers such as Harold Ickes and Henry Morgenthau tarred them with aiding and abetting Hitler.

They argued that America didn't need Britain in order to defend itself from Hitler. This was, of course, a selfish argument. But Americans thought they had a right to be selfish, the same as any other country. The American way of life was not a thing to put at risk by being talked into a war in Europe. Nor would Americans ever want to become part of a gang, giving up their right to steer their own course in the world. That attitude is derided today as "unilateralism," but in 1940 it was a fixture of the American mind.

Garet Garrett, the author of the essays here, was an eloquent defender of the prewar America. Born Edward Peter Garrett on February 18, 1878, in Pana, Ill., he was raised on a farm in Iowa. He attended school through the third grade, and learned afterward from reading books. He left home by jumping a train to Chicago. He became a printer's devil in Cleveland, then a newspaper reporter in Washington, D.C., where he changed his name. Through the first decade of the century he was a financial reporter in New York. He tried his hand at newspaper management and at writing books. In 1922 he began his twenty-year association with the leading magazine of middle-class America, the *Saturday Evening Post.*

Garrett became a voice of the Old Right, the prewar conservatives who opposed military crusades abroad and government programs at home. At the *Post,* Garrett had carried on a seven-year campaign against the New Deal. Roosevelt's revolution, he wrote, had eaten out the substance of the Constitution; the old republic had been supplanted by a welfare state, an idea imported from Europe. Garrett pined for laissez faire, the social rule of the world of his youth. He allowed that sometimes that world had been harsh, and that "only the strong could love it." But self-reliance was nature's way, and it had made America what it was.

Garrett did not want the American republic reduced to bailing out the monarchies or social democracies of Europe, and restoring their busted credit. That is what America had done when it had allowed itself to be sucked into World War I. In *Other People's Money* (1931) he wrote, "We were going to save Europe from Germany, the German people from the Hohenzollerns, little nations from big ones, all the people of Europe from the curse of war forever. . . The Allies did not care what our reasons were. We could be as romantic as we liked, only so we came in on their side; for unless we did, the war was lost. They were not themselves fighting to make the world safe for democracy, nor to end war forever, nor to put destiny in the hands of the little people; they were fighting to beat Germany. . . None of the things we thought we were fighting for came out. What survived was a continuing sense of obligation to save Europe."

In the 1920s private American finance lent Europe, including Germany, a greater amount than the war debts. Government lending continued—to restore the mark after Germany wrecked it, and to maintain the promise that France and Britain would repay their war loans. "Lending is with motive," Garrett wrote, arguing that it was once again a "sense of obligation to save Europe." But Europe was not saved. After 1931, billions of debts were left unpaid—including billions in gold dollars owed to the United States by Britain and France.

In the 1930s the United States passed a law saying that none of the countries that had defaulted on their loans from the U.S. Treasury could borrow in the American capital markets. The law expressed American feeling, but the feeling—and the law—would change.

In 1940 came Britain, "down, fighting for her life and calling for help." Britain's plight, wrote Garrett, "was bound deeply to move the hearts of a people whose racial foundation was Anglo-Saxon."

And so Americans thought again of saving Europe. It was a strategic opportunity for Roosevelt, whose battle to banish the Depression had not gone all that well. War brought a second chance for greatness.

Asked to enlist in a second European war, Americans would demur. But Roosevelt used less direct approaches. In *The American Story* (1955), Garrett wrote that the President was "peculiarly qualified in mind and character. . .to wend his contrary way toward war without a single false step, and at the same time to keep an unwilling people with him."

Roosevelt conditioned the national mind with appealing terms. One of them, from his state of the union speech of January 4, 1939, was "measures short of war." America was going to oppose Germany with measures short of war—stronger than talking but weaker than shooting. "Measures short of war" became a key phrase for two years,

15

then was dropped. What remained was the idea of allies—"the thesis," Garrett wrote, "that never again would the United States be able to stand alone in the world."

The war party said the defense of Britain "was vital to the security of the United States," and that our first line of defense was the English Channel. The antiwar party denied it. "If Hitler had been unable to cross the British Channel to finish England when she was prone on the ground," wrote Garrett, "how was he going to cross the Atlantic to attack America?"

My first collection of Garrett's work for the Caxton Press, *Salvos Against the New Deal* (2002), was put together from bylined articles spread over many pages of the *Post*. If they had not been edited, that book would have been at least 150 pages longer. This book is different. These are editorials, usually no more than one page of the *Post*, and sometimes less. The prose is tighter, and the pieces are not edited.

This book includes about half the editorials Garrett wrote for the *Post*. I have chosen the ones I thought worked together best in a book. But they were not written for that purpose. They repeat things, and they refer to events that were fresh then but are forgotten now. I have filled in some of the holes with footnotes.

The dates on editorials are not when they were written. They are the magazine cover dates, about a month after going to press. The first piece to refer to the December 7, 1941, attack on Pearl Harbor, for example, is dated January 4, 1942.

The first chapter contains three editorials from 1939 and 1940, written before editorials were Garrett's regular job. His work as editorial writer-in-chief begins in chapter two. This is in May 1940, when Germany attacked France and the major campaign began for aid to Britain.

The book begins with Garrett's arguments against involvement—for example, his argument that supplying the Allies would suck America into the war. As it did: first came cash sales, then the lending of weapons from

American arsenals, then the gift of old weapons, then the gift of new ones. To Garrett, the point of no return was the Lend-Lease bill. When Lend-Lease passed Congress, he wrote, the fight against intervention was over. After that his editorials focused on war requirements and aims.

"From May 1941 on, the *Post* was no longer isolationist," writes Garrett's academic biographer, Carl Ryant, in *Profit's Prophet* (1989). "While it regretted the necessity of going to war, it believed the nation would do so." My reading of the editorials presented here is that the *Post* never admitted the necessity of going to war but believed the nation had already done so.

One might look for several subjects on these pages and not find them. One is the Jews. Germany's persecution gave American Jews particular reason to support intervention and American anti-Semites particular reason to oppose it. The America First Committee disavowed anti-Semitism. So did its most famous spokesman, Charles Lindbergh; but when in a speech in Des Moines on Sept. 11, 1941, he criticized American Jews for supporting intervention, he unleashed a storm of criticism. He had broken a taboo, and the whole antiwar movement paid for it. There is nothing in Garrett's editorials about this, nor about Jews in Germany. In the retrospectives of today, it sometimes seems that Americans fought Germany because of the Holocaust. But that came later. In 1940-41, the question was whether to fight for Britain.

There is no argument here about fighting for China, and only one chapter about aid to the Union of Soviet Socialist Republics. When the interventionists won the argument for aid to Britain, they won it for the other Allies, democracies or not.

There is also hardly a mention in these pages of Japan. Garrett lived on the East Coast. But even in Seattle, war news in 1941 was much more about the North Atlantic than the Pacific. The main enemy in mind was Germany, and even after Pearl Harbor the European war would be the higher priority.

Garrett has nothing to say about what Roosevelt knew

in advance of the attack from Japan. But Garrett's editorials are a reminder, as he wrote years later, that "nine months before Pearl Harbor the country, actually and illegally, was at war with Hitler."

To present these editorials is not to claim that the world would have turned out better had America remained neutral. It might have. In *A Republic, Not an Empire* (1999), Patrick Buchanan imagines Germany and Russia grinding each other down like Japan and China did, leaving America unbloodied. In *What If? Eminent Historians Imagine What Might Have Been* (2001), Andrew Robertson imagines a contrary history in which Stalin's tanks rolled all the way to the Pyrenees. We cannot know what would have happened had America stayed out of World War II, nor if, in the end, America could have stayed out. We know only what did happen. On the plus side, America restored political freedom to Western Europe and planted it in Japan. On the minus side, America firebombed Hamburg, Dresden, Tokyo and Berlin, and used the atomic bomb on Hiroshima and Nagasaki. America also became an accomplice to the Communist domination of Eastern Europe for 40 years.

Whether the world would have turned out better or worse may not be the right question. It assumes that American interests are secondary to "world" interests— and that is not an assumption most people made in 1940. If Americans then could have been shown the postwar future at a price of 290,000 American dead, a nuclear stalemate and military commitments in Europe and Asia, they might well have said, "No, thanks."

In Garrett's view, America had assumed the mantle of empire. That the government did it, and the people accepted it, was to him the most grievous cost of World War II.

The editorials preserved here can be read as arguments about America's future. Unlike most antiwar arguments today, they are from the political right. They are common to two closely related schools of thought, the paleoconservatives and the libertarians.

The standard-bearer of the paleoconservatives is Patrick Buchanan, who in 1990 opposed the elder President Bush's Gulf War, in 1999 President Clinton's bombing campaign against Serbia and in 2002 the younger Bush's intention to attack Iraq. In foreign policy, Buchanan follows in the furrow of Garrett; the title of his foreign-policy book echoes Garrett's volcanic 1952 essay, "Rise of Empire," which begins, "We have crossed the boundary that lies between Republic and Empire."

Outside of foreign policy, Garrett and Buchanan are different. Buchanan is a populist who would defend the American worker from the competition of Chinese, and who berates CEOs for moving work abroad. Garrett was never a populist. He defended industry and spent five years editing the magazine of what is now the quintessential corporate fount, The Conference Board. He was a Wall Street journalist and a longtime correspondent of statesman-speculator Bernard Baruch. Garrett extolled the unplanned, organic, Darwinian struggle of business, and the "wild wheels" like Henry Ford who were its mutagens. Garrett's biographer aptly called him "profit's prophet." Nobody would call Patrick Buchanan that. Buchanan is for the old republic, but he is not a champion of laissez faire.

"Laissez faire" is the political property of the libertarians, such as Rep. Ron Paul, who was one of only six Republican votes in the House of Representatives against the Iraq war resolution of October 2002. Libertarians, who trace their genealogy to Jefferson, will find much to savor in Garrett, the defender of exuberant self-reliance and bottled-up government. But there was a strain of Hamilton in him as well. He was for a strong central bank, and for home industry.

In 1940 he wrote, reluctantly, in favor of the draft. When libertarian novelist Rose Wilder Lane chastised him for it, he replied: "Don't abuse me. Argue with me. What is the good of being free if you cease to exist? Survival is an important value, whether you think so or not. Your thesis that Nazism will wreck itself by wrecking production at last may be sound, but if it is it comes later. God knows it has beaten everyone else at production in the last six years; and if you say the machine must have a man, look at these German youngsters. They are not disliking it. Catch that in the pictures. They are a lupine race; they love war." He concluded: "The German power has to be matched, else there is no living in the world."

Garrett was not unwilling for his country to fight Hitler. He was unwilling to *pick* a fight with Hitler. That was because his country was not ready, and when it would be ready, a fight might not be necessary.

That is a cautious attitude toward war, conservative and libertarian both; and it is one of the aims of this book to introduce conservatives and libertarians to Garrett's way of thinking on it.

The other aim is simply to record, for those who love history, a set of arguments forcefully and memorably made for staying out of World War II. Because, of course, we did not stay out; and because World War II was such an immense event, the stuff of a hundred dramas from *Casablanca* to *Saving Private Ryan*, the idea that we might have stayed out has faded. The average American, absorbing his history from high school and Hollywood, might be excused for thinking that the whole argument began and ended on December 7, 1941.

It didn't. And arguments about war will keep coming up as long as Americans struggle with self-government and a world alive in risks.

Garet Garrett, passport photo, 1925

Chapter One
INVITATION

For four years the world had heard rumblings of war. In 1935 came the Italian attack on Ethiopia, in 1936 the Falangist revolt in Spain, in 1937 the Japanese invasion of China, in 1938 the German demand for the borderlands of Czechoslovakia, to which Britain and France agreed at Munich. In January 1939, Adolf Hitler began making demands on Poland and on the Free City of Danzig.

Who Cultivate War, April 8, 1939

Never was a stranger thing than that the American people should be inviting themselves to another world war before it happens.

At frequent intervals those who sample the waters of public emotion heave their questionnaires into the stream—such as, "If England and France were attacked by the dictators, will this country have to do something about it?" or, "Shall the democracies of the world at any cost, stand together?"—and when what comes up is put through the sieve that separates the ayes and noes, the tabulated result shows the steady onset of the idea that we shall have to save the world for democracy again. But you do not need the statistics. You can feel it. There is all at once an intellectual cult of interventionists. The feet of many pacifists are running in the paths toward war. The American character is inhabited by a strong crusader spirit. Many voices, for different reasons, have been calling to it, and it responds.

When the President first called to it, we were not thinking of war, talking of war, or preparing for war. Our thoughts were inturned upon our own economic and social maladies. The New Deal was going badly. That was in October, 1937.

Suddenly, out of the blue, in a speech at Chicago, the President proposed that we should have to help quarantine the aggressor nations of the world. First he borrowed the words to make a terrifying picture of what that day would be like when the aggressors went utterly mad. "If those things come to pass in other parts of the world," he said, "let no one imagine that America will escape, that it may expect mercy, that this Western Hemisphere will not be attacked. . . If those days are not to come to pass. . . the peace-loving nations must make a concerted effort. . . there is no escape through mere isolation or neutrality. . . the epidemic of world lawlessness is spreading. When an epidemic of physical disease starts to spread, the community approves and joins in a quarantine."

We dwell upon this speech because it is the key to much that has happened since. Nobody knew we were going to cast aside the priceless advantage of mere isolation. Nobody knew we were going to forsake the traditional policy of mere neutrality. As for our duty to help quarantine the aggressor nations of Europe and Asia, such a thing had never been debated.

Several weeks ago there was an unseemly dispute as to whether or not the President had said in a certain way to members of the Senate Committee on Military Affairs, under pledge of secrecy, that our first line of defense was France, or, by another version, that France was our frontier. Members of the Senate committee privately said that he said it. The French embassy in Washington confirmed it to the French government. Various responsible persons said they had heard him say it before. Yet three days later he called the newspaper correspondents to the White House and said to them that anyone who said he had said it was a boob and a liar.

Well, but he said it in that Chicago speech. Everybody knew the aggressor nations were Germany and Italy in

24

Europe, and that his peace-loving democracies were England and France. If we were going to help England and France to quarantine Germany and Italy, as if they were our enemies, too, where was our frontier, our first line of defense? It was in France, of course; and all that row of a few weeks ago over how he had said it again was emulsion.

Ever since the quarantine speech, the Government of the United States has been slapping the dictators in the face. When Secretary Ickes[1] had used his heavy hand on Hitler, and the German government protested, the State Department slapped him again by saying, in effect, that the indecencies of Nazism had put Germany beyond the pale of diplomatic amenities.

We ourselves sincerely tolerate that feeling. Just as sincerely we say that the Government should let the flames of hatred alone, instead of fanning them; and in any case, there is nothing to be said for the palm of the hand as an instrument of foreign policy.

After the quarantine speech, the front page of your newspaper began to change. Did you notice it? Rumors, alarms and discussions of war, touching this country, began to compete for the first position with news of our internal frustrations. It was a relief, indeed, to be thinking and talking less about our economic anemia and more about our place in the affairs of the world.

The President went visiting in Canada, and said the United States would never "stand idly by" if Canada were invaded. Probably not; it might have to be taken for granted. So far as anybody knew, there was at that time nowhere in the world a thought of invading Canada.

Then it was South America. The dictators were penetrating South America with their hateful ideologies and their merchandise, and we should be ready to fight for the Monroe Doctrine. So we should. That is not what we are talking about. We are talking about the cultivation of the American mind with thoughts of war. We should sooner think of an American frontier in South America than of one anywhere in Europe. It would make more sense. But it cannot well be one day in Europe and another day in South

America. Or shall we have one in Europe and one in South America too?

In his message to Congress, last January, the President said: ". . .Words may be futile, but war is not the only means of commanding a decent respect for the opinions of mankind. There are many methods short of war, but stronger and more effective than mere words, of bringing home to aggressor governments the aggregate sentiments of our own people."

He could not name the aggressor nations against whom we proposed to take measures. That would be going to far: though, of course, the whole world knew them as well as if he had called them by name.

But they had already been named. Two weeks before these words from the President, the chairman of the Senate Committee on Foreign Relations took a statement out of his pocket and handed it to the press. It said:

"1. The people of the United States do not like the government of Japan.

"2. The people of the United States do not like the government of Germany.

"3. The people of the United States, in my opinion, are against any form of dictatorial government, communistic or fascistic.

"4. The people of the United States have the right and power to enforce morality and justice in accordance with peace treaties with us. Our Government does not have to use military force and will not unless necessary."

This amazing statement produced a sensation. The chairman of the Senate Committee on Foreign Relations is a high officer of the Government; moreover, it was Senator Pittman, whose same-seeing with the President on matters of foreign policy is so well known that few could suppose he would have prepared such a statement without the knowledge and approval of the President.[2]

As one of the American people, we admit that Senator Pittman perfectly states what we feel about the governments of Germany and Japan. Nevertheless, he ought not to have said it; and if he could not help saying it, he ought to have first resigned from the Government. He must have known the effect his words would have not because they were his—if they were his—but because they were bound to be received abroad as an indirect utterance of the American Government. Obliquely in that way the hated nations could be named.

The hypnotic by this time has undergone some change. In the President's Chicago speech it was the word "quarantine." Not to fight the dictators, but to quarantine them. How simple!

The hypnotic now is the phrase, "short of war." Something to be done against the dictators, "stronger and more effective than words," and yet "short of war."

Regard now the spectacle of the great American Government shouting at other governments, "We hate you. The American people hate you. These words as we utter them are futile. We know that. But we will do more than words. We will do everything we can to defeat you—short of war."

There is no such infantile thing. If those who say it do not know better, they are even more dangerous than we think, for they are incompetent.

What are the methods more effective than words and short of war that one nation may employ against another? They will have to be either measures of economic hostility or measures of economic discrimination; and measures of either kind, with the positive and avowed intent to do injury, are measures of war.

Suppose this were not so. Suppose it were, as a senator said in debate on the national-defense program, that "Every time we sell a plane to France, standing between us and the dictators, so to speak, we need one less ourselves." In that light, the thought of measures short of war turns out to be such a thought as that, of all the nations representing the democratic ideal in the world, the one most powerful shall save itself by selling arms to the others. The word for that attitude is one that war at its worst has never yet deserved.

Meanwhile a national-defense program was taking

27

shape, and when it had been submitted to Congress, the foreign affairs of the nation passed suddenly into a phase of ominous mystery. We do not yet know whether the clumsy secrecy was meant to intensify the alarms or was only what it seemed.

The American ambassadors to England and France came to testify at secret sessions of the Senate Committee on Military Affairs and of the House Committee on Military Affairs, and it was made known what they said was too alarming to be disclosed.

The crash of a military plane on the Pacific Coast[3] accidentally disclosed the fact that a French commission was secretly buying bombers in this country. When the Senate Committee on Military Affairs began to ask embarrassing questions, and had already discovered from secret testimony that the President, over the protest of the War Department, had directed that the French buyers be given special access to what they wanted—just then the President called the members of the committee to the White House and, under the pledge of secrecy, told them things that made their blood run cold.

That was all they could tell, and it was perhaps worse to tell that then to have told the truth.

The gong was still vibrating with this alarm when the President, on his way to the fleet maneuvers, said to the reporters that he might have to cut his absence short and return at any moment in haste, on account of something the dictators might be doing in Europe. This was cabled over the world and produced immense astonishment in all the chancelleries of Europe.

The effect of imparting those frightful White House secrets to the Senate Committee on Military Affairs was to produce on the floor of the Senate this humiliating situation—that in a debate on a new program of national defense some senators were in possession of facts they were pledged not to divulge, some found themselves speaking from expurgated versions of secret testimony that had been superseded by other versions, and it was impossible for anyone to make an indisputable statement of what our foreign policy was; wherefore such a thing as an armament policy had to be debated in the dark by the United States Senate, since, of course, an armament policy, rationally, must be determined by a country's foreign policy and suited to it.

But whose foreign policy? Whose armament policy?

We go back to the quarantine speech in Chicago. Toward the end of it, the President said: "It is my determination to pursue a policy of peace. . . yet we cannot insure ourselves against the disastrous effects of war and the dangers of involvement."

My determination.

This is the balcony manner. It is the leader telling his people. Strange as it was then, it has become very familiar since. The national mind now is used to it.

This we may illustrate. From the Washington news leads of the *New York Times*—and it might be any other important newspaper—we take these examples:

February 1— "President Roosevelt told Senate Military Affairs Committeemen at the White House yesterday that the United States would back European democracies against dictatorships in every way short of war."

The President tells the senators what the United States will do!

The point is not whether this news paragraph is accurate or not; the point is that the news so written seems to excite neither wonder nor uneasiness.

Another:

February 3— "President was pressed by Congress groups yesterday to clarify his policy on the sale of arms abroad to aid the democracies."

His policy.

Another:

February 4— "Taking cognizance of several severe attacks on himself and his policies in the German and Italian press, Mr. Roosevelt vehemently asserted that he contemplated no change in the country's traditional foreign policy."

It is not written that the President said there was no

change in the traditional American foreign policy; it is written that he said *he* contemplated no change in it.

Again:

February 5— "Foreign-policy debate in the Senate next week is expected to turn on the question whether the President intends this country to back the French, except for man power, in the event of war."

And so the debate did turn on that question. What did the President intend? In this debate, if you will read it in the *Congressional Record,* you will find the senators asking over and over: "What is the President's foreign policy?"

We seem to have forgotten that the President does not make the foreign policy of the United States. He has not that constitutional power. He can negotiate treaties, but he cannot make them; a treaty is not made until the Senate confirms it. He cannot declare war. Only the Congress can do that.

Nevertheless, he can, if he is so minded, provoke war.

He can create situations and entanglements such as to make war inevitable.

He can, as we have seen, condition the national mind to thoughts of war.

The Constitution cannot save us from a President who turns world hero on our hands. It left that to the people.

There is no division of the American mind on the subject of adequate—very adequate—military defense. But unless we have a definite foreign policy—not Mr. Roosevelt's nor any president's but a national policy—it is impossible to be intelligent about a defense program.

To this we add that while we talk about our military defenses without knowing what our foreign policy is, we are neglecting our natural defenses. The first of these, more important in many ways than armament, is to keep our industrial machine at high key and in full production. This we have failed to do. Our machine is running down. And our second most important natural defense is to mind our own business.

On March 15, 1939, Hitler sent German tanks into Prague. On March 29, the British government, enraged at this breaking of the Munich agreement and by Hitler's territorial demands on Poland, guaranteed the independence of Poland. France was already Poland's ally.

On September 1, Germany invaded western Poland. Britain and France declared war on Germany.

On September 17, the Soviet Union, which had signed a secret agreement with Germany to divide up Poland, invaded eastern Poland. Britain and France did not declare war on the Soviet Union.

On September 21, President Roosevelt asked a special session of Congress to change the 1937 neutrality law, which forbade sales to either side in case of war, by allowing whoever could get their ships to the United States to be able to buy arms from private suppliers for cash.

Design for Freedom, November 11, 1939

We suppose that a nation, like the individual, is both body and spirit, and that it must sometimes happen, under certain circumstances unforeseen, that the body will leave its spirit in the lurch. We believe that is what has happened just now. In no other way can we explain the character of the debate on the so-called Neutrality Law, which was, in fact, a debate on how we should behave on the war in Europe.

Consider the argument for lifting the embargo on the sale of arms, munitions and implements of war to the belligerents.

The first reason was that the embargo law turned out to work in favor of Germany by depriving England and France of access to the arsenals of the United States. If it was lifted, it would be lifted for all belligerents alike, of course, in the name of neutrality; nevertheless, such access would be impossible for Germany. Only England and France would be benefited.

And why should we be wishing to give England and France that advantage? It was not a sufficient answer to

31

say that such was the shape of our sympathies. That was, of course, true. But it was said that England and France were fighting the battle of humanity and civilization; it was said that if the British navy was lost, our own first line of defense would be gone; it was said that if Germany won, the banner of aggression would cross the Atlantic to destroy our happy isolation.

So, lift the embargo. For such reasons lift it and give England and France access to our arsenals in order that they should be able to buy from us the means with which to defeat the enemies of civilization and freedom. But on what terms? Only on such terms as to make sure that we ourselves should not get into the battle; only provided the defenders of democracy, the keepers of our own first line of defense, should come and get the arms in their own ships and pay for them cash down.

The whole of this noble thought was expressed in one sentence by Senator Norris,[4] who said: "It is fortunate, therefore, that in following our legal rights [meaning the legal right to lift the embargo] . . .we are able to enact a law which will more likely keep us out of the war and at the same time puts us on the side of humanity and civilization."

How fortunate to be able to take the side of humanity and civilization, how fortunate to be able to save the principle of free institutions, how fortunate to assist at the defeat of the aggressor before he can make it our turn—and to do it with perfect safety and some profit!

We do not subscribe to any part of the argument. For if the argument were true, it would be our war, too, and instead of selling arms to those on the battle line we should at least be willing to give them without cost and deliver them at our own risk.

Consider then what was said on the other side. What was the apex of the argument against lifting the embargo? Senator Borah touched it—that even though as we lifted the embargo we should forbid American ships to carry arms to England and France, for fear Germany might sink them and involve us in war, even though we should require the buyers to come and get the lethal cargoes, take title to them at the dock, pay in cash, and carry them away in their own ships, which Germany might sink without offense to us, still we should not be safe, because Germany might come and bomb the plants we had turned into arsenals for our customers.

"Why," he asked, "should not a belligerent dynamite or bomb the plant and destroy not merely a cargo on the sea but the entire establishment which is furnishing. . . the cargo? . . .Would not every munitions manufacturing plant and every arsenal in the United States be spotted for destruction? Would not the war be brought into our very midst?"

This was to say that we should abandon our legal right as neutrals to sell arms to whom we like, or to all alike who could cross the sea and get them, for fear the one belligerent who was thereby put at a disadvantage might come and bomb our industries.

Fear is the ignoble matter here—fear of being neutral, lest the wrong side win, in which case we might see the British navy in German hands, with the American fleet needed in the Pacific; fear, on the other hand, of being unneutral, lest we be dragged into the war against our will. If the historian does not gloss this over, our children may not understand it.

What saves it for us is that we know we are not that kind of people. We are not afraid of war. This is not a wee, timorous nation. It has a record. Why then are we involved in this contradiction?

The first explanation we can think of is that the American people have been pursuing a fantasy held out to them by a false evangel of softer living, a more abundant life for less exertion, and, above all, security. The word "security," which was new among us, has worked a deep injury to the American spirit. It has meant everything— economic security, social security, physical and moral security, immunity from war by passing a law in which we abandoned all the neutral rights we had once been willing to fight for—and all the time it meant nothing, for there is no such thing in this world as either immunity or security.

Secondly, the American people have been led to believe they could keep their fancied security and still exert their moral and material power in world politics. They were told there was much they could do, more effective than words and short of war, to uphold the principles of freedom; that they could indulge their moral passions against the aggressor, threaten to employ decisive economic weapons against him, threaten to quarantine him, in fact; and all with perfect safety. For had they not passed a law to keep themselves out of war?

Suddenly all this fantasy breaks down. In place of it is reality. Suddenly it is realized that means more effective than words and yet short of war are perilous means, if they are means at all. It is realized that the American people, the most powerful in the world, have a role to take. They do not know exactly what it is. The body is not armed for it and the spirit has been day-dreaming of perfect security in a world where all law was vanishing but the law of force. The rest is confusion. In confusion there is panic.

The measure of this confusion is that we talk of putting a three-hundred-mile zone of neutrality around a hemisphere, knowing as we talk of it that we have not in being the power to defend it.

If we want it we can have it, but we shall have to prepare ourselves to patrol it, defend it, fight for it. Absolute security we can never have. Practical security we can have if we want it, but in order to possess it we shall have to do more than pass a law, and so long as we think of it as a blessing in any way defended by the British navy we shall neither have it nor deserve it.

What we need for purposes of practical security is first of all a new word. The word is "impregnability," or a state of supreme defense. We need more than a bigger navy. We need two, one for the Atlantic and one for the Pacific, each incomparable. We need an impervious antiaircraft wall. We need to be able to meet not any aggressor but any combination of aggressors.

Then we may be sure that the principle of free institutions as a basis of modern civilization shall have beyond the solace of our words, a time yet to live in this world.

Then we may create a world of our own, or finish the one we started, dedicated to peace and freedom indestructible.

No other nation in the world has the power to do this. To no other had it been possible for destiny to assign that prodigious task. We have all of the means, and though the cost would be very great, our fantasy of security without price has cost us more.

The Senate approved the lifting of the arms embargo 63-20, and the House, voting November 2, 1939, by 243-181. A Gallup poll showed Americans approved the action, 58-42.

That of Our Own, March 23, 1940

We could wish that a neglected book entitled *The Contrast,* by Hilaire Belloc, might be made required American reading.[5] It was written between the World War and this one, when there was time to think. The author's qualifications rest upon three possessions—namely, one of the very fine minds in England, courageous wisdom, and a long, intuitive acquaintance with America. His thesis is that although American culture did descend from European culture, American destiny is separate forever; and that although the United States may belong to Christendom, nevertheless

". . .they are a part of it, subject to a cultural schism, the intensity of which is my whole object to declare. The United States are not merely an enlargement of our European culture, still less a mere branch of it; they create a division of that culture into two—themselves and the rest. The line of cleavage does not lie between them and any other sub-group, such as France or England or Italy; it lies between them and *all* Europe."

And if this truth be forgotten on either side, or if it be overcome by emotions leading America to take part again in Europe's affairs, or Europe to wish it, then, he thinks,

"European and American culture are both doomed to receive wounds which may prove mortal."

First and last, Belloc is European. He knows better than to break with the ancestry of his native environment. Only an American ever thinks of doing that. He says—and this is at the end:

"We of Europe shall solve our own problems. . .Things return to their origin, and our Roman unity should revive. But the process whereby that peace shall be accomplished is not one which could be understood from the standpoint of the United States; it is our own affair; we alone understand it. And let me add this: every public man from Europe, especially every professional politician, who approaches the people of the United States, begging them to interfere in our affairs, is a liar. . . and the fine phrases about peace and justice and humanity and civilization and the rest of it, are hypocrisy and a poison."

When shall we learn again that Europe is Europe, America is America, and these are two worlds?

When shall we believe again that our destiny is unique, parallel to nothing?

Once we knew it. Living by it, we came to be the most powerful people in the earth and made certain great contributions to the thought and life of the world. First was an idea of government. It was our own. We did not send it abroad. Yet it was as if we had released the winds of freedom, dangerously, and what we had done was written in foreign tongues on many banners we never saw or heard of.

There was our idea of neutrality; we were willing to fight for it, and did—for freedom of the seas and for neutral rights above belligerent rights.

We evolved our own economic philosophy, not out of Europe's books but out of our own experience and from our own ways of thinking. We made the astonishing discovery, and formulated the thought, that wages are paid not out of profits, but out of production; which means that wages and profits may rise together, if only you will increase production. That was a new kind of liberation.

There was an American standard of living, the highest

that had ever been known in the earth. There was an American philosophy of labor, regarding the employee-employer relationship as economic purely. Politician, let it be!

There were many American evils, too; we were increasingly conscious of them. But as the good was our own, so was the evil, unlike any other. And the curious fact was that when the envious and marveling world began to send economic experts and labor commissions to inquire how we did it, they saw much more of the good than of the inseparable evil, knowing that evil, after all, is a relative thing, and that if a society, on the whole, has progressed in material well-being to a new level in human history, it can be trusted to absorb a great deal of evil.

Sometime after the turn of the century, a change began to take place. You cannot mark it precisely. It became fashionable to plant Old World seeds. They grew in soft warm places, often in the gardens of the leisure rich, and flourished in academic soil generally. There appeared in the East an intellectual cult of disaffection, with a sneer in its mind for what it named 100 per cent Americanism and a pose of contempt for the wealth that supported it. Everything American was vulgar. Happy the expatriate who could live abroad with his dollars and forget where they came from.

It was not only Europe's culture that was preferred; her solutions also began to be admired. What followed was a new kind of exchange. Europe went on taking economic ideas from us while we, for the first time, were taking political and social ideas from her.

The first wedge was the idea of political labor unionism. We got that from England. It was alien here. Then the doctrine of paternal government with the responsibility to administer human welfare; and the saying that we were twenty-five years behind Europe in social legislation. A country sending its wage earners to work in motorcars might, indeed, be doing less for labor by law than countries where only the highest-paid workers owned bicycles.

All of that was happening when the World War came.

That chapter in world history will sometime bear this caption: "America's Return to Europe."

What we lost at that time cannot be computed. Not the cost of our war exertions. Not the illusions that went in our slogans. Our own center—that is what we lost. That sense of separate destiny on which we had been building departed from us, and we have never since recovered it.

After the war we accepted the role of rich prodigal repentant, with a duty to restore Europe. It was false. We were romantic about it; Europe was cynical. It was a strange balance of trade. During the 1920's we poured billions of material wealth into Europe. What did we receive in exchange? All those Old World ideas, ideologies and hatreds for which the unrugged American intellectual and an envious classroom mentality had been preparing the soil.

Marxism, Leninism, Stalinism, Nazism, collectivism, revolutionary dialectic, the class struggle, youth movements, ideas of a state all-powerful and all-doing, planned economy, status for the individual, anticapitalism, hatred of the profit motive, redistribution of wealth among classes by law, contempt for the parliamentary principle, government by propaganda, deficit spending, manipulation of the currency for political and social ends, repudiation of government obligations—of such is the harvest. Old World harvest in New World soil.

As we reap it, Europe goes to war again. This happens in spite of the doctrines and solutions we had thought so well of as to borrow them. Or do you suppose it might have been because of them?

However, as to that, and notwithstanding the resolve we intone to stay out of it if we can, our interest in the war is such that we cannot let it alone. We permit our emotions to become deeply involved. We see right and wrong. We sat in judgment on the preliminaries. We hissed Chamberlain for the Munich appeasement. Since then we have hated Hitler officially. On Mussolini we reserve opinion. We are so close to it all that a change of war ministers in England is news that runs under four-column headlines in the New

York papers.

Russia's invasion of Finland produces many reactions here; one of them dangerous. Why dangerous? Because people begin saying to one another: "Could we bear to see Scandinavia trampled down by the powers of evil?"

For now beginning to make itself felt is what has been musically named: The Moral Urge Toward War. Out with business, the profiteer and the munitions maker. This is a thing they cannot feel. In whom does the feeling arise? In "some of the best people," says *The New Republic*. "They really are among those who are most sensitive to values, those who live in the world of ideas, those whose consciences and honor are not blunted by too much prudence. . . The impulse to fight is spontaneous and rises from what every one of us has heard and felt. That is the reason it could start a prairie fire. . . The great peril lies within ourselves."

But the peril lies in being not ourselves.

Where are the Americans who were themselves and knew it? Alas, it seems they are not among the best people.

Where is the America that saw only the star of its singular destiny and pursued it? At this moment it would be the hope of the world.

America in the crusading spirit, entertaining the fantasy of descending upon Europe out of the sky to part right and wrong, to overthrow evil, to scatter its simple judgments about, is worse than a peril to itself. It is a peril to the whole world.

Is it war we abhor? We shall never abate war by taking part in the conflicts of Europe.

Is it the plight of small neutral nations that gives rise to the heroic impulse? Well then, instead of thinking to save them by the sword, we had done much better to be willing to fight for a principle we have scuttled—namely, the principle of inviolable neutral rights in time of war. This was the only nation powerful enough to defend that principle against the belligerents. If we had been willing to defend it by force, if necessary—the world knowing for sure that we would—there would now be less terror of the aggressor in the hearts of small neutrals.

Or is peace the matter of our ultimate anxiety? If that is it, then, instead of indulging in the moral urge toward war, we should be putting all the intelligence and imagination we possess to the problem of peace, and how, when the war ends, to assume and discharge the responsibilities of world leadership.

Finland was invaded by Soviet forces November 30, 1939, after refusing to make territorial concessions. In December, Garrett was involved in an effort with Bernard Baruch to raise $50 million on Wall Street for the Finnish government. The effort failed. The Finns were pushed back by the Red Army, and agreed to Soviet terms on March 6, 1940.

Chapter one notes

[1] Harold Ickes, 1874-1952, secretary of the interior 1933-1946. Originally a progressive Republican, Ickes became an acerbic defender of the New Deal. In the Garrett papers at Harvard is a long letter from Ickes replying to one of Garrett's broadsides. Ickes was one of the few New Dealers who outlasted Roosevelt. But Truman was too conservative for Ickes, and he resigned in a huff. His son Harold Ickes was a political operative for Bill Clinton.

[2] Key Pittman, 1872-1940, Democrat of Nevada, Senator 1913-1940. During a drinking spree just before the 1940 elections, Pittman had a heart attack that was kept secret. After he was reelected, it was announced that he had just died. It was long rumored that he had died before the election and had been kept on ice in a hotel bathtub—a rumor that was never disproved.

[3] On Jan. 23, 1939; a Douglas DB-7.

[4] George W. Norris, 1861-1944, of Nebraska, was elected as a progressive Republican. Norris was one of six senators who voted against war with Germany in 1917, and was an opponent of the Versailles Treaty at war's end. From 1928 on, he supported Democratic candidates for President, and in 1937 became an independent.

[5] Hilaire Belloc, 1870-1953, was an English Catholic novelist, biographer, poet, historian, political philosopher and writer of travel and children's books, including *The Bad Child's Book of Beasts* (1896), *The Path to Rome* (1902), *The Servile State* (1912) and *The Restoration of Property* (1936). He criticized Fabian socialism and industrial capitalism and advocated a pastoral state of craftsmen, farmers and small merchants.

Chapter Two
THE CALL

On April 9, 1940, Germany seized Denmark and Norway. On May 10 Germany attacked the Low Countries and France, and Winston Churchill became prime minister of Britain.

In May, Garrett became the Post's *editorial writer in chief, giving him a weekly pulpit. This was his first use of it.*

And They Were Unprepared, June 22, 1940

We trust history to erase or disregard the fact that there was a moment when the thought of having to stand alone in its own hemisphere against the European aggressor made the great American democracy seem to be afraid. Alcibiades explained it when he complained of his Greeks—who were often scared, but never afraid—that he could not get them to act until he had made their flesh to creep. That is a weakness of democracies still. Their emotions are quick, but their minds are dilatory. They trifle with time and are never ready.

For how long did England and France watch the Germans at the work of building the most frightful war machine of all time? They knew well enough what it was for. They could have stopped it. Their resources were in every way superior. At least they could have prepared the invincible defense. But they were unwilling to forgo in time their customary ways and comforts, unable to forget their

41

internal disputes, incapable of bringing their lives, their powers and intelligence under discipline of a single grim purpose, as they saw the Germans doing. So it was that when the terror struck, they were not ready, and began calling to the great young democracy across the Atlantic to save them, or, if not to save them, who had been saved once before, to save civilization.

And what had this romantic democracy been doing? It had been indulging its moral passions. Conscious of having in its hands the balance of all power in the potential sense, with two-thirds of the world's gold in its vaults, with an unlimited surplus of essential resources, it had been saying to the aggressor, "You and who else?" It had been pursuing the fantasy that, merely by threatening to put its weight in his path, it could stop him.

The origin and growth of that fantasy may be said to date from the President's quarantine speech in Chicago, in October, 1937. He said, "Let no one imagine America will escape, that it may expect mercy, that the Western Hemisphere will not be attacked." And what he proposed was that the peace-loving nations should "quarantine the aggressor."

No one asked how or with what means. Had we not our Mobilization Day Plan in the files of the War Department, an army of four million men on paper, and a law all written and ready to be passed, turning the economy of the entire country from peace to war overnight?

Whether the Germans knew that or not, they went on building their war machine.

Nothing came of the quarantine idea. The next shape of the fantasy received from the President was, "Methods short of war, but more effective than mere words." What methods? What measures?

Anyhow the Germans went on building their machine.

Then the President began to say that the old 1937 neutrality law, forbidding the sale of arms and munitions to belligerents, was the reason why he had been unable to awe the aggressor. He wanted it repealed, and in place of it a law that would give him almost unlimited discretion to employ the economic power of the country in foreign wars. The Congress, after a very bitter fight, refused to give him such a law. It was then that the controversy arose over whether he had said to members of Congress, in a confidential White House interview, that our first line of defense was in France, or what exactly he did say to make them think he said that. Yet suppose he did say it, and suppose he had been right. What were we going to put there? A typewritten statistical statement of our potential power? Another warning to the aggressor of what we could do?

The Germans went on building their machine; and when of a sudden they released it fully and went crashing through Holland and Belgium with it, the President announced that we were "shocked and angered." We were. Rising in millions of American hearts that day was the passion to put forth the arm of the most powerful democracy and smite that aggressor. Yet again, with what? With shock and anger. Shock is sensation and anger is emotion, and neither one has ever yet shot a bombing plane down.

It was then, and as if for the first time, that a country hitherto boasting of its offensive power looked to its weapons. That was the moment we spoke of in the beginning—the moment of panic. Its weapons were not fit. They were not fit for self-defense, even. If its entire military strength had been there to meet the aggressor, it could not have saved Holland, to say nothing of civilization. What would happen, therefore, if the Germans should suddenly win, and then turn their frightful machine against us? Could we defend ourselves?

The truth, or quite enough of it, concerning our state of military and industrial unpreparedness now is notorious. Such sayings as that in these days of "swift and shocking developments" a nation must "look to its defenses in the light of new factors," or that the Administration had not at its disposal the means necessary to prepare an adequate national defense—for that matter, a hemisphere defense according to its own thesis—are but suavities and gloze. The Administration did know. Its files are heavy with neglected information. Our foremost authority in industrial preparedness is Bernard M. Baruch, who, as chairman of the War Industries Board, commanded the country's economic exertions in the World War twenty-two years ago. Ceaselessly for three years he importuned the Government and the President personally with oral statements and written memoranda on the necessity to prepare and organize industry for national defense and on the rise and character of the German menace. After the appeasement of Hitler at Munich, he returned from Europe and stood on the White House steps saying, "The condition of American defense is unknown only to Americans. Every foreign power knows what we are doing and exactly what we lack." And to the Government he addressed another memorandum, saying, "I do not know whether the special machinery that is necessary for making powder[1] has been bought. That should be top priority. Next should be the shortage of antiaircraft and antitank guns and semiautomatic shoulder rifles, with a reserve of special machinery. Then airplanes and more airplanes."

And as for the means, there was a dispensation of chance such as will never occur again. For his recovery program the President received from Congress billions to spend in whatever way he would. Under the National Industrial Recovery Act alone, to begin with, he got three billion three hundred million dollars. The Congress did not say what he should do with the money; it did suggest to him, among other things, naval construction, aircraft and mechanization of the Army.

What did he do with it? In the next fiscal year total emergency expenditures under the recovery program were four billions; and of this four billions, less than sixty-one millions were spent for national defense. Billions out of that first free purse and billions since for relief, for social security, for the more abundant life and to make work—save the word!—at a time when in Germany every ounce of human labor was employed and people were on short rations in order to build a war machine with which to destroy the soft-living democracies.

That is not all. Besides the free billions that might have

been spent in works of preparedness, Congress has directly appropriated for national defense in the last seven years
the enormous total of seven billions. Seven years was
Germany building her war machine. In those seven years,
with the money that we might have spent under the recovery program for national defense, plus the seven billions
appropriated for that purpose, we could have made this
continent impregnable. What have we got? A first-class
Navy, yet one not large enough to defend both coasts at
once or to defend the line of neutrality we have cast upon
inter-American waters; hardly more than the fine nucleus
of an adequate air force; an Army waiting for guns and
instruments, with fewer tanks to its name than the number in one German division.

So it is that in a time of the world without reason, no
law extant but the law of force, the richest and most powerful democracy in it, this Cathay that has been sending
insulting messages to Genghis Khan is unprepared to
fight.

But we are going to be prepared. The first thing shall be
unity of mind about it. In unity of mind we adjourn politics.
To adjourn politics means that we shall say of what might
have been, "What's over the dam is forgotten." To speak of
it further would be partisan. Then we are going to begin.
There is nothing the Germans know that we don't know;
nothing they can do but we can do it more so.
Mechanization? We are the famous mechanizers. We are
going to defend this hemisphere. We are going to have a
power of defense that will enable us to attack an aggressor
on his way hither. We are going to have an air armada of
fifty thousand planes, and bases everywhere, and the per-
sonnel and everything.

When? As soon as possible. We are going to "speed up to
a twenty-four-hour basis all the existing Army and Navy
contracts," without saying why they were not speeded up
before. We are going to resurrect the old spirit of industry
and embrace it and then require of it, says the President,
"the ability to turn out quickly infinitely greater supplies."
Infinitely greater.

And toward all this going-to-be and going-to-do and infinitely-greaterness, an immediate appropriation of how much money?

Roughly, one and one-half billions.

Less than one-half the size of the first free purse for the recovery program. Less than 2 1/2 per cent of the national income, whereas Germany, to build her war machine, had been spending at least one third of her national income for seven years.

We mention the sum and scale it thus only as a measure of discrepancy. Money will not buy preparedness. The price of defense is sacrifice.

Regard the German machine. Money did not build it. Nor did credit. It represents grueling work, heroic privation and what people did without, including butter. They could have butter or they could have guns; not both. It is a monstrous thing, and yet so it was done. And so only may the power of defense be achieved. It is evident that even yet we are wishfully thinking. We think we can prepare our defense by passing an appropriation. But what is it we are willing to consume less of in order to produce armaments? By how much are we willing to lengthen the hours of labor? How much profit, income, comfort and pleasure are will willing to surrender? To work harder or to consume less—it is one or the other. In the heroic mood we should do both.

The difference between a totalitarian state and a democracy is that in one the people are commanded to do it and in the other they must be persuaded. In England and France they could be neither commanded nor persuaded enough.

We have the billions and they are nothing. We have the resources. We have the labor. What has been wanting is grim leadership calling the grim spirit in us to rise again.

Garrett sent a copy of this to Bernard Baruch, noting that it was his first editorial in his new job. "It won't do you any good with the precious administration," he wrote, "neither will it do you any harm with the country you love." Baruch wrote back, "I do not want you to think whether anything will do me any good or not. We have all to think of what is best for the country. I think we are up against it."

His first editorial got high-level feedback—from the prickly and combative Secretary of the Interior, Harold Ickes. In his August 17 editorial, Garrett wrote: "We have now a letter from Secretary Ickes in which he blames us severely for an editorial entitled And They Were Unprepared, *printed June twenty-second. It was unfair, he thinks, because, for one thing, we did not say, as Mr. Ickes says, 'It was the Republican Party that systematically blocked defense measures in Congress.' It follows from this that the Republicans were to blame for the country's shocking state of unpreparedness; it was their fault, not the President's, that he was caught bluffing with an empty gun.*

"We waive that dispute. If the country was unprepared, that was a fact. If the President was unable to persuade it to prepare adequately, that also was a fact. Given these two facts, any high-school essayist on foreign policy would know better than to insult, threaten and provoke on one side with most powerful and fanatical aggressor of modern times, and on the other side the Japanese at the same time, and at last actually to intervene in the conflict with futile measures."

Garrett's promise to adjourn politics was a bad idea and, fortunately, one he soon gave up.

Will We Do It? July 6, 1940

W e do not believe the great ways of thinking and feeling that have made this country what it is can be overthrown. They may be betrayed. Therefore we say—saying it bluntly as a challenge—that for a time already too long the American people have been out of character in their emotional premises, in their reactions to evil and in their choices of mentors and leadership. And if the principle of free government were really in danger in the world, it would be owing less to the rise of the totalitarian powers than to the softness of a people upon whom freedom has conferred incomparable gifts.

Not the first bad sign, perhaps, but certainly a very wrong turn, was when the country followed the magicians who said there was an easy way out of depression. Repudiation of debts and contracts, debasement of money, inflation, confiscation, redistribution of the national income by law, then recovery, the more abundant life, less work for more pay and security forever—all of that was wishful thinking.

Such was the beginning of a headlong flight from individual responsibility. It was the beginning of a dangerous habit of soft living unearned. We presented the spectacle of a people trying to consume more than they produced and able for a while to do it because they had been so rich. We had the finest industrial machine in the world, and for seven years we have been consuming it. Do you know what that means? Take a single fact as it was stated by Mr. Hoover, that according to a recent census of machine tools in the United States, 70 per cent of them now are more than ten years old, whereas in 1932 only 52 per cent of them were more than ten years old. And no move had been made to enforce an embargo up to June fourth.

All this time certain hungry nations commonly called the have-nots, and first among these the German people, were working twice as hard as we were, consuming not more but much less than they produced, in order by heroic self-denial to create a surplus. We were purposely destroying our surplus, saying it was ruinous. They were putting theirs into war machines, with intent, when they were ready, to turn them on the soft democracies and take from them what they wanted.

We knew it; we watched them doing it. Behaving as if our power were still intact, we warned them not to do what they were intending to do. Yet they went on as if we had said nothing. They knew what we had done to our strength, that we had let our armaments rust.

From here on it is painful. When the war the Germans had been preparing was imminent, what did this country, the richest, most powerful republic that ever lived on earth—what did it do? It adopted the thesis that its own first line of defense was in France. It would not itself go to the battlefield. Never. Yet the aggressor had to be stopped; the free governments of the world must stand together. Therefore, it would sell food, supplies, planes and war munitions to France and England, provided they came in their own ships to get them and paid cash; it changed its neutrality laws accordingly, and argued as it did so that it was helping to save democracy, keeping itself out of war, and doing business, all at the same time. And such was the leadership that the people followed, apparently unaware that if the thesis were true, their country's behavior was pusillanimous.

The thesis was false. Our first line of defense was not in Europe. It was here. American civilization, that is our own possession. It could not be saved in Europe or defended there. We are its sole defenders and it can be saved only here.

Well then, the war came, and suddenly it appeared that the strength of the aggressor had been fatally underestimated. Thereupon a great voice was heard in many places at once, as if it were the American voice, saying we must rush to the side of the Allies with material aid—with credit, munitions, anything but men—because it would be cheaper and more intelligent to do that than to let the war come to us, and because (we quote it exactly): "The success of the Allies is vital to us."

We do not believe that was the American voice. It was the voice of fear, to say no worse of it. "Vital" is not a word to be misunderstood. It means something essential to life. Was it the American voice saying the life of this American republic was at stake on the outcome of a war in Europe, even such a thing as the fall of the British Empire? Never had the American spirit a voice like that.

May came. The historian who examines the American newspapers for the month of May, 1940, may wonder how much of ourselves we saw in that mirror.

What had happened? The power of the German war machine had been revealed, its triumph was a definite possibility, the fall of the British Empire was imaginable; and the American mind passed through the strangest experience of its life. The emotion was that of dread, acted upon by hysterical mentorship. If we may speak of the national mind, certainly never had its behavior been so unimportant, so weak against the impact of deformed ideas crashed forth before they were born, such as the idea that we should forsake our political traditions and name Mr. Roosevelt on both party tickets, because that would be a demonstration of unity, meaning mass-mindedness, and it would be dangerous in this emergency to change leadership!

The President's own first contribution was a defense message, hastily prepared, in which he suggested how easy it would be for the aggressor to get here with bombs unless we were prepared to stop him en route, which we were not. He imagined that adequate American preparedness would require 50,000 airplanes and then asked Congress to increase the regular Army and Navy appropriations by a sum not much more than the amount it was voting for the WPA program. Less than two weeks later he was saying to reporters at a White House press conference, as reported in the *New York Times*, "that there was no reason for the country to become discomboomerated. The women of the country would not have to give up their cosmetics, lipsticks and chocolate sodas in consequence of the preparedness program. . . The whole idea is that the present state of international affairs calls for an outlay of about a billion and a quarter dollars over and above the two billions that were being spent on the military and naval establishment." Three days later he was saying, in another message to Congress, that "the almost incredible events of the last two weeks" made it necessary to appropriate another billion for defense.

While the Germans were doing without butter and buying one cigarette at a time in order to have guns, we were changing our automobiles once a year. "We have not manufactured a big gun in many years," says General Marshall, our chief of staff, "but it would take about two and a half years to make a sixteen-inch gun and carriage" for our coastal defense.

We are not prepared to fight the aggressor. Yet we defy him. He shall not make us give up any of our social gains, says the President. He shall not upset the normal American way of life. American women shall have their cosmetics still, in spite of him. Preparedness the easy way!

If the Government knows what the problem is and comprehends it even dimly, it is treating the American people as if they were children unable to bear reality. If it does not know, its incompetence, hitherto an economic disaster only, may come to be remembered as a calamity.

The problem is not that we stand alone in this hemisphere, with not one powerful friend in the world to help us defend it. When was it that we stood not alone here? Where was that powerful friend in the world ever willing to help us defend American civilization? We are sick of hearing that the British navy all this time has been defending our Monroe Doctrine. More than once we have been willing to fight the British navy for it. Our part is to stand alone for as long as we have the hardihood, the spirit and the fortitude to do it, and when we haven't, we may as well stop talking about American destiny.

No. The problem is that a balanced distribution of power in the world has been upset. A new and frightful power has appeared, an offensive power moved by an unappeasable earth hunger, conscious of no right but the right of might. It does not threaten this country with invasion: at least, not yet. It does threaten the Western Hemisphere by economic and political designs in the Latin American countries, and this, for us, is an ominous fact. But the larger aspect of what has happened is that the world is in a state of unbalance. Until an equal defensive power has been created in the hands of people who prefer peace to war, there will be no safe living in it, no security for free government.

Who shall create that equal defensive power and restore the balance? You have only to ask the question to get the answer. There is one country in the whole world that can do it. In that simple sense it is the United States against Germany, now or later. And that is not to speak of war. It is the minimum price of peace.

The cost of doing it, in terms of self-discipline, harder living, more work, may be terrific. This is the truth that we have so far declined to face. It might well cost us, not some billions more or less to be voted by Congress, not a 10 per cent increase in the income tax, but possibly a quarter of our total national exertions for several years. There is no easier way. A thousand airplanes a day, if necessary. That is the American voice. It is possible. But how many of us realize what we should have to do without for a thousand airplanes a day? What we will, that we can do.

On June 6, 1940, the Navy Department announced that fifty Curtiss-Wright bombers were being sold to France.

Quo Vadis? July 13, 1940

This is written on June tenth. With no notice to the American people or to the Congress that is supposed to interpret their will, this country entered the war four days ago. Stranger than the fact was the passive acceptance of it.

While the Senate was debating, with intent to kill it, a resolution that would have conferred upon the President of the United States certain extraordinary powers, the President seized those powers and involved this country in the European conflict by an act of physical intervention.

This he did by sanction of his own will. The Congress did not know what he was going to do and debated it after the fact. The people, whose war it will be, first read it in the newspaper headlines.

What we now write is to complete the record. We have no idea what the next consequences will be or what will have happened by the time these words appear. But as in time to come it may be bitterly remembered, so now be it said that in the one hundred and fifty years of its existence the house of constitutional republican government was betrayed, even as the builders feared. Unawares to the people, the exalted Executive principle could involve them in a war. We dare to look at the truth and to ask why the house of our fathers had to be half surrendered before it was attacked. We do not here touch the question of whether we should go to the side of the Allies. What we are saying is that if the American people may be involved in a world war unawares and without a specific act of Congress, then much else has happened to them of which also they are unaware.

We do not believe the people had ever thought of going again to the battlefields of Europe. They had been misled to think this country somehow could put forth its economic strength and not itself become involved. That is what they were thinking when they were polled on whether we should be giving more aid to the Allies. The idea that we could help to destroy the aggressor in Europe and not get hurt was a propagated fantasy and produced on many minds the hypnotic effect that may or may not have been intended.

To accomplish his purpose, it was necessary for the President to outwit the law. First was a statute, enacted in time of peace, permitting the military establishment to sell to any foreign government with whom we are at peace on a certain date surplus munitions and war materials for which there was no other market, and to exchange motor vehicles, airplanes, engines and parts for new and similar equipment. When that statute was written, nobody could have dreamed that it would ever be used by the President as a pretext for opening this country's arsenals to either side in another world war.

Secondly, it was necessary to beat the prohibitions of international law and especially Article VI of The Hague Convention of 1907, to which this country put its name, which is still in force, and which reads: "The supply in any manner, directly or indirectly, by a neutral power to a belligerent power, of warships, ammunition or war material of any kind whatever, is forbidden."

Observe here the very strict distinction. The private citizen of a neutral country may sell arms and war material to a belligerent power; that is permitted. American industry, acting privately, could sell airplanes and guns to the Allies. But for a government to do it is an act of intervention. The government that does it is no longer neutral. It has taken part. It is, in fact, at war.

The President of the United States could not himself, on his own will, declare war. Only the Congress has the constitutional power to declare war. But he hit upon a device for getting the country into the conflict without declaring war.

As commander in chief of the armed forces of the United States he declared the Navy to have a surplus of airplanes, at a moment when there was a panic of anxiety over the shocking inadequacy of the country's air defenses. As commander in chief he ordered the Navy to deliver this alleged surplus of planes back to the factory they came from, in exchange for new planes yet to be made—and this under a previous stipulation with the airplane factory that as fast as it received the planes from the Navy, it would hand them over to the Allies.

We had no surplus of airplanes; so far otherwise, we very urgently want more than we are yet able to make for ourselves. Nor were these obsolete planes, for if they were, of what use could they be to the Allies in battle? Thirdly, then, the make-believe that in the end it became simply a transaction between the private American airplane industry and the Allies, because the Navy, on delivering the planes to the factory, quit title to them, was only clever, and far beneath the dignity of a great people.

The next day it was guns. As commander in chief, the President would declare obsolete or surplus a lot of U.S. Army guns, including thousands of the 75 mm.'s the French were greatly in need of, sell them to the American gun makers, who would sell them at once to the Allies, undertaking to replace them later in the American armory out of new manufacture.

That way, as reported in the *New York Times,* "In his press-conference discussion of national-defense plans President Roosevelt refused the role of prophet when asked how far this government was prepared to go in supplying the Allied powers with guns, ammunition and aircraft." And how about bombs to go with the bombing planes? That question was asked because only the Government itself manufactures the bombs. Therefore there could be no subterfuge of turning back bombs to private manufacturers in exchange for new and better bombs later. The reporters could not quote the President directly at this point. The *New York Times* reporter wrote: "It was remarked, however, that the law does not require surplus munitions to be returned to the factory whence they came, but merely specifies that they may be exchanged for other munitions." Which means, if it means anything, that the President was thinking the Government could manufacture bombs to go with the airplanes, sell them to somebody who would sell them to the Allies, and itself take anything in exchange.

Then what of warships? What of turning warships back to the shipyards that made them on an undertaking by the shipbuilders to sell them to the Allies and make new ones for the U.S. Navy? The reporters asked the President that question. The *New York Times* reporter wrote: "He explained that he had been unable to get to that question, so far."

How far on this line would the Government go? Only the President could say, and he declined to be prophet.

What else might the Government do? If the people would know that, let them read the cryptic words of newspaper reporters writing under the censorship imposed by the White House press conference.

What a text is there! Government by Executive inspiration. War by Executive impulse.

We shall survive the war. But how? As a government of the people, by the people, for the people? Or as a state that has embraced in the new world what it had wished to destroy in the old?

For it is war. Since the first week of June this country has in fact been at war with Germany. Take it as a simple fact. Suppose we were at war and a government that had been neutral in form, but not in feeling, suddenly opened its arsenals to our enemy, exactly as we have opened ours to the Allies.

Would we regard it as an act of war? We would. What would we do about it? We would declare war on that government, and if for strategic reasons not actually at once, then certainly in our hearts and minds, for a future settlement.

If it should turn out that to strip this country of armaments and send them to Europe at a moment in history when our existing power of national defense was pitifully inadequate and the crisis in Europe was such that no one could say how many hours remained of the British Empire, or that the aggressor might not win, capture the Allied fleet and dictate a peace before enough American aid to turn the battle against him could possibly arrive—if it should turn out that this had been a tragic blunder, beyond recall, then the leader who had done it might wish that his page in the book of fame would refuse to receive ink, for it would be written of him that in his passionate zeal to save civilization in Europe he had forgotten his own country.

On June 10, the day the preceding column was written, Italian forces in Libya attacked British forces in Egypt, beginning the war in North Africa.

On June 12, Roosevelt agreed to Vannevar Bush's proposal to create a National Defense Research Committee to mobilize scientists for the war.

On June 22, the French surrendered. Russia had just seized Latvia, Lithuania and Estonia, and on June 27 it marched into the Romanian province of Bessarabia.

Britain was alone against Germany and Italy.

At this low point of American feeling, Garrett wrote the next piece to remind countrymen of their strength. Change a word or so, and it could be a call to save the world. In Garrett's hands, it was something much different.

There is a Star, July 20, 1940

When the star of world supremacy crossed the Atlantic during World War I, and stood in the American sky, we regarded it with a kind of skeptical wonder. In a little while we were hanging our hat on it.

Almost the first commensurate idea was to build what President Wilson described as incomparably the greatest Navy, not as a weapon so much as a lesson. We did not build it; and the reason why we did not was that then, for the first time and suddenly, other naval powers found respect for the American doctrine of limited armaments. Followed the Washington conference of naval powers, the 5-5-3 treaties,[2] and the pacifist jubilee at the spectacle of our warships being towed out to sea and sunk. We were unbelievably naïve. It was more than a few warships we buried; it was incomparably the greatest Navy.

Our next commensurate idea was to rebuild Europe for a millennium of peace and prosperity. Our exertions during the war, prodigious as they seemed, had not prepared the European imagination for this Aladdin's-lamp era. Not only did it appear that our wealth was inexhaustible; the amazing fact was that access to it was free, only for the asking. We solicited the whole world, especially Europe, to come and get it. The only cost at all was the cost of engraving pieces of paper called bonds, promising sometime to pay us back, and in many cases we paid the engraver, too. Our war debtors came and settled with the United States Treasury by signing such pieces of paper and went gleefully home with more millions in their hands.

We seemed to be doing it with the greatest of ease, even to prosper by it, and it was incredible. Europe began to send her engineers and economists to see how we did it at all, and if it was real. The Germans alone understood what they saw. The machine did it. We had raised machine power to a new dimension. They went home with an idea of their own, which was, as they said, to rationalize German industry; and they borrowed American money to begin it with. From this at last came the German war machine.

The Aladdin's-lamp era blew up, of course. We had the engraved IOU's and the world had our wealth. Then came the depression, and with it a slump in our moral power. There was nothing new in the experience of a depression, but what happened to our morale had never happened before.

We forgot the star. Our resources were intact, our physical powers were not less, but we kept saying to ourselves that a riddle devoured us. Want in the midst of plenty. What was wrong with that system? There was no want such as other people know. Plenty was anything we had resolved to make it. All we had to do to get out of the depression was to take our lesson, write off the loss and go to work.

In view of what was overtaking us, it seems almost puerile to have treated the depression as an extreme national emergency, for whereas then it was only that our mechanism of internal economy had lost its rhythm, now suddenly the world that we live in is in a state of perilous political imbalance, and the great work ahead of us is to restore its equilibrium.

In the whole world, as we have said before, there is one people able to create a defensive power equal to the new power of frightful aggression that has destroyed the basis of international peace and civility. We are that people. It is our work. That is what the star means. That is why it stands there in the American sky. Unless we do it, we shall lose the star. It will become a German star. Until we do it, there can be no rest but in unease, no leisure but in dereliction, no peace but by abnegation.

It is too late to debate whether our foreign policy shall be that of the turtle or the bald eagle. The eagle is our symbol. A solitary people, devoted to peace, yet dangerous to any degree. Not an isolated people. A hemisphere people. Long ago that die was cast in the first shaping of things.

It is now that our true business with destiny begins. That it will make demands upon our moral and physical resources hitherto unimagined is inevitable. Let us look, therefore, at what we are and what we have.

First, we are the most nearly self-contained nation of modern times, an empire entire, possessing of our own in plenty practically every essential thing, including now rubber, which can be made from petroleum. We have no food

58

problem, no umbilical cords to defend. Fewer than one-third the people now engaged in agriculture could produce an abundance of food.

Statistically measured, we have more than two-fifths of all the ponderable, natural, dynamic wealth in the world. We produce more than two-fifths of all the steel in a steel age. We have nearly 60 per cent of the world's oil. That is to speak of materials. What else?

We have the finest and most highly engined machine craft. Our genius for the technics of mass production is incomparable. Other nations learned mass production from us.

Where else is a Ford who could imagine making 1000 airplanes a day, give him a standard design and let him be? It is only American industry that is able to say to its Government: "Tell us what you need, give us priority of materials and transportation, and it shall be produced, anything and in any quantity." We can make 1000 tanks a day; a warship a week if need be. Give the machine-tool industry the specifications and let it alone, and we can make guns with the fingers of women.

Our productive power is equal to that of all Europe, and may be increased, so far as we know, without limit.

Is it something that does not exist? That, too, shall be produced. We have private industries whose research laboratories are unequaled in Europe.

Mechanized warfare suggests that as a people, more than any other we have the feeling of machines in our hands, as you might take for granted, seeing that we have and use three-quarters of all the automobiles in the world. We are probably, too, the most air-minded race.

Finally, as we lie between two oceans, our geographical advantages in the military sense are such as to give us great natural odds against any aggressor.

How could a people with such gifts as these, such possessions and potentialities, entertain even weakly the thought that their free institutions are in peril or that human liberty on this continent is in danger, by reason of the rise of an aggressor principle in the old world? The tone is wrong. This is not the eagle's cry. Let it be said, rather, that danger cometh to any European power or combination of them that dares to think of touching human liberty on this hemisphere or to any that challenges our sovereignty in it.

Addressing the 1940 class at the University of Virginia, the President said young men and women were asking very earnestly what was to become of their country; and they were asking because they had been reading and hearing that the ideals of individual liberty on which it was founded were decadent.

Yet they belong to a people who have not to wonder, but only to resolve, what shall become of their country. If its free institutions are in danger it is because there is wanting the American voice that said to the Holy Alliance of European powers one hundred and seventeen years ago that we should regard "any attempt on their part to extend their system to any portion of this hemisphere as dangerous to our peace and safety"—Monroe's message to Congress, 1823—and again in 1895 to Great Britain: "The United States is practically sovereign on this continent and its fiat is law upon the subjects to which it confines its interposition. . . Why. . . It is because, in addition to all other grounds, its infinite resources combined with an isolated position render it master of the situation and practically invulnerable against any or all other powers."

Whether or not we shall defend the Monroe Doctrine is not the question in its right form. We have been defending it ever since we expelled the old world. Shall we now surrender our sovereignty in this hemisphere? That is the question.

The star is not here to guide us. Nor is it an omen of anything that must come to pass. It may rise to its zenith or go away; and that will be as we succeed or fail with the task our fathers prepared. If it has moved at all in the last ten years, it has been only to decline a little, and that was our fault.

What it means as a sign is that the new world was the magnificent intention of a historical process that comes now to a crisis. The part for which the American people were cast is to save that intention. What does the saving of it require? Only that we shall find again the simple faith and whole will to exert the power we have been building since the beginning, in haste, heedless of waste and ugliness, always as if we were in a feud with time, not knowing what the power was for. Now we know. The rest is foretold in writing we cannot read.

This is Garrett's argument to defend America first. It was not a reluctance to fight Hitler, but a reluctance to fight for Britain or for Europe instead of for America.

While Yet There Is Time to Think, Sept. 7, 1940

In a kind of hypnosis, produced partly by propaganda designed for people who believed themselves to be cynical and immune, partly by a sincere crusading evangel carried on by those whose emotions, as we think, have overcome their reason, but mainly by a Government whose foreign policy, to call it such, has been compounded of a spirit of moral grandeur, inspirational heroics, delusions of a military power not in being, false promises and panic, this country now goes where it does not look and looks where it does not go.

If it should come awake one morning to read in the newspaper headlines, or hear by the radio, that it had walked backward into war, it would take it no doubt as having been somehow inevitable from the first, and yet nobody would be able to say quite how or why it happened.

As the hagfish enters the body of its victim unawares and slowly displaces it by devouring it, so it is that ideas that were clear and virile in the beginning have been devoured by new meanings, with no change in the word shells, until now you may be called anti-American, a fifth columnist or an appeaser if you doubt that the only way to keep America out of the war is to get into it, that to save ourselves we have to first save the British Empire, or that our first line of defense is and always has been the English

Channel.

The *Post's* position cannot be misunderstood. Before the blitzkrieg started, we said: "What we need for practical security is first of all a new word. The word is impregnability, or state of supreme defense. We need more than a bigger Navy. We need two, one for the Atlantic and one for the Pacific, each incomparable. We need an impervious antiaircraft wall. We need to be able to meet not only any aggressor, but any combination of aggressors. Then we may be sure that the principle of free institutions as a basis of modern civilization shall have, beyond the solace of words, a time yet to live in the world."

And that is our position still.

Now the Congress has voted a two-ocean Navy; for this proper sea power, for an approach to adequate air power, and for an army of 2,000,000 men, it has voted in a few weeks extraordinary appropriations rising to ten billions of dollars. We are not interested in the sums. We shall have to spend a great deal more than ten billions to create a power of defense equal to the power of aggression that has made this all at once a pirate world without law, the lean and hungry nations, as Mussolini says, out to take what they can from the fat ones by force. That, too, we have said.

It is defense we are thinking about, not war. And what concerns us now is that this distinction is becoming blurred.

What are we preparing for—defense or war?

Either the Executive Government itself does not know or it is unwilling to clarify the situation with a few positive words. We suppose the reason why it cannot do this is that it is already too much involved in its own confusions. Pursuing the insidious formula of measures short of war, conceived, to begin with, on a gross underestimate of the aggressor's power, it was carried headlong into acts of physical intervention for the consequences and implications of which the country was in every way unprepared, to say nothing of the fact that it acted without the consent of the Congress and beyond the awareness of the people.

In his message to France on June fifteenth, the

President said: "The Government of the United States has made it possible for allied armies to obtain, during the weeks that have just passed, airplanes, artillery and munitions of many kinds, and. . . this Government, so long as the Allied Governments continue to resist, will redouble its efforts in this direction."

That was the United States Government speaking, acting, pledging itself to assist in the war against Hitler in the utmost, short only of an actual declaration of hostilities. It was already too late to save France. Moreover, nothing we had been able to send her, even our total military power, including the Navy, could have saved her, which was a trifling reality the Government was unwilling to comprehend.

Only six weeks later, the Secretary of War is speaking directly for the Administration.[3] He is saying what it thinks. The Administration thinks there is a very grave danger of an invasion of this country by Hitler before we can be ready to meet it. But this is the same Administration that stripped the American defense of rifles, artillery, munitions and airplanes and sent them to the Allies. It is the same Administration that would have delivered to the British Admiralty the whole of our mosquito fleet[4] in building if the Congress had not found a law to stop it. It is the same Administration that has ever since been trying to find a way to deliver U.S. Navy destroyers to the British. If what it thinks is true—that there is grave danger of an invasion of this country by Hitler before we can get ready—then we have not a rifle, a gun, an airplane or a rowboat to spare, nor any industrial capacity. On the day the Secretary of War was making his statement before the House committee the New York newspapers carried pictures of National Guardsmen training with imaginary machine guns devised by plumbers out of gas pipe.

We can imagine circumstances in which the highest strategy would call for taking the war to the enemy. We cannot conceive of circumstances in which it is permitted in sanity to slap danger in the face before you are ready to meet it—to name an enemy who has not named you, to attack an enemy who has not yet attacked you, before you are ready to fight him.

Our enemies, the Administration keeps telling the people, are Germany, Italy and Japan, naming them. Not one of them has made a gesture of war toward us. For all the think and feel about Hitler, he has not attacked us. He says he does not intend to. We do not believe him. Nobody in the world now believes him. Very well. But the American Government has attacked Hitler, first by words, then by measures short of war, then by giving a pledge to his enemies to assist them by all physical means to the utmost.

In June, the American Government entered the war against Hitler by acts of physical intervention, all the worse because they were futile.

In July that same Government is telling the people they are in grave danger of being attacked by Hitler before they can be ready for him. "Hitler does not wait," said the Secretary of War to the House Committee on Military Affairs—and the National Guardsmen in New York training with gas-pipe guns!

What a triumph for statecraft! What strategy!

What a face for a great nation!

These are the conditions under which there has been created in this country a war psychosis, misled by cries of "Stop Hitler Now!" and "Defend America by Aiding the Allies." We had nothing to stop Hitler with in Europe. A Government that either did not know that, or made believe it was not so, now is saying that if he decided to invade the United States soon, as there is very grave danger that he may, we are not ready to stop him here. Nevertheless, it goes on to declare against him an economic war—a Pan American economic bloc against his European bloc—for which it also is unprepared, not having thought it through, not having calculated the cost.

We do not believe that an invasion of the United States is among the imminent possibilities. The word of the Government for it does not greatly impress us. A Government that had been so wrong about his power to overcome in Europe and about the power of France to resist could very well be wrong again. Nor do we believe that fifty or sixty destroyers from the U.S. Navy would save the British Empire. That would be but another futile act of futile intervention, much more likely to infuriate an enemy we are not prepared to meet than to save a friend.

We are bound to be emotionally torn by the spectacle of the British Empire fighting for its life. That is a feeling that lies deep in us and is shared even by those who can think in a realistic manner. The fall of the British Empire would be a mighty human disaster. Yet we part with those who say, or who believe, it would mean the end of American civilization, and part with them again when they would in any degree weaken the American defense to repair the weakness of Great Britain's, for which Great Britain, not we, are responsible. We add here two reflections—first, that Great Britain would be stronger if she had stood alone; second, the enemy is governed by logic, not emotion.

We stand, therefore, in our first position. Let us jealously mind our own defense in the great manner of a great people, resolved to let it alone. Let us build at any cost a dreadnought defense power such as no aggressor, nor any combination of aggressors, will dare to challenge. Thus we forfend war.

And meanwhile, for this will take some time, let us look very hard at the state of facts. The German thing has conquered Europe. That will still be true whether the British Empire stands or falls.

Who is going to put the German thing back? The British? They are not able.

Shall we do it? Unless we are willing to go to Europe and destroy it there, we may as well make our minds up now that we shall have to live in the same world with it, maybe for a long time, whether we like it or not. None the less, for that reason, only all the more, we should, we must, create on this continent the incomparable power of defense. After that we shall see. For after that we shall be again what we were, safe and free and dangerous.

*On August 26, Roosevelt met with a secret British mis-
sion to share defense technology. In September, the British
presented U.S. scientists with the magnetron, the key part of
the radar systems they had been using to detect German
planes over the English Channel.*

*On September 2, without asking Congress—but with the
secret approval of his election opponent, Wendell Willkie—
Roosevelt announced that fifty of the Navy's old destroyers
would be transferred to Britain in exchange for eight bases
on the Atlantic.*

*German planes had been raiding air bases in Britain
since August 8. They began mass bombing of London on
September 7. The next day, Roosevelt declared a state of
emergency and formed the Office of Production
Management to coordinate the production of war material.*

On Going to War, October 19, 1940

How should a great nation go to war, if it goes? The
answer is unhesitating. A great nation should go to
war in a proud, forthright manner, saying what it does and
why it does it, keeping faith at the same time with both its
own laws and the laws of the world.

What have the American people and the American
Government been saying in their moral indictment of the
aggressor? They have been saying that the aggressor
makes war without declaring war, that he breaks the faith
of treaties, that he tramples down the inconvenient law of
the world—and this, of course, is intolerable.

But for all its power of moral judgment, how, in fact,
does this great, proud nation of ours get into a European
war against Hitler?

In November, 1939, after the war started, the Congress
enacted and the President signed a law beginning: "To preserve the neutrality and peace of the United States. . ."
That is the American Neutrality Law, forbidding American
ships to enter combat zones; forsaking, therefore, the old
American doctrine of freedom of the seas as no longer
worth going to war for; and forbidding the sale of arms and

munitions to belligerents, except for cash, and then only provided title is passed at the dock and the belligerents take the stuff away in their own ships—this is the famous cash-and-carry formula.

It is notorious, nevertheless, that the American Government is not neutral. The people are bound by the Neutrality Law, but the Government itself has systematically violated it by acts of intervention that were, in fact, acts of war. Then why has the law not been repealed? Because, from the point of view of the executive will, that was not expedient. The executive will was resolved to intervene. The people were not. The people believed what the Government said, that it was keeping them out of war by measures short of war, and when measures short of war had led to acts of war they could be sooner persuaded to condone a policy of subterfuge and degradation of law than to accept all at once the status of belligerency.

So long as it insists that its legal status is that of a neutral, the United States is in honor bound to keep Article 6 of the Hague Convention XIII, 1907, which is solemnly signed. This international treaty reads that "the supply in any manner, directly or indirectly, by a neutral power to a belligerent, of warships, ammunition or war materiel of any kind whatever, is forbidden."

The American Government's first violation of that treaty was by artifice. Army and Navy planes were returned to the factories that made them, for trade-in, on condition that they be sold immediately to the Allies. It was a legal fiction only that this was not a transaction between the American Government and the belligerents. Then artifice was abandoned, because it limited the action, and the American Government next out of its own arsenals supplied Great Britain with fifteen shiploads of arms and munitions.

In further violation of the Hague Convention and in violation also of the first rule of the Treaty of Washington, 1871, which says that a neutral nation is obliged "to use like diligence to prevent the departure from its jurisdiction of any vessel intended to cruise or carry on war," the

American Government went on to release a part of the U.S. Navy to join the British against Hitler.

This was the famous matter of the fifty destroyers delivered to Great Britain in exchange for rights of use and leasehold in certain air and naval bases in this hemisphere. The President did this as an act of his own will, without the knowledge of Congress, and presented it to the Congress as a *fait accompli*. To go to the aid of Great Britain with fifty destroyers or any other part of the U.S. Navy, provided only the Congress and the people were willing, it would not be necessary for the American Government to break the faith of treaties. It would be necessary only for it to embrace the status of a belligerent, in place of the status of a neutral. Then what it did would have been perfectly lawful, according to the law of the world. But it was easier to break the obligation of treaties than to bring the country to a belligerent status.

In this destroyer transaction the American Government not only violated the country's international treaty obligations; it violated at the same time two American laws. First, it violated the cash-and-carry provisions of the Neutrality Act. Great Britain did not come and get the destroyers at an American dock. They were delivered to her at a Canadian port by American sailors. Secondly, it violated an older piece of statute law, and this is a curious story. In June, by accident, the Congress discovered that the Government by executive will had released to Great Britain a number of small fast torpedo boats, called the mosquito fleet, then building for the U.S. Navy. The Congress was about to accept this as a *fait accompli* when it found on the statute books a law that had been passed in 1917, positively forbidding such a thing to take place. That law reads as follows:

"During a war in which the United States is a neutral nation, it shall be unlawful to send out of the jurisdiction of the United States any vessel built, armed or equipped as a vessel of war, or converted from a private vessel into a vessel of war, with any intent or under any agreement or contract, written or oral, that such vessel shall be delivered to a belligerent nation," under pain of fine and imprisonment.

No one could possibly mistake the meaning or intent of that law; and when the executive Government was confronted with it, the sale of the mosquito fleet to Great Britain was canceled.

All the same, the executive will was resolved to send the fifty destroyers, and did send them; and when the President notified the Congress of this *fait accompli,* he pinned to his message an opinion from the Attorney General concerning the law which had saved the mosquito fleet and which Congress had thought made any secret sale of warships impossible. Go back and read the law again before reading what the Attorney General said. He said the law meant only that a vessel built with intent to be delivered to a belligerent was forbidden to leave the jurisdiction of the United States; he said the law did not apply to a vessel already built and built without that intent. The profound absurdity follows that the law would forbid the transfer to Great Britain of a little unfinished torpedo boat and not the transfer of a fleet of destroyers, a fleet of submarines, a cruiser or a battleship, already built and belonging to the U.S. Navy.

So you see how a great, proud nation like this might get into a war on the placing of a comma or on the upside-down reading of a clause suspended between two points of punctuation. Why was it necessary for the executive Government to procure the legal department to interpret away the meaning of the law? Because only the Congress could repeal or change the law, and this it would have refused to do. That it would have refused is certain, for only a few days before, it had particularly affirmed the law as it was.

In its anxiety to intervene in the war, the executive will was all the time running far ahead of both the Congress and the people. To do what it was resolved to do, it was obliged to go around the law if it could, to outwit it when it couldn't, or in the extreme case, to break it. And not only could it do this with impunity, by reason of having a submissive majority in the Congress; when it had cleverly succeeded, all those who had wished to have the thing done in spite of law shouted their applause.

Remark you, this occurs not only in the streets but in the Congress; there the lawmaking power itself is heard applauding the executive will for putting the law in its place.

You have the spectacle of the Congress defending the *fait accompli,* beyond any law. To a member of the minority who is saying that the sale of a part of the United States Navy to Great Britain is in violation of both international law and the law of the United States, a member of the majority retorted that, if the opposition is so jealous for legality, let it introduce a resolution to ratify the acts of the executive will and then everything will be lawful.

On the part of the submissive majority there is the sentiment expressed by one, saying, "Just any way so England got the ships is all I wanted." Or the thought now commonly heard, even in the Congress, "Why stand upon law against an aggressor who knows not law?"

There is the Secretary of War saying, "It is not a question of complying with formalities like declaration of war. Nations do not declare war now. They wage war."

There is the Secretary of the Navy[5] saying of the transfer of the fifty destroyers, "As for the deed bringing us closer to war, that isn't so. We were in bad with Germany long before this."

What was the moral case against the aggressor? That he made war without declaring war, that he broke the faith of treaties, that he was contemptuous of the inconvenient law of the world—and that this was all intolerable, for if ungoverned will should prevail over law there would be a time without law, and a time without law would be a time of chaos.

How ready we are to see what is taking place in the world. A moral debacle of frightful proportions. All law between nations breaking down. Without it, the arch will fall. The idea is that the American Government shall be a Government of laws, not a Government of men. You may read it engraved over the doorway to the United States

Supreme Court. But is not the meaning of it in the American heart eroding away?

The most ominous event in the history of the American Government has been the sudden rise in the power and authority of the executive will. It does not begin now in the emergency of national defense. It began in the economic emergency. With it has come a cynical attitude toward the law, a contempt for the lawmaking principle, and a version of the democratic process that reduces it to the sound of huzzah.

In the name of great deeds for the general welfare, it began with acts of confiscation and repudiation which the Supreme Court said were immoral but sovereign, that is to say, above any law; then the brain trust and a thousand lawyers hired by the executive Government to beat the Constitution it was sworn to uphold, the attempt to pack the Supreme Court, a letter from the President to a member of Congress hoping a little matter of constitutionality would not stand in the way, surrender by Congress of the public purse, the stamping of laws unread as they came from the hand of the executive.

As the light of the legislative power grows dim the flame of executive power burns higher, until for one day the Senate for a moment stops aghast at what it finds itself debating. It has already accepted an act of war as a fait accompli, hoping only that the war will stay away; and now it is debating a proposal to give the President power, in time of peace, to suspend all laws, in the name of national defense. Absolute Government by executive will. One senator says he could not have imagined living to see this day. And that is all. It is an unreported incident.

What we attempt to account for is the fact that a great, proud nation, facing the awful grandeur of war, has lost the clarity of the idea it would fight for. A habit of violence toward the inconvenient law disinclines it to see the enormity of violating the law of the world and the faith of its own treaties in order to move against a lawless aggressor. It finds itself involved in moral contradictions, double meanings, the confusions of dialectic.

In his message to the Congress to notify it that he had delivered fifty destroyers to Great Britain in exchange for air and naval bases, the President said: "This is not inconsistent in any sense with our status of peace. Nor is it a threat against any nation."

That is the characteristic kind of half-saying that has so befuddled the national thinking. To acquire the air and naval bases was not inconsistent with a status of peace, nor a threat to any nation. That half is true. If we had bought them with money, the statement would be entirely true. As it stands it is half untrue, for to send in exchange a part of the U.S. Navy to fight against Hitler was inconsistent with a status of peace; it was more than a threat against any nation; it was an act against Germany, an act of war.

The only justification for sending the ships would be the conviction that the battle of Great Britain was our battle too. That is not our conviction. We resist it.

But if that were our conviction, we should be ashamed of a status of peace.

If that were our conviction, we should be denouncing the law and idea of neutrality as pusillanimous.

And if we believed that to be the conviction of the country, the fact that it would break the faith of its treaties in order to clothe its acts against Hitler in a fiction of neutrality sooner than accept a status of belligerent would fill us with humiliation.

And so it is that this great, proud American nation would go to war, if it went—to a war that it is already in, but stays out of—under a Government that is no longer a Government of law entirely, nor quite yet a Government of men, but one of a middle kind in transition, that must for that reason say what it is not doing and do what it is not saying.

From going to war, or from going toward it, there will be a coming back. Will the keystone hold or will the arch have fallen? And if the arch were fallen, what would victory mean?

On September 26, 1940, in response to Japanese moves on French Indochina, Roosevelt forbade all shipments of steel and scrap iron outside of Britain and the Western Hemisphere. Japanese had been buying shiploads of scrap steel on the West Coast.

On September 27, Japan signed the Tripartite Pact with Germany and Italy, formally joining the Axis. Each pledged to defend the others if attacked by a power not presently at war—which meant, in practical terms, the United States and Russia.

Chapter two notes

[1] The original says "power," but Baruch wrote Garrett that the word had been "powder."

[2] The Washington Naval Treaty of 1922 limited capital ships to 525,000 tons each for the U.S. and Britain and 315,000 for Japan, for a ratio of 5-5-3.

[3] Henry L. Stimson, 1867-1950. A pro-intervention Republican, he had been secretary of war for William Howard Taft and secretary of state for Herbert Hoover. Roosevelt named him secretary of war in 1940.

[4] These were PT boats. In June 1940 the Senate Committee on Naval Affairs was chasing after a rumor that the Navy was planning to give old destroyers to Britain—a true rumor, as it turned out later—and the Navy officer there to testify was asked if there were any other vessels being given to Britain. The next day the acting Secretary of the Navy told the committee chairman that 11 motor torpedo boats and 12 sub chasers, called "the mosquito fleet," had been disposed of. Even though the wooden boats were new, the Navy had decided on a new design, and was giving them to the British. The acting Navy secretary tried to take responsibility for this benevolence himself, but when it was pointed out that it was illegal for him to give away U.S. vessels to a foreign power, the White House announced that it had ordered the thing. When Rep. Francis Case, R-S.D., pointed out that *that* was against a 1917 law, President Roosevelt called the mosquito fleet back. It was one of the antiwar forces' few victories.

[5] Frank Knox, 1874-1944, was publisher of the Chicago Daily News in the 1930s and Republican nominee for Vice President in 1936 with Alf Landon. One of several Republican interventionists brought into the Roosevelt administration, Knox was made secretary of the Navy in 1940. He had been an Army officer in World War I and a Rough Rider in 1898.

Chapter Three
SACRIFICE

This editorial, on changing the New Deal's mindset about work, is one of Garrett's best.

Work, August 10, 1940

It is Saturday morning in Indiana. The two owners of a machine shop are at the drawing board designing parts for heavy turret lathes. They have many urgent orders. The machine parts they make are needed for the national defense. But the shop is silent. Why? Because the men have already worked their statutory forty hours for the week, and anything more than that would be overtime at penalty wages.

Legally and artfully we have lightened the yoke; yet it may be that God's second arrangement with Adam shall not be so easily broken.

France was in flight from the curse of work. The hours of labor were foreshortened by law, wages were raised by law, the workers controlled the speed of production, and disputes about it were settled sometimes by locking the boss in until he gave up and sometimes by locking him out. Now France is a slave nation.

In Great Britain the rise of labor to political eminence as a self-regarding class was one of the magnificent social gains of the century. Now Great Britain is fighting for her life.

In Russia, where labor was puppet king, the hours of

toil have been lengthened by decree. Why? In order that a proletarian state, like any other aggressor, may increase its military exertions for purposes of conquest.

In the moment of going to war, Mr. Mussolini's swollen adrenal glands caused him to betray all the silly ideologies in which the aggressors had clothed their intentions. The war, he said, was a war between the lean and hungry nations that had got the power, and the rich, soft nations that had lost it; and now the lean and hungry ones were going to take what they wanted.

How did they get the power—the lean and hungry ones? Their natural resources were inferior.

Look back at what was taking place in the world. The principal great powers were eight. Three were richer than the other five together. They had higher standards of living, a softer culture, more than two thirds of the world's material wealth, not to speak of their social gains, but they were all in flight from work. These three were the United States, Great Britain and France, now commonly called the democracies.

The five were the lean and hungry ones. And what were they doing? While the three were limiting and reducing their hours of labor, the five were extending theirs. While the three were saying the machine was to relieve man of toil and if only they could think of a law to distribute in a social manner the plenty the machine had made possible, everybody could have more with less and less work, what were the five saying? They were saying the machine was to enable people to perform more work, not less. It was their means to power.

The first consequences were economic. The five, especially Germany on one side and Japan on the other, working harder and consuming less, pressed cheaper goods on all the markets of the world. The three were unwilling to meet this competition. To protect their higher standards of living and their social gains, they put tariff barriers against those cheaper goods. The American tariff was specifically designed to equalize differences in the cost of production, for of course it was unfair that goods produced by people working sixty to seventy hours a week at low wages should be permitted to compete with goods produced by people working forty hours a week at high wages.

But the lean and hungry nations, especially Germany, worked all the harder and consumed still less and sold goods over all tariff barriers; and they did it because they had to buy the materials they needed for the war machines they were building.

What follows is the dire consequence. Tariff walls are an economic protection but of no military value whatever. What a pleasant world it would be if you could stop the aggressor with a prohibitive tariff, or by a tariff law equalize a disparity of military power!

Work inherits the earth. The power of the aggressor is an idea externalized by work. What the dictator commands is labor. Note where it was where the social malady of unemployment became chronic. Not in the lean and hungry countries. It was the problem of the three rich countries, and most acute in the richest of all, our own. Only a rich country can afford unemployment.

In his annual message to Congress, January 4, 1939, President Roosevelt said: "The first duty of our statesmanship today is to bring capital and man power together. Dictatorships do this by main force. . . However we abhor their methods, we are compelled to admit that they have obtained substantial utilization of all their material and human resources. Like it or not, they have solved, for a time at least, the problem of idle men and idle capital."

We are looking at it, but in an oblique manner, not seeing it for what it was. We kept thinking and writing about it as Nazism, Communism, a philosophy of state, or what else, whereas it was a very old thing. Those who will intelligently and purposefully perform the most work will possess the world. Either they will dominate it economically or they will take it by force, and there is no help for it. But we made no such deduction. Neither did Great Britain or France.

We went on slowing down our industrial machine, killing our surplus, limiting the hours of labor, dividing the

work, subsidizing youth to keep it in school and off the
labor market, giving pensions to the elders in order to
retire them sooner from the labor market at the other end
of the scale, spending more than a billion a year in unemployment relief—and then, when all of this notwithstanding, the more abundant life with still less work did not
appear, the brilliant little doctors at Washington began to
write and lecture on the strange case of a young country
that was prematurely and suddenly old. We were arriving
at what they called a static economy. Never again would
there be work enough for everybody. That was the best
thing they could do who did not know what they were
doing. The Government did not know. The people did not
care too much to know, because the evangel of an easier
life, everyone who had not had enough now to have more by
less exertion, was extremely attractive.

For a free people it is the law of necessity that acts in
the place of a dictator. But it is a very hard law, and it is
human to rebel against it. Here was a Government saying
there was an easier way, saying there was already plenty
and surplus if only it were properly divided. Leave that to
the Government. It would plan the economic scheme and
administer it. On borrowed money, and it may be on borrowed time, it undertook first to restore old values and
then stabilize them, to regulate production, to support the
wage structure, the price structure and the capital structure, all at one time. For purposes of this balanced economy there was apparently a surplus of labor. That was said
to mean only that the wage earner had been working too
hard to support the private-profit motive. The thing to do,
therefore, was to shorten the hours of labor; less work for
the same pay, and everybody to have more than before.

First, the revolt against necessity, the fantasy of producing less and consuming more, the surrender of self-
responsibility to a Government that said it knew this
magic—and then the flight from work.

We have always been a very hard-working people, and
for that reason we have been able to accumulate an enormous surplus of wealth. The existence of that surplus and

the free distribution of it by the Government, downward through the social structure, created for a time the delusion that the magic was true. But it could last only until we had devoured, used up, worn out, our surplus wealth.

We were coming to the end of it. Our standard of living was beginning to fall, simply for the reason that we were not performing enough work to maintain it, and thoughtful minds were already in a state of acute anxiety as to the sequel, when suddenly the country was faced with the unexpected necessity to prepare a national defense beyond anything hitherto imaginable.

The emergency is one that involves our destiny; it may be our survival as a free people; it calls for us to work harder, perhaps, than we have ever worked before. Yet almost the first thing the President said was: "There is nothing in our present emergency to justify making the workers of our nation toil at longer hours than those limited by statute." And he has been saying it ever since. The statutory hours of labor are now the lowest point we have ever known. That is the position the Government takes; it becomes naturally the fixed position of organized labor.

Billions for national defense. We vote them—like that! Billions to any number for the American destiny. But no harder work. No increase in the hours of labor. Not that.

Would that it were so. Would also that it were a world without war or aggressor in it. The reality is bitter.

We cannot buy defense. There is nobody to buy it from.

We cannot spend these billions we are voting unless by our own labor we produce the ships and planes and guns and machine equipment they are for; and to produce them in time, or at all, we shall have to work harder.

We cannot prepare an adequate national defense and at the same time afford our present standard of living unless we enormously increase the production of all things.

We cannot increase it by voting billions. It can be increased only by more work.

Above any law that we can make, there is a jealous law of work. It was passed at the gate of the Garden of Eden, with man on his way out. Man's entire history since then has been the story of his struggle to overcome it. He has had the cunning to invent for himself a race of mechanical slaves and still he cannot beat it.

The Mental Bottleneck, September 14, 1940

Now comes a vogue for saying that if man power is going to be drafted, so also it should be done to wealth. Conscript wealth for the national defense. This sounds at first both fair and plausible. But we wish those who keep repeating it would think it through. We do not know what they mean and we wonder if they know themselves.

Suppose the man who is drafted happens to have a net worth of $25,000. Shall his wealth be drafted with him? That cannot be what they mean. He will have been drafted to defend free institutions, and one of these is the institution of private property. That is to say, he will have been drafted to defend his own, and it would not be fair to demand of him also that which he defends.

Then they will say that what they mean is idle wealth. That is the kind of wealth that shall be conscripted. But this man's wealth may be idle. He may have buried it in a tin can, which was one of the things he was free to do, and would not in any way make it fair to demand it from him.

Probably what they think they mean is that the wealth of the rich may be drafted. Conscript great wealth for the national defense. Thus you come to the old idea of a capital levy—old in Europe, but new here. It presents difficulties which have never yet been solved, even in theory. Suppose you strike a horizontal line through one of the lower income-tax brackets and say that everyone above that line shall hand over to the Government a certain proportion of his wealth—a tenth, a quarter or one third. How shall it be liquidated and be made available to the government? Shall people sell their stocks and bonds and shares of proprietorship and give the proceeds to the Government? That seems very simple. But to whom could they sell? Such liquidation would either wreck the financial structure or oblige the Government to support it with borrowed money. Maybe then, instead of trying to liquidate their own investments, the people should turn them over to the Government direct. But what could the Government do with them until it had sold them? And to whom could the Government sell them?

But it is unnecessary to consider the difficulties or the implications. So long as we mean to keep the free system of private property, the idea of a capital levy is absurd. To realize how absurd it is, you have to ask but one question. Why should the Government bother about the golden goose at all when, with no trouble or risk whatever, it can take the golden eggs? All the goose is for is to produce the eggs— that is to say, income. If the Government owned all the great wealth there is, the goose entire, it could get only the income, which would be probably less than it was before, whereas there is no limit that we know of to the amount of income it may take by taxation, leaving only enough for the bare living of the goose that produces it.

Drafting income for the national defense, or for war, is perfectly feasible. And if that is what they mean, the answer is that income is already subject to conscription, and has been for a long time. When we shall begin really to pay for the defense program, it will be drafted pale.

But there is a difference between drafting income and drafting capital. The income from wealth is helpless. That, we say, can be drafted. Capital, by distinction, is wealth in the dynamic character, possessing and exercising powers of discretion, judgment and will. Recently there has come against it the accusation that in the national emergency it bargains hard and selfishly and threatens to be recalcitrant; and the feeling that would justifiably rise if this were true has been fat to every cauldron of hate that is bubbling. This we shall try to clarify.

More than three months after the beginning of the defense program, with billions lying on the table to be spent, the Government was still higgling with industry over profit. First, the Congress passed a law to limit the private profit on Army and Navy contracts. Then the question was how that profit should be calculated. If a manufacturer had to invest a million dollars in new machinery and plant, which would be worthless when the contract was completed, at what rate would he be permitted by the Internal Revenue Bureau to charge depreciation as cost before counting a profit. "Amortization" was the word. Amortization wrongly calculated could ruin the manufacturer in the end, though his apparent profit had been 10 or 12 per cent while performing the contract. On the other hand, amortization overestimated might make him rich. And beyond all this was an x factor in the form of an excess-profits tax yet to be imposed, at whatever rate the Congress might deem necessary.

Well, that a matter of profit more or less should be holding up the defense program was intolerable. The public would not long be patient, and once public opinion began to act, it would be likely to assess the blame in a brutal manner. Recriminations began, but whereas on the part of industry they were guarded, for fear of offending the Government, on the popular side they were loud and harsh. It began to be said that capital was on a sit-down strike, refusing to take contracts for the national defense until it was permitted to write the kind of contract it wanted. And all this made fertile ground in which to cultivate the thought of compulsory military service for capital.

The unfortunate fact is that the relations between business and Government are shot with animosity and distrust. Business could not forget that the New Deal set out to conquer the free competitive profit system. Now, for the country's sake, the Government needs the confidence of business and cannot command it.

In his fireside chat on the emergency, on May twenty-sixth, the President spoke of his seven-year "offensive on a broad front against social and economic inequalities," and that it "should not now be broken down by the pincers movement of those who would use the present needs of physical military defense to destroy it." That was a bad beginning. Suspicion implanted beforehand. There had been no pincers movement.

He went from there to say that of all the social and

economic classes that had become beneficiaries of the New Deal, not one should be obliged in this emergency to surrender its advantage or profit—not agriculture, not labor, certainly not the underprivileged class; the whole new system of social security should be extended, in fact, the emergency notwithstanding. "Private industry," he said, "will have the responsibility of providing the best, speediest and most efficient mass production of which it is capable." But let it beware! "The American people will not relish the idea of any American citizen growing rich and fat in an emergency of blood and slaughter and human suffering!"

You would not expect this oblique and gratuitous aspersion to re-create a basis of confidence between industry and Government. It was largely fear that made the manufacturer unwilling to accept contracts on faith, subject to laws and regulations yet to be enacted, and leave his skin in the hands of the Government. He, therefore, insisted on a contract that would let him out whole, with some hope of profit over. The Government on the other side of the table was controlled by its old suspicions, and deeply resolved that whatever else happened, there should not come out of this what the President had called a "new group of war millionaires."

In that atmosphere they debated the fictions of amortization, the principles of cost accounting, the life cycle of machines, legal filigree, writing contracts and tearing them up—and all the time the national defense was waiting! For more than three months it waited. There was talk of bottlenecks in engines, bottlenecks in machine tools, here and there, retarding the program, but the first and worst bottleneck of all was Washington.

Our acquaintance with the American citizen is various and fairly wide. We do not know the one that would grow "rich and fat in an emergency of blood and slaughter and human suffering." We suppose that his frequency in the world of business and industry would be about the same as that of the criminal in the total population.

It is our conviction that never before has American industry been less minded to profiteer in defense, never more anxious to do its part effectively, with or without profit. It knows very well that even an extraordinary profit is likely in the end to prove illusory and that it will be lucky to save its hide. We think its behavior will compare not unfavorably with that of organized labor, whose gains, the Government says, both in wages and leisure, shall be immune.

Nevertheless, labor is for pressing them. The United Automobile Workers of America, CIO, beginning a drive to organize the aircraft industry, says: "The campaign will be carried on with complete realization of the needs of our national-defense program. . . Unionization of the aircraft industry and the establishment of fair standards for labor will make strikes unnecessary."

So much to be fair. And yet fairness is not the last word. Profiteering or recalcitrant capital, like profiteering or recalcitrant unions, should be and would be swept away. That is not all. The imperatives of defense are such that the very word "profit" would become hateful if too much insistence upon the use and principle of profit began dangerously to impede the work of preparedness.

This we are saying to both capital and labor. There would not be time to argue about it. There would be only time to take the alternative way. And the alternative way would be total compulsion first of capital and then of labor. Thus the end of the free competitive system, and in place of it, by any name you like, the totalitarian state. And that would be a sequel perhaps not very displeasing to some of those who keep saying that we should be drafting wealth for the national defense along with man power, on democratic grounds of equality and justice.

This might be thought a strange editorial from Garet Garrett, defender of individualism. But when the nation of liberty was threatened, he was a nationalist. He saw no contradiction in calling for sacrifice in which "people lose themselves" to defend their country.

84

The Spirit Would, September 21, 1940

We have had so many letters on the editorial, Work, in the August tenth issue, that we feel obliged to return to the subject and make the emphasis unmistakable.

First, however, a word about the letters. Roughly estimated, four out of five were commendatory, and of these it seems enough to say that the point of view had no consistent relation to any political, social or private economic interest. It is not the first time that we have observed this behavior of the American mind in situations of stress, hence our deep respect for the final verdicts of public opinion.

We had uttered a very hard truth. We had challenged the President's assertion that there was nothing in the present emergency "to justify making the workers of our nation toil for longer hours than those limited by statute"—namely, the legal week of forty hours. The emergency, as we said, is one that involves our destiny, it may be our survival as a free people; it calls to us to work harder than ever before, whereas the fact is we are working less than ever before, under a limitation of law.

We could hardly have expected the reaction of union labor to be favorable. Yet one of the very fine letters we received was from a man responsibly representing union labor, who wished it were possible for every person in the United States to read what we had said, and who himself wrote: "We cannot win this race against a totalitarian form of government by men and minds which are only geared to indulge in the pleasurable things of life and to work accordingly. You must put iron through the crucible before you can make steel."

Immediately, however, we are more concerned with that one letter in every five that was adverse. In nearly all of that kind it was evident that what the writers expected and took to be inevitable was what the President suggested in his fireside chat on the national defense, in May, when he spoke of those who by a kind of "pincers movement" would take advantage of the emergency to destroy, if they could, the social gains of seven years, and of others who might be thinking to grow "rich and fat in an emergency of blood and slaughter and human suffering." Were we on the side of these? Were we assisting the pincers movement?

One wrote: "I don't believe you want labor to go back and work six days a week." Another: "If you think we are going to go back to that, brother, you are nuts." Another: "Your reactionary editorial is well in accord with the ideas of those who hope the defense program will furnish the excuse to abolish every social gain made since 1932." Again: "If at the worst every airplane should cost 20 per cent more, what of it? War and war materials are made for waste." And again: "Mr. Knudsen[1] flies home every week end. He is a wise man and knows he can do a better job in five days than in seven."

Mr. Knudsen, we understand, gives his time to the Government. He is probably rich. He can afford to do it. But every man who has skill in his hands is in that way rich and has something he can afford to give to his country.

There was a third group of letters expressing bewilderment. Why talk of increasing the task of those who work while there are still millions unemployed? The answer is that unemployment is a sore and separate problem, one that we had not solved before. Generally speaking, the unemployed are not those who have in their hands what the national defense requires of labor—at least, not what it requires at first.

Let us now speak of one thing at a time—of social gains, to begin with, meaning all those ameliorations of our terms with life which in a free humane society take place naturally and inevitably as people progress in wealth. They are made possible not by law, as many seem to think, not by any kind of progressive legislation, but by work well done before, by the thrift and self-denial of those who consumed less than they produced in order that their children might have more. One of the social gains was the forty-hour week, decreed by law. But so was the forty-four-hour week before it a social gain, without any law, and the forty-eight-hour week before that, and all that shortening of the hours of toil took place naturally, and was bound to take place as the productivity of labor was increased by science, technology and invention.

There is no social gain of the last seven years, or the last seventy, that we would annul. But whether we would or not, has nothing to do with it. Social gains such as society can afford are irreversible. Never do people go back if they can help it. But social gains that cost more than society can afford, especially those that are founded on a doctrine of dividing what there is instead of producing more, are bound in a little time to annul themselves. If we have been critical of any of the social gains of the last seven years, it was upon the ground, not that they were undesirable or in time unattainable, but that they were imposed and not evolved, and that we were not at the same time providing the means wherewith to sustain them. If that was true, the time would come when people would have to go back, having devoured their surplus, and then there would be serious trouble, for it is true that people rebel more at going back than at not having gone forward.

We said it again and again, and we affirm it still, that the total amount of work being performed—which is to say, production—was not enough to support what we were calling our social gains. It was not enough to sustain the standard of living to which we had become accustomed. We were living an illusion. We were consuming more than we produced. Our machines were wearing out; we were eating them up. With the population increasing, the trend of production was downward. Obsolescence was increasing at an alarming rate. The employed, with the shortest work week and the highest hourly wages ever known, were supporting the unemployed and did not realize it. Taxes had been raised to the point of diminishing returns, so there was very little further to go in that direction. And the Federal Government, which had been shoring it all up with borrowed money, had stopped trying to balance its budget.

Suddenly there is the necessity to divert at least one fifth, probably one quarter, of our total productive power to

87

the creation of weapons to defend our place in the world, and to do it in a wasteful manner because it must be done in haste. We cannot eat and wear and enjoy armaments. For purposes of living, they are a total loss. Every airplane, warship, gun and tank must be in lieu of something we might otherwise have produced toward better living. We cannot prepare this mighty defense and go on living as before. We cannot prepare it at all and maintain anything like our present standard of living without doing much more work.

It is an ordeal we face. There is no easy way through. To say beforehand what we will or will not go back to, what we will or will not give up, or to think we can do it by borrowing money from ourselves and taxing the rich and passing a law against profit, is only to look away. To debate equality of sacrifice is folly. There is no time for it. If the household is worth defending at all, it is worth defending as it is and as a whole. If it should fall, it would fall as a whole, social gains and all.

The pincers are German pincers. Whether we like it or not, we are obliged to meet the competition of the aggressor, in military terms immediately and in economic terms thereafter, else we shall not be able to keep our world.

What that means is work, more and more work, forgetting the hours. And as we think of work, it is more than the task of the hand and the bench and lathe and throttle. It is more than activity of the mind added to that of the hand. There will come a time for self-denial, certainly. And then those will indirectly contribute work who forebear to consume it in the form of pleasurable satisfactions and devote the equivalent to national defense, as, for example, by lending their money to the Government, thereby supporting the public credit.

Labor unwilling to give up more hours, capital unwilling to forget its profit, wealth unwilling to part with its income, cannot be supposed to represent the American spirit in this time of crisis. We disbelieve it. We believe, to the contrary, that all are willing. It is only that the all-demanding, all-compelling, selfless passion of patriotism has not been lighted. The leadership capable of lighting it has not existed.

Who has yet sacrificed his leisure, his pleasure, his profit or advantage to the national defense? Of whom has it been demanded?

Not for anything it does for them do people love their country. It is what they do for their country, giving and dying for it, that makes them love it with a fierce and jealous love. We seem to have forgotten that. Only in sacrifice do people lose themselves and find that unity of feeling toward which the American spirit now gropes its way, and gropes because it is not led.

The first conscription bills were introduced June 20 and 21, 1940, as the French were signing the papers of surrender. The U.S. Army, then 255,000 men, would be increased to 500,000. Roosevelt endorsed the idea in his acceptance speech July 19 for the Democratic nomination. Wendell Willkie, the Republican challenger, did the same in his acceptance speech August 17. The anti-interventionist side was split. Charles Lindbergh supported the draft. Historian Harry Elmer Barnes opposed it as "the first step to American fascism." Garrett supported it, but with strong misgivings on the purpose for which it was done.

Conscription, September 28, 1940

When the paper it is printed on has become friable with age, a writer of American history may open the *Congressional Record* of August 22, 1940, and read the following caption in small capitals: "A MATTER OF PERSONAL PRIVILEGE UPON HAVING BEEN HANGED IN EFFIGY BEFORE THE CAPITOL FOR FAVORING THE SELECTIVE SERVICE ACT AND AID TO ENGLAND SHORT OF WAR."

The senator who thereupon rose and addressed the chair had this to say about it: "Mr. President, yesterday I had the unique experience of being hanged in effigy in front of the Capitol of the greatest democracy in the world. I think perhaps it might be considered something of a compliment for the stability of our institutions for this information to reach the dictators abroad, because I can hardly imagine a member of the German Reichstag being hanged in effigy in front of the building of that assembly in Germany."

Women in crape, calling themselves the death watch, were sitting in a row outside the Senate chamber when another senator rose and said to the chair: "Mr. President, let us assume that you have come here from another planet and that you are seeking to know what governments are free; you wish to know what governments on this planet are peopled by free men. Philosophical student as you are, Mr. President, you would not look to the Army and the Navy. You would visit the parliament. Freedom of debate in the people's forum and the absolute freedom with which the people criticize their parliament betoken liberty and a free government."[2]

That writer of American history whom we imagine to be turning these pages when they are yellow and have the honorable smell of archives will know what the sequels were. He will know what survived of the old American forms and the shape of what else came; he will know what fears and anxieties turned out to be false and which were true. It may be clear to him, therefore, that what Congress was really debating in the guise of "Bill (S.4164) to protect the integrity and institutions of the United States through a system of compulsory military training and service."

History was taking place. Everyone knew that. The debate moved on a very high plane. Party lines disappeared. Feeling was intense, but seldom bitter. Extremes of passionate conviction were treated with the utmost respect. Altogether it was a performance worthy of the American Congress in its best tradition and a memorable justification of the free parliamentary method. Yet notwithstanding the wonders of the modern news system, it was imperfectly reported. Speeches that would have been printed in full fifty years ago, before we knew so many ways of saving time, received day after day less newspaper space than the war communiqués from Europe.

The subject was not conscription. That was only the
title. Certainly the draft is no new thing among us. The volunteer is our ideal defender. But then you come to total
war or total defense, and the volunteer method is unscien-
tific. In the modern case of war, the system of selective
compulsory service is what Woodrow Wilson said it was—
"not a conscription of the unwilling but selection from a
nation that has volunteered en masse." The rational arguments for it are invincible.

Nor was it simply a question of whether or not the
necessity for adequate preparedness, and preparedness in
time, required the conscription of man power, for if the
principle of conscription be not denied, then whether you
shall resort to it beforehand ought to be a matter of judgment, based upon facts concerning the nature of the emergency and the imminence of danger.

It is true that conscription in time of peace—that is to
say, beforehand—was entirely new. That had never been
proposed before. It is true also that much of the debate did
turn upon that point. Nevertheless, those who kept saying
that conscription in time of peace was a step toward military dictatorship, the beginning of the end of our form of
representative government, the first phase of a dictated
unity in the totalitarian manner, were expressing, we
think, partly their distrust of the Executive Government
and its foreign policy and partly their inability to accept
the Government's view of the emergency. If they had been
persuaded that war was inevitable and at hand, even
these, we are sure, would have voted for conscription.

But the anxiety of the Government to pass at once to
conscription without having first exhausted the possibilities of volunteer enlistment, its haste to commit acts of
physical intervention under the fiction "short of war," the
sensational war propaganda it sanctioned, including the
Bullitt[3] speech to make the people's blood run cold, which
had the visa of the State Department—these and many
other signs and omens, all messengers of war clothed in the
arguments of defense, were bound to produce forebodings
that could hardly name themselves. Estimates of the size

of the Army that might be needed ascended in a spiral manner, from around 750,000 to 1,2000,000, then 2,000,000, then 3,000,000 or 4,000,000. What would such an Army be for—defense or war? Were we going to war again in Europe, saying we wouldn't, as we did in 1917? Many of the parallels were ominous. "If we build up a big Army," said one senator, "and in the meantime send our destroyers to aid Britain, I can see a very real prospect that our battleships, our airplanes and our Army will follow the destroyers."

This fear of being dragged backward into war unawares and unprepared ran through the entire debate, and was, we think, well-founded. And yet there was a deeper fear theme. There was something to be feared more than war.

Senator Ashurst[4] said: "When once we put this continental European system upon our people, we shall have done it forever. That is the reason there is so much solemnity in this hour. That is why men on either side of this question are earnestly seeking the truth. . . When you have put a draft upon the people in time of peace, you have touched at Saguntum,[5] you have sown dragon's teeth. . . You will not be able to criticize your Government. You will not be free to criticize your lawmakers when once a military caste is imposed upon you. If you impose this continental European system you will walk out of this chamber having taken from your people more liberty than you ever gave them. . . that I warned my countrymen not to allow themselves to be bound, gagged and shackled by a system European in its nature, which has devastated and destroyed Europe."

Senator Ashurst voted for the draft in World War I. He would not have said then what he said now. There is the difference, of course, that in 1917 the draft was a war measure; we had got into it. But was that the only difference? If that were so, the senator would be saying that a nation may raise an army by conscription as a war measure and still be free, but the same nation may not raise an army by conscription as a preparedness measure, in time to train it, without sacrificing its freedom forever.

War we abhor and dread. The ultimate fear is fear of defeat. Next to that, and still greater than the fear of war, is the fear that in order to overcome the totalitarian principle, or not to overcome it, we shall have to surrender our liberties, such in the extreme example, as the liberty to hang a senator in effigy on the Capitol lawn.

There is fear that liberty as we know it, the liberty we are willing to fight for, is now incompatible with its own defense. What a paradox! If, as a fact, the necessity for conscription as a preparedness measure does exist, it is an unlimited necessity, only beginning there, and no one can say for sure what it will demand and swallow up.

There is the fear, even in the hearts of those who are unreconciled to conscription, that Gen. Charles G. Dawes[6] is right when he says: "At this time when our Government is preparing to be able to meet totalitarian attack, it must proceed with totalitarian speed and efficiency under a powerful central control. . . German civilian industrialists who had been called upon by the German government to assist in military preparedness have been co-ordinated and made responsible directly to Marshal Goering, of the German army. By this method Germany has applied Napoleon's sixty-fourth maxim of war—'nothing is more important than a central command, under one chief.' This has resulted in remarkably efficient civil co-operation in German military preparedness."

Only under military principles, he says, can the American preparedness program move to succeed. A military system adjusted to civil administration.

And all of that is what the Congress was debating, touching it obliquely, fearful of its being either true or untrue, in relation to "a bill to protect the integrity and institutions of the United States through a system of compulsory military training and service." The first of these institutions is liberty; and liberty does not inhabit a military system, except that a people are free, in the first place, to impose it on themselves.

We cannot alter the fact. The principle of free government is in mortal competition with the ruthless totalitarian principle. This competition will continue, even beyond the war into peace, for purposes of economic conquest, so long as the totalitarian principle endures. We cannot believe it will endure for long. If it be not destroyed, it will defeat itself. Meanwhile, however, no one can be sure of what will or will not happen to free government. That will be not as we wish but as necessity may dictate. For in the extreme case even freedom is subject to necessity, and one of its rights would be the right to conscript itself.

SACRIFICE

Chapter three notes

[1] William Knudsen, 1879-1949. He emigrated from Denmark at 21, became president of General Motors during the 1930s and agreed to recognize the United Auto Workers in 1937. He was one of the "dollar-a-year-men" Roosevelt brought in to run the war effort. He made a bid to be czar of war production, but was squeezed out by Donald Nelson, another dollar-a-year-man, and moved to the Pentagon.

[2] The two quotations are approximations of the words in the *Congressional Record*, p. 10,749 and 10,724, but express the essence of it. The "hang in effigy" quote is from Sen. Claude Pepper and the "from another planet" quote from Sen. Henry Ashurst.

[3] William Bullitt was named the first U.S. ambassador to Soviet Russia, in 1933. The experience made him a passionate anti-communist—too passionate for Roosevelt— and in 1936 Roosevelt named him ambassador to France.

[4] Henry F. Ashurst, Democrat of Arizona, 1874-1962. Ashurst was chairman of the Senate Judiciary Committee 1933-1941 and was one of the hard-core supporters of Roosevelt's plan to pack the Supreme Court.

[5] It was the fate of Saguntum, 219 years B.C., to offer heroic, futile resistance. Hannibal conquered it.

[6] Charles G. Dawes, 1865-1951, chief of procurement for the American forces in World War I; formulated the Dawes Plan for postwar reparations; elected Vice President with Calvin Coolidge in 1924; won Nobel Peace Prize in 1925; ambassador to Britain 1929-1932.

Chapter Four
THE STATE

As the Roosevelt administration rushed to help Britain, the anti-interventionists raised the alarm not only about getting into the war, but how the decision was being made. To Garrett, that decision seemed to come from one man, Franklin Roosevelt. And that was part of a larger problem—the swelling of the power of the Executive that had occurred all through the New Deal, and even before.

This Was Foretold, August 24, 1940

In Philadelphia, one hundred and fifty-three years ago, the founders sat. Their task was to reconcile government with liberty. The great ends to be served were two. One was to protect the people against their rulers. The other was to protect the people against themselves—for was it not the lesson of history that people, being liable to passion, suggestible, dreading responsibility, tending by power of majorities to oppress minorities, were wont to sacrifice or surrender their liberties?

"But there is a natural inclination in mankind to kingly government," said Benjamin Franklin to the Convention. "I am apprehensive, therefore, perhaps too apprehensive, that the government of these states may in future times end in monarchy."

They understood what Franklin was saying. They knew what the problem was. The problem was how to limit the power of the executive, who might be called magistrate or president; limit his access to the emotions of the people, lest he persuade them by promises and by eloquence to make him monarch; and at the same time limit the power of the people to act directly upon their own government, lest in fits of sudden feeling or aberration they should act unwisely upon it, to their sorrow. They solved the problem by creating the delicate political mechanism of checks and balances which was the American contribution to the art of government.

The popular principle was established in a House of Representatives, elected directly by the people.

The conservative principle was set up in a Senate, elected not directly by the people but by their several state legislatures.

How to elect the President was long and anxiously debated. If he were elected by the people directly it would be too easy for him to shake hands with Demos and override everything else. If he were elected by the Congress, as some preferred, an ambitious man would be tempted to corrupt the legislative principle and so again make himself monarch. It was decided at last that he should be elected not by the people but by electors chosen by the people. How long his term should be and whether or not he should be chosen for re-election, which would be dangerous, were questions of extreme difficulty. Finally, the term was made four years and the question of re-eligibility was left open.

There was yet a judicial principle to be established. So there was ordained a Supreme Court, the members not to be elected at all, but to be appointed for life by the President, subject to the approval of the Senate.

Nowhere an absolute power. The President could veto a law passed by a majority of Congress; by a two-thirds vote the Congress could pass it over his veto. The Supreme Court could declare a law unconstitutional; the Congress could then amend the law and pass it again, or, if that did not avail, it could move to amend the Constitution; and the Constitution could be changed only by the will of the people. Sovereignty was at last in the people, only that they were bound by the Constitution not to exercise it in an unreflecting or capricious manner.

And it was shrewdly provided that never should the sword and the purse be in the same hand. The President was commander-in-chief of the armed forces; but control of the purse was delivered to the House of Representatives— that is, to the popular principle, which was right, because so long as the people themselves kept the purse in their hands it was certain that they could never be taxed beyond their consent or be made to pay for more government than they wanted.

This was not a democracy. The founders dreaded democracy almost as much as they feared despotism, believing, indeed, that one would tend to produce the other. What they had devised was a system of limited, representative, Constitutional government. In the Papers of Dr. James McHenry there is this quaint footnote of an incident that occurred after the founders had finished their work: "A lady asked Dr. Franklin, 'Well Doctor what have we got a republic or a monarchy. A republic replied the Doctor if you can keep it."

We have not kept it. Step by step, we have moved from being a republic toward becoming an unlimited democracy, until now the word republic has been almost expelled from our political speech.

What then were the steps?

The first was universal suffrage touching all matters whatever, local, regional and national, whereas in the beginning the right to vote was qualified by state laws, generally requiring a modicum of property interest in the commonwealth.

The second was that the business of electing the President was brought closer and closer to direct vote of the people, until now in fact it is direct; it has become a fiction that we choose electors to elect a President.

The third was the election of senators by direct popular vote, instead of by vote of the state legislatures. Thus the conservative principle was destroyed. There is no longer in the scheme of government a conservative principle as such.

Fourth was the graduated income tax. That kind of

taxation was strictly forbidden by the Constitution, and the Constitution, therefore, had to be changed to permit it. The justice of the income tax, everyone to pay according to his ability, is not easily impugned. Exercised in a reasonable manner, under restraint of a conservative principle in government, it might well be the ideal tax. Nevertheless, it makes possible—only would say, inevitable—a vast extension of beneficent government; secondly, it makes possible for an Administration seeking its own power to promise, and to effect, a redistribution of the national wealth in favor of the groups and classes that support it, and so corrupt the electorate. It was for precisely that reason that the Constitution originally forbade the Federal Government to lay taxes except in a uniform manner.

What followed in natural sequence was that inevitable extension of beneficent government, a very great rise in the power and prestige of the executive principle, and then bureau rule over the people by administrative law.

Such were the steps. They were taken slowly at first, with long and thoughtful debate; then faster and faster, sometimes without any debate at all, even without looking. And now, almost unawares, we arrive at the doctrine of indispensability—the doctrine of one leader above all, infallible, who knows better than anyone else what is good for people and how to do it. That idea had been heard before in the extravagance of campaign oratory; never before in this country has it been asserted by the leader himself.

The objects to a third term for President, we think, are not absolute. There is no law against it, only a tradition. If Washington had served a third term and refused a fourth, the tradition, we dare say, would like against a fourth term and not against a third. But this new doctrine of indispensability, which might be only immoderately egoistic, becomes sinister in relation to a background of seven and one-half years during which there has taken place a centralization of power in the Federal Government and a subordination of that power to the will of the executive such as hitherto had been thought impossible under the

Constitution. The sovereignty of states has been systematically eroded by new legislation, by reinterpretation of old law and by a kind of Federal bribery. The Congress, which is the legislative principle, has surrendered or delegated such powers to the President as formerly it had jealously defended. As the power of the President has been exalted, all other powers have been diminished, to a point at which even the judicial principle has been annealed and made responsive to the executive will. Finally, control of the purse was surrendered when Congress began to vote billions to the President to spend in his own discretion.

Briefly, during these seven and one-half years the Roosevelt Administration went further to intervene in the economic and social life of the country, to control it, to plan it, and to administer it, than any other government in the world not already totalitarian in character.

As he was receiving into his hand from an obedient Congress the new instrumentalities of power, Mr. Roosevelt himself remarkably said: "In the hands of a people's government this power is wholesome and proper;" in bad hands, he added, it "would provide shackles for the liberties of people."[1]

And now what is he saying?

He is saying that he alone is the people's government. He alone can be trusted to exercise that power. He is saying that he accepts the nomination for a third term because he is convicted of a duty to keep the government from passing to other hands. The power is too much to lay down. It may be abused. It may be used to provide shackles for the liberties of people.

That is not all. If the power now changes hands the people may lose their liberties in a worse way. The President says that in what he has done to awaken the country to the menace of the aggressor he has been opposed by "appeaser fifth columnists." And: "If our own government should pass to other hands next January—untried hands, inexperienced hands—we can merely hope and pray that they will not substitute appeasement and compromise with those who seek to destroy all democracies everywhere."

That is to say, if the Republican Party wins, the country may be betrayed.

For shame! The pity is that Mr. Roosevelt does not believe it as he says it.

A President of the United States who has arrived at this state of mind is no more a Democrat than he is a Republican or himself a fifth columnist. There is among us no word that defines him, nor ever before was the want of it felt. He is the one whom the founders feared and partly foretold—I, Roosevelt.

To Garrett, President Roosevelt's executive order of September 2, 1940, to send fifty destroyers to Britain was an event of ominous meaning. Aid meant war, and war was the province of Congress. And Roosevelt had not even asked Congress. His attorney general, Robert Jackson, who would be appointed to the Supreme Court the following year, argued that the president did not need to ask Congress, and that a law that had been passed by Congress that prohibited what Roosevelt had done did not apply. The president could do what he liked, and there was nobody empowered to stop him.

Your Government, October 12, 1940

Irresolute, gazing at what is carved on the lintel, the American people now stand at the third threshold. They read:

NEW AMERICAN WAY OF LIFE BY THE DEMOCRATIC PROCESS. ENTER.

There is a voice saying: "It is your Government that bids you enter. Trust your Government. Has it not brought you the easy way to this point? Would you go back to the hard life of individualism and self-responsibility? Remember what your Government has done for you, and count it all twice, for it shall be doubled."

Beyond that threshold is not any American way of life, new or old; beyond is a New Europe.

What your Government has done for the people may be

noted as a statistical fact. At least one family in every four through the entire country now draws sustenance from the United States Treasury. What, at the same time, your Government has done to the people cannot be expressed statistically. We undertake to set some of it down.

Your Government has perfected in this country the European political art of doing with words what the sleight-of-hand performer does with objects. The words are the same, but the meaning is changed. What now is the meaning of democratic process? It means the surrender of individual responsibility to the executive will of Government. This liberty may commit suicide, as it has done in Europe, and it is still the democratic process. If that is debatable, we waive it and go on.

Neutrality was the people's resolve. What has happened to it?

A very subtle intelligence disguised as your Government devoured the meaning of neutrality within the shell of it, pretending all the time to have been guarding it. Now, cynically, it exhibits the empty shell. And what are you going to do about it?

Your Government has encouraged one kind of foreign propaganda in this country. Witness, for example, this cool paragraph from a Washington dispatch of the United Press, dated August tenth: "The criminal division of the Department of Justice plans to start preparation next week of official documents exposing the propaganda operations of Germany, Italy, Russia and Japan in the United States. Propaganda of other foreign nations, including Great Britain, does not threaten our security, it was said at the division."

Your Government has secretly collaborated with the British government by thought and act in a manner which, even if it had not been intended to involve the United States in the European war, could have had no other effect or meaning.

Measures short of war. What, at first, did you understand that formula to mean? That England and France should have access to the private industrial resources of the United States, which would be internationally lawful, would not involve the Government at all, and would be still a tremendous advantage to the Allies, with Germany blockaded? But your Government understood it to mean much more than that; the British government understood it to mean much more.

The imperious intelligence acting as your Government was resolved to intervene. The British knew that all the time, and kept saying that it was not the direction of American policy that was in doubt; only the speed with which it could move. For each act of intervention the public mind was prepared by propaganda. The first acts were a sampling, the adventure oblique. Some Army and Navy planes returned to the makers for a trade-in, with the stipulation beforehand that they should be delivered immediately to the Allies. This was an act of war by any neutral interpretation of international law and treaty, covered only, saved from overtness, by a legal subterfuge that quieted the first alarm.

When the Congress had accepted these acts, your Government abandoned the legal subterfuge and went on to strip the American arsenals, until fifteen shiploads of arms and munitions out of America's own inadequate defense equipment had been delivered to Great Britain— 80,000 machine guns, 700 field guns, half a million rifles— and every fourth man in the British home army had in his hands an American gun. Your Government did not tell you this. Afterward the Committee to Defend America by Aiding the Allies[2] told you.

With the Congress quiescent, your Government perceives that it can go much farther. By act of executive will alone it forms a military alliance with a country at war— namely, Canada—and proceeds to deliver American armaments there. This is done in the name of national defense and is so accepted. The end forgives the way of it. Nevertheless, it is a momentous fact that the President of the United States, in time of peace, on his own responsibility, can meet with the Premier of Canada in his private railway carriage and make offhand a military pact with a country that is at war with Hitler. It passes.

Having done all this, step by step, from beginnings that were not resisted, this now power-happy intelligence representing itself to be your Government has the daring to present to the American Congress what in Europe is called a *fait accompli.* We have in our language no exact verbal equivalent. The *fait accompli* is a thing done, concerning which the executive will says afterward, "So what of it? What are you going to do about it?"

The *fait accompli* is by nature an act of violence. It may be either political or physical violence. This *fait accompli* we are talking about was first of all an act of violence committed against the American principle of free, constitutional, representative government.

Suddenly, and again on a railway train in the dramatic European fashion, the President summons the reporters to the vestibule of his private car and tells them he has released a part of the United States Navy to go and fight against Hitler. He reads to them the message, prepared on the train, in which, by courtesy, the Congress will be notified of what he has done. With this message he sends an opinion from his Attorney General. The opinion is that what the President has done, the *fait accompli,* is beyond the reach of Congress. It cannot even vote on it.

Two days later, Winston Churchill makes the statement in the British House of Commons beginning: "The memorable transactions between Britain and the United States which I foreshadowed when I last addressed the House have now been completed." He is referring to the fifty destroyers the American Government has released to go and fight against Hitler. And he adds that British crews are already there to receive them, at the western side of the Atlantic—that is to say, at Canadian ports—by "what one might call the long arm of coincidence" (Laughter at this in the British house.)

What does that mean? It means that before the American people knew it, before the American Congress knew it, the British government knew that your Government was going to release a part of the United

States Navy to go and fight against Hitler, and then present it to the Congress and the people as a *fait accompli.*

So you see what else your Government does. As it leads the country to war, saying it will keep it out, it tells you only what it thinks it will be good for you to know, and cannot always afford to tell you the truth, because you may not have been enough accustomed to the idea. As, for example, when the news was out that your Government was negotiating with Great Britain for air and navy bases on the fringe of this hemisphere, it told you that this had nothing whatever to do with the fifty destroyers for which the British had put forth a great propaganda in this country. Simply, that was not so.

In the opinion your Government got from its legal department, kissing away the law, the Attorney General said that such things were customarily submitted for ratification by a two-thirds vote of the Senate. "However, the acquisitions which you are proposing to accept"—air and navy bases in exchange for fifty destroyers—"are without express or implied promises on the part of the United States to be performed in the future. . . It is not necessary for the Senate to ratify an opportunity that entails no obligation," nor, he added, any necessity for the Congress "to appropriate money."

Here your Government has involved itself in both sophistry and misrepresentation. The only reason why it is not necessary for the Congress to appropriate money for the development of these air and navy bases is that the President took care beforehand to get a large sum of national-defense money voted into his hands, to do with has he would. He has the money.

As for there being no obligation incurred, the obligation is merely this—namely, that we defend the British possessions in this hemisphere. Title to those bases does not pass. The United States has only a leasehold, the right to use them. As it will be obliged to defend its own bases, so at the same time it will be defending British possessions. In truth, the only reason why this treaty of Anglo-American military alliance was not submitted to the Senate was that the President feared, and privately said, that the Senate probably would not consent. Well, now it is a thing made done. The Senate cannot touch it.

For the British we have only further admiration. They wanted the destroyers very badly. But they wanted much more. They wanted their possessions on this hemisphere to be defended, and here was Uncle Sam going to do it and give fifty destroyers to boot; and even more, they wanted the American Government to put forth its hand, as the Irish say, farther than it could draw it back, or, in the word of the British press, to "take the plunge."

In that same speech, announcing the memorable transaction to the House of Commons, Winston Churchill cheerfully said: "No doubt Herr Hitler will not like this transference of destroyers. I will have no doubt he will pay the United States out if ever he gets the chance."

Thus is was reserved for the British government to announce to the world the fact that the United States had got into the war, so far into it that it could not back out.

We are not thinking of any of this in the arguable terms of defense strategy. We are not thinking at this moment of the destroyer transaction as an irreversible act of war, which it was, short only of a declaration of hostilities against Hitler. Whether or not it was sometime inevitable has nothing to do with what we were saying.

There is a disaster worse than war. We are concerned only with how it was done. We are thinking of how your Government, instead of telling the people what it meant to do or what it was doing until it was done, by indirection, by subterfuge, by cleverness, by beating the law, uncontrollably pursuing its own will, did involve this country in the European war it was resolved to stay out of.

We return to the threshold where the people stand gazing, still with some irresolution, at the insidious carving on the lintel. Why do they hesitate? Because against the voice of your Government is another, the voice of all the people who have ever possessed freedom and lost it, who have ever achieved self-government and grown weary of it, saying:

Beware of measures short of dictatorship, for they are

like measures short of war.

Beware of personal power in the worshipful image.

Beware of this European doctrine of indispensability, and of the saying that to challenge it is treasonable.

Beware of the *fait accompli,* for it is the last warning.

Beware of the next step, for there is only one more.

On June 28, 1940, the Republican Party nominated Wendell Willkie for President. Willkie, a utilities lawyer with almost no history in the Republican Party, was the most interventionist of any of the candidates, a list that included former president Herbert Hoover, future nominee Thomas Dewey and midwestern senators Arthur Vandenberg and Robert Taft. Willkie, who arrived at the convention with only a handful of delegates, had won on the sixth ballot. "Had the foes of intervention coordinated their efforts, they might have stopped the Willkie boom," wrote historian Justus Doenecke in Storm on the Horizon *(2000).*

The Democratic Party renominated Roosevelt in July, breaking the tradition set by George Washington that no President would ever serve a third term. Thus was created a race between two pro-intervention candidates, each wooing an electorate sympathetic to the Allies but suspicious of war. Willkie played it down the middle, supporting the destroyers-for-bases deal but criticizing how it was done.

Within the Form, October 26, 1940

More than two thousand years ago Aristotle wrote of a revolution within the form. It is then, he said, "by small degrees only that one thing takes the place of another; so that the ancient laws will remain while the power will be in the hands of those who have brought about a revolution within the state."

Within the Republican form of American government democracy grew. It entered by another name. Jefferson, now revered as the founder of democracy, did not call himself a democrat. He was a republican and his party was the Republican party. Later it cast away that name, and the conservative principle took it up.

You cannot say precisely when it was that the sense of distinction between a republic and a democracy was lost. What you now see, however, is one word on all the clashing banners; Republicans, Democrats, liberals, radicals, Communists and revolutionaries all acclaiming democracy, and all alike holding themselves out to be its only true and devoted defenders.

Does this mean that we have such a curious thing as a total defense of democracy? On the contrary, it means that the American significance of democracy, too, has been lost. The word itself has become a political hotel, under no management, offering a once-respectable address to any and all ideas, harlotry not forbidden.

Many voices using the same word to mean different things produce an effect of utter confusion; and yet it is not entirely so. Much of this confusion is purposeful. A sequel is taking place—that one Aristotle indicated when he wrote of an oligarchy degenerating into a democracy and a democracy degenerating into something like tyranny, or what we now name dictatorship.

As it was that within the form of republican government democracy grew, so now it is that in the mask of democracy there is rising, very cautiously still, yet higher and higher, the hideous head of absolute government. With skillful ease it turns to the gaze of the people only its benign aspect; and when people, even by that appearance, are startled, it says to them: "Your government is the same as before. It is only conditions that have changed. Everything, nevertheless, is within the form." And of all the voices that pay worshipful homage to democracy and flatter the people, this one is the most suave and disarming.

In a mid-glory moment of the New Deal, candor possessing him, President Roosevelt admitted that in the new instrumentalities of executive government he had created that there was such power that if ever it fell into bad hands it might serve to shackle the liberties of people.[3] From that danger he now is resolved to save them. The power shall not pass, not yet. That leaves to be answered only those

109

who say it is too much power for the government to have, since it was bound to lead to the doctrine of one man's indispensability, and this is toward dictatorship. And he answers them gently in his University of Pennsylvania speech, saying: "No dictator in history has ever dared to run the gantlet of a really free election."

If that were true, it would amount only to saying that a certain thing is improbable because it has never happened, with no point whatever in saying it but to make grace for one daring to run the gantlet of the no-third-term tradition. However, no answer to dispel apprehension is without welcome. Be the weight of these reassuring words what their weight is. We do not estimate it. But in the dish of simple balance we place against it two other weights so very unlike that we may say one was intended for this purpose and one was not.

The first is a legal mind stating analogous facts, as follows: "In Italy and Germany the current dictators rose to power peacefully and entirely within the form, if not the spirit, of their constitutions of their respective countries. After they had been elevated to power through the endeavors of their party associates, all they had to do to make themselves supreme was to gather into their own hands complete control over administration of the laws, using that control to crush all opposition." This is Julius C. Smith, member of a special committee of the American Bar Association, on the extraordinary use of administrative law, addressing the Florida Law Institute last November. His subject was Totalitarianism and Administrative Absolutism.

He cited the doctrine, here new, that administrative agencies of government, making and executing their own laws, are not meant to be impartial, but are created in the interest of one side or to advance a policy; and from this the rise of an administrative power now saying that the remedy of appeal from its decisions to a court of law has generally "no practical content." And at the end he said: "Is there any labor leader, any businessman, any lawyer or any other citizen of America so blind that he cannot see that this country is drifting at an accelerating pace into administrative absolutism similar to that which prevailed in the governments of antiquity, the governments of the Middle Ages, and in the great totalitarian governments of today? Make no mistake about it. Even as Mussolini and Hitler rose to absolute power under the forms of law. . . so may administrative absolutism be fastened upon this country within the Constitution and within the forms of law."

For the second weight, the one we said was not intended to be used in this way, we are indebted to the Attorney General of the United States, the Hon. Robert H. Jackson, brilliant legal advocate of revolution within the form. What we have here is not the evisceration of a word like "democracy," but a sudden inversion of meaning, all the more startling because it was so easy to do. The meaning of free government is turned upside down and still makes perfect sense.

When the President, in that same University of Pennsylvania speech, spoke of people having fought and worked to win the privilege of free government, no one could have supposed he did not mean it in the traditional sense, unchanged since the beginning of the written history of government—namely, a government under which people are free; a government under which the rights, liberties and immunities of the individual are founded in law; a government that is itself limited by law—for unless the power of government be limited there is no freedom. And yet these two words, "free government," taking them literally, can mean also the very opposite. They can mean that government shall be free, not people. We get this from the Attorney General.

In June, last, he addressed the Institute of Public Affairs at Charlottesville, Virginia, on how to make democracy efficient. Were people saying that government was already too big, too powerful, too concentrated, and that its power to control and regulate ought to be limited? His answer to them was to say it was not yet big and powerful enough. Democracy could be made efficient only by more government—more power and more freedom of government to punish individual conduct wherein it interferes with the main objectives of democracy, more power to coerce minorities, more power to prevent "some freedoms."

The restoration of federal power was a subject on which he could speak with some assurance, for that had been his special task. "In 1933," he said, "we were not a nation—that is, judicially speaking, we were forty-eight nations, and our Federal power had been interpreted away until the Constitution was but a little stronger than the old Articles of Confederation. . . Our representative democracy has been made a nation in the last four years. If it is able to organize its economy to support its defense today it is in no small measure due to the greater liberty of action won in little-publicized court decisions too technical perhaps for complete public understanding. The National Government has won its long fight to free itself of unwarranted limitations. . . We have restored the vitality of a free government on which a narrow legalism was inflicting a kind of rigor mortis. . . We have won for peacetime programs powers that in 1917 were felt could be used only in war emergency. . . The lines of future liberal policy are clear. We must move at an accelerated pace."

Then he looked at the people's freedom. What would happen to it? How could it be reconciled with this new freedom of government?

Well, the essence of democracy, namely, "control of the government by the consent and will of the governed as expressed by its majorities"—that should be preserved, of course, but—

"Once a decision is democratically arrived at, I see no reason why it would not be consistent with democracy to provide means to execute that decision with as much expedition and efficiency as the decision of a dictator."

For that once, the rising head of absolute government, turning its benign face to the people's gaze with skillful ease, turned a little too far, and thanks to the zeal of the Attorney General, there was the glimpse of the averted features.[4]

To freedom, the right only to arrive at general decisions

by a majority vote; to the government, means equal to the means of a dictator. What have you then? You have what Thomas F. Woodlock[5] has named a totalitarian democracy, within the form of a government that was designed, as the founders thought, to make that sequel impossible. You have the kind of government De Tocqueville imagined when he said that once it appeared in a democracy it would be bound not only to oppress the people but to strip them "of several of the highest qualities of humanity."

Chapter four notes

[1] In his message to Congress, January 3, 1936. A more complete quote: "But the challenge faced by this Congress is more menacing than merely a return to the past, bad as that would be. Our resplendent economic autocracy does not want to return to the individualism of which they prate, even though the advantages under that system went to the ruthless and the strong. They realize that in 34 months we have built up new instruments of public power. In the hands of a people's government this power is wholesome and proper. But in the hands of political puppets of an economic autocracy such power would provide shackles for the liberties of the people."

[2] The CDAAA was founded by William Allen White, an internationalist Republican and editor of the Emporia, Kansas, *Gazette*. He founded it at the personal suggestion of President Roosevelt, who used it as a transmission belt for White House's political line on the war. Garrett paid close attention to this group for about seven months.

[3] Garrett wrote in "National Hill Notes," the *Saturday Evening Post,* Feb. 29, 1936: "In the entire book of the New Deal's self-revelation and self-exegesis there is a certain paragraph that would reconcile all of its acts, not one with another but with one principle of contradiction. It is the passage in the last annual message in which suddenly the President speaks of the new instruments of governmental power that have been created, and then says of this new power that it is such that as in other hands 'would provide shackles for the liberties of the people.' But it is in his hands. Well, conquest of power for purposes of all-doing—that in itself could be a controlling policy, and such a policy, impossible to acknowledge, would involve many inconsistencies of immediate policy, because the peaceable course to the seizure of great political power is a zigzag path."

[4] In May 1940, Roosevelt had sent Jackson instructions and authorization to begin wiretapping, which was forbidden by federal law. It was still going on in January 1950, when Roosevelt's order was disclosed in the spy trial of Judith Coplon.

[5] Thomas F. Woodlock, 1866-1945, wrote the "Thinking It Over" column on the *Wall Street Journal* op-ed page 1930-1945.

Chapter Five
CONSENT

Garrett, who had been despondent four years earlier, when Alf Landon failed to mount a principled opposition to the New Deal, was let down again.

Not on the Ballot, November 2, 1940

We wonder how many people realize that they are going to vote next Tuesday on the fate of free government in this country. There will be nothing about it on the ballot.

In an empty sense only has the presidential campaign now at its close represented a contest between two political parties. The Republican Party took as its candidate a former Democrat. Many Democrats, without forsaking their clan, but with intent to save it, have embraced the Republican totem. Conservative and liberal principles have not been in conflict; the liberals have it in either case. In the premises of national defense there has been no disagreement at all; and on questions of foreign policy methods and expedients have been more in dispute than convictions. Therefore, one who would might say that happily in a time of crisis there is no deep cleavage of thought and feeling.

But that is not all. The crisis is compound. There is a crisis within a crisis, one tending to obscure the other. There is the crisis we did not create and cannot control, rising from our imperiled position in the middle of a world at

115

war; and there is the other crisis which, as we believe, involves the fate of free government. In this other crisis lies the field of struggle. It is a struggle between people and government. The candidates as we name them are Freedom and Status.

This is the struggle we have been writing about for nearly eight years. During all that time we have held against the New Deal on two grounds, one minor and one major.

On the minor ground we have opposed its economic fallacies and fantasies.

On the major ground we have said that the rising power of the executive will, the progressive degradation of the legislative principle, contempt for the restraints of constitutional law, were bringing to pass a revolution in the relations of the individual to the state; that people were being beguiled with promises and presents to surrender their individual responsibilities to an all-doing government, thereby exchanging freedom for status; that the sequel, if not averted by a return to the hard and jealous precepts of liberty, was bound to be absolute government, some form of elective despotism. Again and again we have said that free government must be a limited government, as the Constitution intended—that is to say, a government not above the law but limited by law; that unlimited government, no matter how benevolent and righteous its intentions, would in the end devour freedom.

Never did we say this but to become aware that people were increasingly interested in what government should do, in what it should do for them, forgetting what government should be, which to us seemed very important. And never did we say it but to be bitterly reproached for thinking and writing with political bias, in a partisan spirit, by people who entertained the delusion concerning themselves that they were Democrats, concerning the New Deal that it was the Democratic Party, and concerning that we were clothed in Republican sackcloth. Yet what we were saying had been always the orthodox doctrine of American democracy.

Until the advent of the New Deal, political freedom knew no party. The rights and immunities of the individual were written in the constitutional law. Political parties might rise and fall, change their clothes, swap their principles, but that government should be servant, not master, was thought to be settled for all time. Even so, it was the Democratic Party that would not so much as tread on the shadow of freedom; it was the Democratic Party that resisted with foreboding any extension of governmental power touching the sphere of the individual.

It was Thomas Jefferson, founder of American democracy, who said, "The natural progress of things is for liberty to yield and government to gain ground."

Government was the natural enemy of freedom. What had destroyed liberty and human rights in every government under the sun? Government did it. There was a natural impulse in government to centralize, consolidate and extend its powers. Therefore, he said, the spirit of resistance to government was so valuable that it should always be kept alive. It would be often exercised when wrong, yet better so than not to be exercised at all. He believed in the common man and doubted him, too, saying: "When all government, domestic and foreign, in little as in great things, shall be drawn to Washington as the center of all power, it will become as venal and oppressive as the government from which we separated; . . .and the blasphemers of man, as incapable of self-government, become his true historians." There he says "when," not "if," so you may take it to be either warning or prophecy.

Since Jefferson, the material world has changed in a way he could not have imagined. You will think of that. But for all the change in social and economic conditions another great Democrat, one hundred years later, was saying: "The history of liberty is a history of the limitation of governmental power, not the increase of it. When we resist, therefore, the concentration of power, we are resisting the processes of death, because concentration of power is what always precedes the destruction of human liberties." That was Woodrow Wilson in 1912.

A Democrat believed that the laws that limited and governed free government were immutable, like natural laws, and there could be no liberty but by keeping them the hard way.

Twenty years after Woodrow Wilson, another fine Democrat, Hatton Sumners, chairman of the House Judiciary Committee, was saying it was the development of people, not government, with which Nature concerned herself. Government from the top, relieving people of the necessity to govern themselves, was destroying the self-reliance of the individual. That was the easy way, and the way of death for free institutions. "We have jazzed off into the jungles. We have lost our way. We were looking for a boulevard to go out on. There is no boulevard leading out from where we are. We are going to have to cut down the trees and go out over the stumps."

What happened to the magnificent Democratic doctrine?

The New Deal expelled it from the Democratic Party. After that there was no Democratic Party. The voice of Jacob and the hands of Esau were now Jacob.

The New Deal, not the Democratic Party, subdued the legislative principle, overcame the restraints of the judicial principle, and raised the power of executive government to a new dimension, extending its ministrations, functions and authority to a point at which, as even President Roosevelt said, the government could, if it would, shackle the liberties of the people. Thus liberty, by yielding, has lost its immunity and come to rest upon the goodness of government. And this in the name of the Democratic Party!

And now it is a former Democrat, leading the Republican Party, saying the American government shall be again the people's government, instead of the American people being the government's people.

What of the spirit of freedom during all this time. Why was it so passive?

It is not a convincing answer to say the New Deal was holding out attractive new fashions in freedom—economic freedom in place of political freedom, freedom from individual responsibility, from insecurity, from inequality, from the terrors of everyday economic pressure.

Political freedom is heavy, too heavy for some people. It may require of them more fortitude and sacrifice than they are willing to pay. One of the fine passages in the literature on the subject is from the Russian, Nicolas Berdyaev.[1] "The path of freedom is difficult and tragic, more beset than any other with heroic responsibility and martyrdom. The paths of necessity and compulsion are easier, less tragic and less heroic. That is why the historical process shows so many derogations from the path of freedom to that of compulsion."

No one who knows the history of freedom will be wholly optimistic. Only those who have fought for freedom may be trusted to defend it. These hand it on. Those who inherit it may take it for granted and so lose it, or they may weary of it and surrender.

In the modern world, free government is new. Its life has been a century and a half. That means only that it was lost and found again.

"For a thousand years after the days of the last republicans of Rome," says Bryce, in *Modern Democracies,* "the most civilized people of Europe cared nothing for politics and left government in the hands of their kings or chiefs. . . No one thought of trying to revive free self-government in Italy or Greece or around the coasts of the Aegean, where hundreds of republics had bloomed and died."[2]

He asks if such lapses are again possible, and he is not sure. His answer is that although those particular conditions will of course not recur, yet others might be imagined to produce the like effect. "The thing did happen, and whatever has happened may happen again. People that had known and prized political freedom resigned it, did not regret it and forgot it."

Jefferson's faith in the common man's power to govern himself was a passion, a religion in fact; anyone who said to the contrary was a blasphemer. Nevertheless, he was bound to say that this was the natural progress of things— for liberty to yield and for government to gain ground. It is a thing he would remember to have said if he were looking at the world today.

Everywhere freedom in surrender, in retreat or on the defensive against government. Everywhere the parliamentary principle in decline or fallen. Everywhere the sign of absolute government rising. Even here. But the struggle has not yet been lost.

A week later Garrett went to press before the election for an issue of the magazine that would appear after it.

Burma Road, November 9, 1940

The people have elected their leader. It was a free election, such as could not have taken place at this time, perhaps, anywhere else in the world. All the forms and images received due homage. And yet we say the spirit of self-government was never before so sick in the American body. If you ask what the people voted for, the answer is one word.

They voted for a man.

The question presented to them was this: To which of two men will you commit the welfare and policy of your country? That question they have answered. They have made their choice. They have satisfied the demands of what by a new fashion now is called the democratic process, but they have left the meaning of self-government in the ditch. To become acutely aware of it, you have only to ask what the people voted on—not *for,* but *on.*

The grave question, the one to which every other consideration ought to have been treated as subject, was not presented to them at all. That question was: Shall the American people pursue the path of glory to battle and empire, or turn back?

They had not deliberately set their feet in that path, meaning to do it. They were led into it, and led so adroitly that they turned into it without looking. Yet in that unpremeditated act of turning into it was the beginning of the end of their own New World. It was the beginning of

New Europe in this hemisphere. The path they took, the path of glory, leads to world responsibilities, world entanglements without end, world politics, world power. That may be the American destiny. If it is, we do not quarrel with it. What we say is that when such a question is to be decided, once and for all in the life of the nation, and people do not decide it for themselves, all that survives of self-government is a memory. Many millions of Americans, seeing what had happened, did want to turn back. They wanted to fortify America and stand alone. It was feasible to turn back. But did they vote on it? No. The question was not submitted.

The campaign was conducted as if the executive will of the American Government, acting beyond the consent of Congress and beyond the law, had not intervened in the war; as if the formula, "measures short of war," had not already got the country into it, or as if, having got into it, still for us it could be a limited war. It was conducted as if for more than a year isolationists and interventionists had not been locked in mortal struggle. To intervene or not to intervene? Did the people vote on that? No. That question, too, was avoided.

During the campaign, the war party definitely perfected its propaganda. It substituted for the idea of defense the idea of offense. Every propagandist for war became a strategist, saying that to defend itself democracy dare not wait for the aggressor to come; it was time for democracy to march forth. To march or not to march? Did the people vote on that?

A panic of apprehension passed through the country at the sight of the headline: JAPAN JOINS THE AXIS! That was in September. It was after the Axis power in Europe had faced airplanes and fighting ships released by the United States Army and Navy to go and fight against Hitler, besides guns and explosives provided out of the American arsenal. What would you expect the Axis powers to do, short of declaring war on the United States? They would create, if they could, a counter menace in the Pacific.

Japan may or may not have wished to join the Axis. At

any rate, she did not join until she understood that the
United States was going to share Great Britain's Asiatic
naval base at Singapore, which would mean, of course, an
American obligation to defend it. There was another shud-
der of apprehension at the news that after consultation
with the American Government, Great Britain had decided
to reopen the Burma Road. Probably one American in thirty thousand knew at that moment exactly where the
Burma Road was, and then only by reading about it in the
news dispatches; a year before he had been unaware of its
existence. Nevertheless, the reopening of the Burma Road
by Great Britain might be the spark that would ignite war
between the United States and Japan.

What did that mean? It meant that the United States
and Great Britain had been actively collaborating in war;
it meant that this collaboration had assumed the aspect, if
not the actual character, of a military alliance.

The people had not been told what was taking place.
The Congress had not been told. The President did it all by
executive will, one thing at a time, and the news came
afterward, not in any case, perhaps, all of the news, but as
much only as was necessary for the people and the
Congress to know.

These entangling commitments are not in the form of
treaties. The reason why they are not is that if they were,
they would have had to be signed by the Senate. As acts of
the President, therefore, they could have been reconsid-
ered; they could have been as easily repudiated by the people as Mr. Wilson's Versailles Treaty. But fancy submitting
to the people such a question as, "To save democracy in the
world, shall we defend the British Empire in Asia?" or, to
be specific, "In defense of democracy, are the American people willing to go to war with Japan over the reopening of
the Burma Road?" No, no. Such questions make a kind of
sense in the high austerities of world politics. They make
no sense to people. They were told, instead, that as they
voted they would please or displease Hitler.

The entire defense program was voted by Congress during the campaign—astronomical sums of money, war

powers to the President in time of peace, conscription.

But what were we going to defend? The United States and its possessions, this hemisphere entire, anything in the world calling itself a democracy, or, on grounds of high strategy, the British Empire in Europe, Asia and Africa, considered as first line of American defense? That ought to have been the very first question. Imagine a defense program without knowing for sure what you are going to defend. But beyond the sense of that, when you consider what must be involved in the decision, who will have to fight and die for it, whose country it is, you might think that with all the facts submitted, it could be left to the people. Was it? Did they vote on it?

Three weeks before election, Turner Catledge, of the *New York Times,* made a notoriously true report on the state of mind and feeling in Washington. "The question," he wrote, "is no longer whether, but when. . . Whatever the personal views of those who share it, the sense of the inevitable as regards our being drawn further into the war is one you cannot escape here at the nation's nerve center. Furthermore, the feeling is not based essentially on any probability of result in the presidential contest. . . If, therefore, one should construct a composite of the expectations of the next few months as they prevail today in Washington, he probably would wind up with a prophesy something as follows: That soon after the election the United States Government will begin to move more openly toward assistance to Great Britain . . .toward some sort of joint working arrangement regarding the Far East. . . definite if not straightforward moves to relax the credit restrictions imposed by the Johnson Act and the Neutrality Law. . .disclosure of some of our own technical secrets, particularly that of the airplane bomb-sight. . . the transfer for British use of some of our first-class fighting equipment."

At the same time David Lawrence was saying in the *United States News:* "Slow motion in foreign policy decisions until the elections are over. Then United States policy will be to give England every needed aid. . . more ship transfers. . . more responsibility for the protection of

Australia and New Zealand."

"Soon after the election the government will," says one. "Slow motion until after the election," says the other. Do you realize how cynical, how derisive of self-government, these phrases are? Every correspondent in Washington was saying more or less the same thing, and the people were indifferent and without wrath. They were choosing a man. Did they vote on repeal of the Neutrality Act? Did they vote on repeal of the Johnson Act, which forbids nations that defaulted on their old World War debts to the United States Treasury to borrow money in the United States? Did they vote on acting with Great Britain to open the Burma Road, though it could cost us war with Japan?

Did they vote on going forth to war—soon after election?

What the result would been if they had, we do not pretend to know. That question, we believe, is foreclosed. There is no probable turning back. The only event we now could trust to keep the country from marching would be for the war to end. We do not say it will not be a good war, and well done as Armageddon, "the battle of that great day of God Almighty." We do say, as a last word, that having wearied of the responsibilities of self-government so far as to surrender them, the people now must reap what they never intended to sow. We say that if they can be led into a good war they were resolved to stay out of, so in the same way they could be led into a bad war.

The thought of fortifying America, instead of saving the world, may have been a selfish thought, yet we loved it. The dream of keeping a New World of our own may have belonged but to the youth of our destiny, yet we believed it. Say not it was impossible. An America strong enough to save the world was strong enough to stand alone. Yet this will be, whatever else, the second unselfish war in the history of the warlike human race. The other, too, was ours.

Roosevelt's total was 27.3 million votes, about 5 million more than Willkie got. The electoral vote was 449 to 82. Willkie had done better than Alf Landon four years earlier, but not nearly enough.

One of the reasons Roosevelt won was his promise to stay out of war. On October 30, 1940, in Boston, he said, "I have said this before, but I shall say it again and again and again: Your boys are not going to be sent into any foreign wars." He said this many times.

In his first speech after the election, he warned that if England fell, Americans would be living at the point of a gun. "We must be the great arsenal of democracy," he said.

Chapter five notes

[1] Nicolas Berdyaev, 1874-1948. Born in Russia, he was expelled by the Soviets in 1922 and lived as an expatriate in Europe—at this writing, in occupied France. Berdyaev defended an aristocratic view of freedom. In *The Realm of the Spirit and the Realm of the Caesar* (1949), he wrote: "In reality, freedom is aristocratic, not democratic. With sorrow, we must recognize the fact that freedom is dear only to those men who think creatively."

[2] Viscount James Bryce, 1838-1922, was British ambassador to the United States 1907-1913 and author of the Bryce report on German atrocities in Belgium, 1914. *Modern Democracies* was published by Macmillan in 1921.

Chapter Six
MEANINGS

The election was over, but the battle continued—and not to the advantage of the anti-interventionists. Wrote Wayne S. Cole in his 1983 study, Roosevelt and the Isolationists, 1933-1945: *"By the time Roosevelt began his third term, isolationists were widely viewed as narrow, self-serving, partisan, conservative, antidemocratic, anti-Semitic, pro-Nazi, fifth columnist and even treasonous. That image distorted the truth, but it formed nonetheless. Roosevelt and his followers helped create that jaundiced view. . ."*

It was brilliant propaganda based on the careful selection of words. What was an appeaser? A defeatist? Aid short of war? Here Garrett appeals to his readers: "Let us make up our minds."

Strategy, December 14, 1940

In the last three or four weeks of the presidential campaign it was very remarkable that a positive expression by either candidate against taking the country into war was sure to receive quick and prolonged applause. We take leave to note also the fact that as this manifestation of the popular will became unmistakable, the activities of the Committee to Defend America by Aiding the Allies and the propaganda of the war party abated to almost the vanishing point. Even the famous matter of the bomb sight was let lie, although, after the destroyers, that was the next most urgent thing on the White committee's[1] program.

At a White House press conference three days before election, the President was asked, according to the *New York Times,* "if it was true that the American Army bomb sight, which is regarded here as the world's best, was being produced by American manufacturers for the British," and Mr. Roosevelt replied that "he did not have the faintest idea."[2] That the commander in chief of the armed forces of the United States should not have the faintest idea whether or not a very important secret military device was being delivered to a foreign country seemed to be incredible. Be that in parenthesis.

During the period we speak of, with popular sentiment against war asserting itself in the only way it could, all the Washington correspondents were saying that immediately after election the agitation for more active participation in the war would be resumed with vigor, and along certain definite lines—namely, more naval vessels to Great Britain, the bomb sight, some of the big bombing planes, some way around the Johnson Act, which forbids our defaulting war debtors to borrow money in this country, and repeal of the Neutrality Law.

To Frederic R. Coudert, of the subcommittee on policy of the Committee to Defend America by Aiding the Allies,[3] we are indebted for a forecast of what was going to happen to the Neutrality Law. It would be attacked on the grounds, firstly, that it is beneath the dignity of a great nation because it surrenders to fear both our conscience and our national rights; secondly, that anyhow we have broken it and would not keep it if we could; thirdly, in view of the unnatural things we are actually doing, it is ridiculous; fourthly, we have already provoked Hitler exceedingly and no fiction of neutrality can hide us; fifthly, the formula "short of war" is an ambiguous term; and lastly—these are Mr. Coudert's words—"We have said 'A,' and he who says 'A,' says 'B.' "

All of this he set forth in a speech, September tenth, before the Section of International and Comparative Law of the American Bar Association. "To exclude our ships," he said, "from the high seas, to insist upon the payment of cash for belligerent purchases and other limitations upon our national rights, is a little absurd in view of the fact that we are now taking definite and positive steps to defend one of the principal belligerents—Canada. Not only that. We have obtained cessions for leases for military posts which can only be useful in the event that Great Britain is beaten. We have given in exchange a part of our Navy, and we have promised every aid in our power, qualified by the ambiguous term, 'short of war.' "

We would trust Mr. Coudert to make the best possible case for going to war to save Great Britain—the moral case first, as it should be, and then the case from the point of view of the American self-interest. "It is so obvious as to seem axiomatic," he says, "that if Britain is saved we need not fear the intrusion of alien systems in South America." Therefore, in saving Great Britain, we are defending the Western Hemisphere in Europe, or, as we defend the Western Hemisphere in Europe, so also we save Great Britain; and it sounds very plausible.

We ask one question: We have asked it before. When we have saved Great Britain, who is going to reconquer Europe? Great Britain alone cannot do that. She has not the man power to do it. If she expects to do it, she is counting on American man power in the end. Unless those who talk of going to war to save Great Britain are willing to visualize the spectacle of an American expeditionary force crossing the Atlantic to destroy the German thing on the soil of Europe, we say to them they have not thought this business through. Either we are going to reconquer Europe or we are not going to do it.

Let us make up our minds. If we are not going to do it, then our problem is to defend the Western Hemisphere where the Western Hemisphere is, and to shape our weapons accordingly.

And America, January 4, 1941

The very eminent Committee to Defend America by Aiding the Allies held a prize contest for war posters.

With ceremonial publicity the first prize was awarded to one showing a tortured tree in a desolate landscape. The lettering in the sky was, "Lest We Regret," and upon the foreground: "HELP BRITAIN AND DEFEND AMERICA."

And defend America! We doubt if these tireless war bringers were conscious that their thought had capsized itself by a psychic law of gravity. They were probably too intent upon a new feat of propaganda. They were changing slogans. Measures Short of War had been used up. They were going to substitute for it, Stop Hitler Now.

By measures short of war the country had been led backward into war. We are in it now. The people are loath to believe this. Because it has not yet touched them, they are still hoping it isn't true. The problem of the war party, therefore, is to make them face it.

"We must now answer a fundamental question," says Doctor Conant,[4] president of Harvard University. He is speaking by radio, November twentieth, under the auspices of the Committee to Defend America by Aiding the Allies, at the obsequies of Measures Short of War. Do we agree that the aggressor powers must be defeated? Well, then, he says, "the words 'all possible aid to the Allies' mean exactly what they say. There are no reservations in our pledge. It then becomes a matter of strategy, and strategy only, when, if ever, material aid must be supplanted by direct naval and military assistance."

Five days later, the Committee to Defend America by Aiding the Allies issues a new statement of policy, saying: "The American people must face squarely the realities of this day and hour." And then: "Also we say regretfully that no one can guarantee that the United States can avoid active military involvement."

Thus is launched the final undertaking, which is to condition the American mind to the idea that for the American way of life we shall have to fight and die—not here where the life grew, not on its own soil where it could be invincible, but in Europe.

The conditioning process began with the first slogan, and while the chemistries of persuasion were acting, until they had completely worked, any suggestion of military involvement was repelled with indignation. The very reason for taking measures short of war against the European aggressor was to avoid war by keeping it away.

The idea that America's own first line of defense was in Europe met with much more resistance. It came at first with such a shock that the President denied having said it to the senators who were repeating it in an panic of anxiety, and declared that anyone who said he had said it was a boob or a liar. Within six months, nevertheless, it was a settled point in American foreign policy. Then followed unneutral acts on the part of the Government, trial acts of intervention, acts that were legally acts of war, and the one saying covered them all.

The first measure short of war was to repeal the arms embargo of the Neutrality Law. The Congress did that, but the President demanded it. The common understanding, the understanding of Congress, was that lifting the arms embargo meant only to give England and France exclusive access to the private industrial resources of the United States as cash war customers. What excluded Germany was nothing in the law, but only the fact that England and France controlled the sea. That was the beginning. The formula thereafter was extensible to any degree, and Congress was powerless to control it.

As a measure short of war, the American Government, in an open message to France, pledged itself to see to it that the Allied armies should receive from the United States ever-increasing quantities of "airplanes, artillery and munitions" for so long as they continued to resist the aggressor. The President alone did that.

As a measure short of war, the American Government released to the British a fleet of mosquito torpedo boats in building for the United States Navy, but was obliged to cancel the arrangement on the discovery by Congress of a law forbidding it.

As a measure short of war, the American Government released Army and Navy airplanes to the British. The President alone did that.

As a measure short of war, the American Government delivered to Great Britain out of its own arsenals shiploads of rifles, artillery and munitions. The President alone did that.

As a measure short of war, fifty destroyers were released by the United States Navy to go and fight against Hitler. The President alone did that.

As a measure short of war, the American Government entered into a military alliance with one of the belligerent nations—namely, Canada. The President alone did that.

As a measure short of war, the American Government divided its defense program fifty-fifty with Great Britain, by what the President called a rule of thumb. The President alone did that.

As a measure short of war, a number of our largest bombing planes together with our secret bomb sight have been released to go and bomb Germany. They were released in exchange for airplane engines that were on order in American plants for the British.

As a measure short of war, the United States has temporarily weakened its own defenses in order to deliver immediately to Great Britain planes, ships and guns in being, all to be replaced out of future production.

By these and other measures short of war we have arrived at what is in effect an Anglo-American military alliance; and the only people in the world who do not know it are the American people.

By measures short of war we have arrived at the verge of total participation, still without looking at it. One more act would oblige us to take the plunge. A single symbolic act is wanting. We have not yet sent in the flag.

The Committee to Defend America by Aiding the Allies now begins to condition the mind for that. It its new statement of policy it says the United States must provide ships to save the life line between Great Britain and the Western Hemisphere, "merchant vessels to fly the British flag," and then be prepared under all circumstances to defend that life line, which would mean, of course, to convoy the merchant ships. That would take our flag in.

It goes on to say that the United States shall have a clear naval understanding with Great Britain "which will permit the two fleets to be placed in the most advantageous position to protect the Atlantic for the democracies and to stop the spread of war in the Pacific." That would surely take the flag in. Once the flag goes in, we shall know what a conscript army is for. We shall also know the answer to the question with which we have challenged those who hold for defending America by saving England and avoid thinking it through to the sequel. The question is: Who is going to reconquer Europe?

England alone cannot do that. She can hope to do it only with the aid of American man power. That is what Winston Churchill has been saying in a cryptic manner. To say it bluntly would be a blunder. Everything but men. That is what Great Britain has been asking for. Everything but men. That is what the American Government has been promising. But this is form and formality.

The only British official who has mentioned men, if he did—meaning by men an American expeditionary force—is Lord Lothian, the British ambassador.[5] And it was an oblique incident. In November, immediately after the American election, he was returning from London to his Washington post, and he had left behind him, in London, the Ediphone recording of a speech to be broadcast to the United States. When the speech came through on the air, the Columbia Broadcasting System's listeners were astonished to hear him say, "But we also need planes, men and ships, if we are to be sure of defeating the Nazi threat to liberty." Immediately came a cable, not from Lord Lothian, who was on his way, but from the British government, saying that what he had said, or meant to say, was "planes, finance and ships." The Columbia Broadcasting System so corrected it, but with this explanation: "There seems little doubt from our playbacks of the recording that Lothian said, 'planes, men and ships.'"

It was perhaps a slip of the diplomatic tongue. But a writer like H. N. Brailsford, in *A Message from England to America*,[6] can make the free authentic statement: If

England survives the blitzkrieg, he says, she must "contemplate the invasion of a continent solidly organized by its German masters." What such a feat would require in the way of a perfectly equipped army he did not care to guess; in any case it "is well above the total that England alone could furnish, even with the help of the Dominions. . . We do not forget that the German Reich has nearly twice our population, nor that it can harness for its own military ends all the industries of a subjugated Europe. . . Our own population is too small; our wealth, deeply drained already, insufficient. The stake is not merely our survival, but the liberation of Europe and the peace of the Americas. Then, may we hope for the comradely aid, in men and money, of the United States?. . . On the day it declares war upon this malignant principle, and sends out its volunteers to fight shoulder to shoulder with our young men, civilization has a future and mankind may dare to hope."

And America!—our men and our money for "the liberation of Europe and the peace of the Americas."

It is what we said could never, never happen to us again. We passed a law against it. We were resolved to be forever free of this thralldom to Europe. That was our true first line of defense, and a phrase destroyed it.

Here is Garrett's thought on the possible meaning of our non-alliance alliance with Britain: What if Britain lost? That was a thought worth thinking in the winter of 1940-41, when Britain stood alone.

If England Should Yield, January 25, 1941

Everything else having been said for going all out to save Great Britain because, whether the European war is our war or not, the British navy is our shield and armor, the last argument now is forthcoming. If Britain should yield, the disaster for us would be not simply that we should lose the protection of the British navy. Far worse than that. The British navy would be turned against us.

This shocking thought is released with an air of wishing

it were not so, or as if such a thing ought not to be said out loud except in the extreme case. For of course it may seem to have disillusioning implications. However that may be, the inescapable fact is that a defeated Britain could not be neutral. It would have to embrace the Axis. That would be true whether it was peace by defeat or peace by negotiation. In either case, the Churchill government would first be swept away. In place of it would be something like the Vichy regime, supposing Britain were defeated as France was, or, if it came to peace by negotiation, then there would be a government made up entirely of British appeasers. Is it likely, is it conceivable, that the British appeasers would feel in any way bound to think of our interests? Certainly not. Is it not plain that their best chance of getting favorable terms for the British Empire would be to invite Hitler, and to help him, carve out his empire elsewhere? Somewhere else at our expense? So ends the argument; and if it helps at all it helps too much.

This British navy that might be turned against us includes the destroyers that were delivered to Great Britain by the American Government. How fantastic it would be if we should have to face them as unfriendly or hostile craft, flying the swastika, perhaps? Logically, the same argument must hold for armaments of every kind. It follows, therefore, that having gone so far with the thought of saving England, we shall have to go on and on, with the fearful thought added that if we fail to save her, we may one day find the weapons we forged for her pointed at us. Did that not happen to Great Britain when Hitler employed against her British-made weapons surrendered by France? France was England's ally. England is not America's ally. So far, she could say she is only America's customer.

Before releasing the fifty destroyers to go and fight with the British navy against Hitler, whereby our own defense was weakened, the American Government received from the British government the solemn pledge that if the waters around Great Britain became untenable, the British navy would never be surrendered or sunk. It would be sent away to continue the fight elsewhere.

That was in September. Do the all-outers remember what they said then? That pledge was a momentous thing, they said. It meant that whatever else happened, America would not lose its shield and armor. That alone was worth fifty destroyers.

The truth was, and the truth still is, that such a pledge is worth exactly nothing. The Churchill government would keep it if it could, but the Churchill government is not Great Britain. There is no possible surety, even from day to day, that a nation at war will not make peace. If Great Britain could save herself by making peace at our expense, she would. We can think of no reason in law or morals why she shouldn't.

What we have to look at is the fact that any peace she might make, now or in the near future, would be at our expense, because in aid of Great Britain the American Government has committed acts of war. We are not prepared to accept the consequences if, as Churchill said, Hitler should see a chance to "pay us out," and, secondly, our position would be weaker than if we had been thinking and acting entirely in our own defense.

The anti-interventionists were accused of many things, including being pro-Nazi and fifth columnists. President Roosevelt called them "defeatists."

Definition, February 1, 1941

What is defeatism? Who are defeatists? Appeasers are defeatists, if you mean those who could wish their country to buy its peace with the aggressor, either with things of its own or the things of other people, as at Munich; but they are defeatists, too, who cry down as appeasers those who are jealous to defend America first.

They are defeatists who hold that by selling, lending, leasing or giving our economic strength to Great Britain, we may hope to save the American way of life without having to fight for it ourselves. If the American people are not willing to fight and die for their way of life, they have already lost it, whether they know it or not. We do not shrink from war. That is not our history. Only let it be our war, not a foreign war.

They are defeatists who say, with the *New York Times,* that what "protects our young men from the danger of battle," what gives us "such security as we now enjoy," is "the bodies of British civilians exposed of their own free choice to mutilation and death" who "could end the war by surrender," but would sooner die than yield. If that were our bulwark, we should be ashamed to speak of "protecting our young men from the danger of battle."

They are defeatists who say our future security is dependent upon the outcome of the Battle of Britain. Our security now and for all time is entirely dependent upon ourselves.

They are defeatists who say the "only guaranty of peace for America and of freedom for the peoples of the world, including America, is a victory for British arms." There can be no guaranty of peace, now or ever; and if American freedom now is dependent upon a victory of British arms in Europe, American history has been a mistake. Let us erase it. Let us repent in time to save the British Empire, if we can, and accept the reward of dominion status.

They are defeatists who say this country must defend democracy in Europe to save the American way of life. When we were ten millions, smelting bog iron with charcoal, with no engines, no machines, only very crude tools, we expelled Europe from this continent in order to create the American way of life, and then dared the world to touch it. Now we are one hundred and thirty million, the richest nation on the earth, with an industrial power equal to that of all Europe combined—and afraid.

They are defeatists who talk of making America the "nonfighting ally of Great Britain." What is a nonfighting ally?

They are defeatists who have doubted the power of America to stand alone in its own hemisphere, to defend itself against any aggressor or combination of aggressors,

137

to make its own world impregnable.

They are defeatists who dream of defeating the aggressor without fighting him.

They are defeatists who say an Anglo-American alliance is the only alternative to Fascism.

They are defeatists who would lean upon the gratitude of nations. For what would England be grateful? That we had wrought and sold to her the weapons to fight a war that was said by our Government to be our war too? She would remember only the saying she overheard in Washington, "It is as if the British were our mercenaries."

They are defeatists who have brought to pass that state of facts acknowledged in the words of the Committee to Defend America by Aiding the Allies: "We are opposed to appeasement, believing that a negotiated peace would inevitably be at the expense of the United States." That is true. But why is it true? Because we are not yet prepared to accept the consequences of the acts of war and enmity we have committed against Hitler. The weapons we have forged for England might be turned against us. We have no status in the war. We are not Great Britain's ally. And yet Great Britain, owing us nothing, could let us down. Any peace she might negotiate could be at our expense. What a triumph of foreign policy!

They are defeatists who, having involved this country in a war for which it is not prepared, now call upon its fortitude to face the fact that if England falls, we shall have lost the war vessels, the planes, the weapons and munitions delivered to her by the American Government out of its own arsenals, its own equipment, its own defense production, at the cost of weakening the national defense—and the possibility that we shall stand at war between two enemies, one in the Atlantic and one in the Pacific, neither of whom had attacked us.

They are defeatists who develop the beautiful thought that if America will now put her strength forth in the world, instead of keeping it selfishly to herself, the principle of evil can be chained down. Then all the free and liberal and liberated people will collaborate to bring to pass a just peace and a new world, and live and let live together happily for a millennium. There is no such world in reality. Suppose we had reconquered Europe for democracy, and the principle of evil were chained down. What should we do about the peace? Leave it to Europe? We did that once. It cannot be imagined that Europe would leave it to us. In any case, somehow, there would be the peace, because the war had stopped, and we should have some responsibility in it. Should we stay there to police it? Or should we come home and stand ready to go back to mind or mend it when something went wrong?

These, too, are defeatists, we say, because they would give America to save the world.

The And-Americans, February 1, 1941

A long tradition of free speech had created in the American mind a habit of credulity toward the world. The war bringers entered that tradition and betrayed it. This is to speak not of their convictions, right or wrong, but of their principles and methods. It was propaganda in the scientific Old World technique, deeply conceived, powerfully organized, clothed in American garments.

Any American citizen had a perfect right to preach a second crusade in Europe or to advocate a London-Washington Axis. The few who did that in a forthright manner could be met on the field of honest controversy. But the and-America strategists who controlled the war propaganda knew better than to name their objectives in the beginning. Therefore, they advanced under such hypnotic phrases as "measures short of war," and "defend America by aiding the Allies," which gathered up in an emotional mass all the hatred of Hitler, all the natural feeling among us for Great Britain, all the abhorrence of war and all the hope there was of keeping the war away. On the ground they occupied they could not be attacked precisely for the reason that it was false ground. Anyone who challenged their slogans had to prove a meaning that was not literally there and one which they plausibly disclaimed.

Measures short of war were to keep the country out of war. If you doubted it you were a fascist, fifth columnist or appeaser.

It was perfect strategy. Yet there was a point of weakness in it. A time would come when it would be necessary to introduce a trestle phrase by which to pass from the false premise to the true one. It would have to be a phrase strong enough to bear not only the engine but a long train of cars in which many innocents were riding in good faith, and at the same time a phrase not too alarming. That time did come and we propose to leave here a record of the curious thing that happened.

The great engine of this propaganda was the Committee to Defend America by Aiding the Allies. Soon after the election in November it issued a new statement of policy, saying among other things that active military involvement was possible. That was not the trestle. It was the opening of the switch by which the train left the track it had been running on. Two or three passengers noticed that was happening and publicly jumped. Apparently William Allen White, the chairman, was not looking.

The trestle was produced not by the chairman, who suddenly found himself on it and was scared, nor by the full committee, but by a little knot of and-America strategists. It was in the form of a message to the President, with 170 signatures urging him in his fireside chat on the great emergency to say it was "the settled policy of this country to try to do everything that may be necessary to ensure the defeat of the Axis powers." No longer measures short of war. But everything! Everything to defeat Hitler would mean war.

Roy Howard, of the Scripps-Howard Newspapers, sent a telegram to William Allen White asking him to define the position of his committee on war. Mr. White replied from Emporia, saying: "The only reason in God's world that I am in this organization is to keep this country out of war." He was still for measures short of war, within the law—within the Johnson Act forbidding loans to Great Britain, within the Neutrality Act forbidding American ships to carry war goods to belligerents, and if he himself were making a slogan for the Committee to Defend America by Aiding the Allies it would be, "The Yanks are not coming." He begged that his committee be not condemned because there were some martial-minded people in it, and added that "Any organization that is for war is seriously playing Hitler's game."

This left the Committee to Defend America by Aiding the Allies stalled on the trestle. The only thing its strategists could do was to repudiate the chairman's statement and threaten to repudiate him. From the trestle builders and the martial minded he received violent telegrams, calling him pallid and ineffective and wishing him happiness in the embrace of the appeasers. What other pressure came upon him we do not know. We know only that two days later another message was sent to the President, saying there were a few names to be added to the petition urging "Everything that may be necessary to insure the defeat of the Axis Powers," and among the names thus added, in an obscure position, without comment or adjunct, was the name of William Allen White.

By this time the Committee to Defend America by Aiding the Allies was split between supporters of aid and supporters of war. William Allen White resigned on January 1, 1941. He remained as honorary chairman until May, when he insisted that his name be removed. By that time, the argument had passed beyond the issue of aid, and the committee faded out.

Smearing, February 15, 1941

The national mind is a conglomerate of individual minds. If it is impossible for the individual mind to arrive at a grave decision by a straight line, which we know to be so, then that must be true also of the national mind, only of course much more. If the question to be decided by the national mind is one that involves war, the conflict which in the individual mind is settled by inner voices takes the form of a raging public dispute, and it follows that an enormous amount of passion will be released. Nevertheless, as we prefer free government, defined as government by discussion, there is no other way. Moreover, those who possess strong convictions have not only the right but the duty to put them forth, always subject to one restraint. We have no right and it is indecent to impugn one another's motives.

This, we think, has been the weakness of the work of Rush D. Holt,[7] the discontinued young senator from West Virginia. It has been his obsession that the one controlling war motive is a greed motive; that a man is a member of the Committee to Defend America by Aiding the Allies because he owns shares in General Electric or an interest in metals. He points to such a man as Lewis Douglas[8] and thinks it is a sinister fact that he has money in chemicals. We no more believe that Lewis Douglas would wish to involve his country in war because he has American Cynamid shares than we suspect Rush D. Holt of taking money from Hitler. No one can have been more antagonistic than the *Post* to the work of the war bringers and to their ways of thinking and feeling; yet we do not for a moment doubt their sincerity or their patriotism, according to their own lights; and least of all do we suspect their motives to be in their pockets. Nor can we believe, with the President, that there exists in this whole country any group of men who would clip the wings of the American eagle to feather their own nests. We should hate to believe that the individual who would do it is not extremely rare.

This kind of smearing becomes at length puerile, as no one is immune, and the smearers begin to smear one another. Even the Committee to Defend America by Aiding the Allies divided to smear itself, with Mayor La Guardia saying William Allen White had "done a Laval" by insisting that measures short of war really meant to keep the country out.[9] As we disagree, violently if need be, let us keep to the argument and remember that we are Americans all.

One of the attacks President Roosevelt made on the anti-interventionists is that they were standing in the way of "unity."

Unity, February 22, 1941

Immediately after the election there was a feast of unity. All the ugly partisan words that had been uttered during the campaign were declared to be unsaid. Bundles of dead printed matter that would otherwise have gone to the junkman were committed to public bonfires, as a gesture. We were going to show the dictators that the people of a democracy could think and feel as one. And while that emotion was running it seemed that in the entire country there was but one voice—a voice saying, "Support the President."

Two months later, with a bitterness of debate rising over H.R. 1776—a bill[10] in which the President was demanding from Congress a grant of unlimited powers— people were asking, "What has happened to our unity?"

Nothing had happened to it. Something else had happened.

For an invincible national defense, to be immediately created at any cost, there was still complete unity of public opinion. Hatred of the aggressor was still a national attitude. Sympathy for Great Britain was still a controlling emotion.

But upon this very extraordinary unity of mind and feeling the Government undertook to impose, by its own will, an Anglo-American policy that would be almost certain to involve us in the European war as an active belligerent, and at the same time demanded for itself full totalitarian powers. For these fateful departures, beyond any consent of the governed, the President expected instant and patriotic unity. He spoke of using against the obstructionists, if necessary, "the sovereignty of government to save government."

The impassioned debate that followed was not a sign of disunity. It was a sign of a surviving sense of sovereignty in the people. So long as we have a government of the people, by the people, for the people, that is where sovereignty resides—in the people, not in government.

There is no such thing as sovereignty of government separate from the free will of people. And if the people, from whom the government derives its powers, may not debate whether or not they shall go to war, what their government shall be and what it shall do, and impose their will upon it, then we are coming to the end of a long delusion.

Unity is not the problem. It is never been the problem. Unity is not the sound of a word nor may it be established by any intimidation of slogans. The government with all its power cannot command unity. Either it is a fact of the willing spirit or it does not exist.

If war comes, there will be unity. We take it for granted. When war comes, if it does, the *Post,* for all it has said against war, will be found supporting the Government that got us into it, because that will be the only Government there is. The time to debate war and the policies that lead to it is before. Afterward there is but one side.

MEANINGS

Chapter six notes

[1] The Committee to Defend America by Aiding the Allies.

[2] This was the Norden bomb sight, which used a mechanical analog computer.

[3] Coudert, who later broke away to join the more clearly pro-war Fight For Freedom Committee, was also the legal adviser to the British consul general in New York.

[4] James B. Conant, 1893-1978, president of Harvard 1933-41, director of the National Defense Research Committee during the war (with a role in the atom bomb project), later ambassador to West Germany and a writer on education. Conant declared about this time, "This is in essence a religious war—a war to my mind between good and evil."

5 Philip Henry Kerr, 11th Marquis of Lothian, 1882-1940, was British ambassador early in the war.

[6] Henry Noel Brailsford, *From England to America: A Message*, New York: Whittlesey House, 1940.

[7] Rush Holt, 1905-1955, "the boy senator," was elected to take office Jan. 3, 1934, but was not sworn in until June 21 because he had to wait until he was 30. He had some fetching political lines. During the conscription debate on August 22, 1940, he denounced those who would draft men but not raise taxes. "According to their theory," he said, "they can take a boy out and kill him, and that is democracy; but if they are required to put their hand in their pocket and take a dime out before they kill him, that is regimentation." Holt lost the Democratic renomination in 1941. His son, also Rush Holt, Democrat of New Jersey, was elected to the House of Representatives in 1999.

[9] Lewis Douglas, 1894-1974, Democrat of Arizona, served in the House 1927-1933, and was Roosevelt's director of the budget, 1933-34. In 1941 he was president of an insurance company; after the war he was ambassador to Great Britain.

[9] Fiorella La Guardia had written an open letter Dec. 26, 1940, coming out against White. "When the going was good for the Allies, you and others were strong in saying what you would do," La Guardia wrote. "Now that the going is bad, you are doing a typical Laval. . ." Laval was the French foreign minister who had given in to the Germans.

[10] The Lend-Lease bill, described in the chapter after next.

Chapter Seven
REMINDER

Memories, March 1, 1941

Twenty-four years ago, this romantic country, singing hymns to peace, was passing under the sign of Mars. The analogies and disparities both are striking.

In November 1916, President Wilson had been re-elected by a very close vote; and it had been remembered ever since as an ironic fact that the most effective slogan on the Democratic Party's campaign posters was: "He Kept Us Out of War."

The war had then been going on for more than two years, and there was a powerful war party that had been saying all the time it was our war too; that Great Britain was fighting our fight, and that we should go to her side in defense of humanity, civilization, freedom. That was not President Wilson's view of it. In fact, he had rejected it, and had said against it that there was such a thing as being too proud to fight—a phrase that many times came back to mock him.

The American Government was neutral. To avoid war, it had sublimated many German outrages, beginning with the sinking of the Lusitania, in which 114 American lives were lost; and it had with great difficulty obtained from the German government a pledge to keep submarine warfare within the laws of humanity, at least so far as neutrals were concerned. The only advantage of the Anglo-French allies was that by reason of controlling the sea they had exclusive access to the American money market, where they floated very large loans, and to American industry as a supplier of munitions. But all of that was strictly within both the letter and the spirit of international law.

President Wilson's mind and nature were hard-shaped against war. Peace was his controlling passion; to be the peacemaker was his grand ambition. This the world very well knew.

A few weeks after he had been re-elected he received from the German side a peace note, suggesting negotiations or at least an exchange of views; and this he transmitted to the Anglo-French allies, who flatly rejected it. Thereupon, in mid-December, he addressed to all belligerents alike a note of his own, asking them to say what the war was about. Were they not all saying the same things? Were they not all talking about humanity, civilization, freedom and right? Was the moment not come to be explicit and to talk of peace, perhaps?

The American war party's reactions to the President's act were extraordinary. *The New York Times* said: "The war must go on. The people of the United States must assume whatever responsibilities its further prosecution thrusts upon them." Fifty distinguished prelates, professors and laymen joined in an appeal to the Christian spirit to resist any effort to promote a premature peace. This appeal was signed by George Wharton Pepper, Dr. William T. Manning of Trinity Church, Dr. John Grier Hibben of Princeton University, Dr. Henry C. King of Oberlin College and, among others, Billy Sunday, the evangelist.[1]

The reactions in England, of course, were bitter. Hall Caine, the novelist,[2] then with the British propaganda service, reported them to the *New York Times*. "We began," he said, "by regarding the President's note as a blow to the moral sense of the allied nations, and of Great Britain in particular. No added enormity on the part of Germany would seem to us to justify America in calling upon the Allies, either directly or indirectly, to call a truce to the war in order that the German barbarity may destroy American lives no more."

It occurred to the British that in his zeal to promote peace, or, as would now be said, to appease Germany, President Wilson might take some steps to hinder the export of American munitions and foodstuffs to the allied side; and, this, they said, would be little short of taking the other side; it would, in fact, be war in disguise, and so regarded. The American ambassador to London was in agony; and all the other American friends of Great Britain, both here and abroad, began to make apologies for the President.

The Senate upheld the President's act; it was proper for him to ask all the belligerents alike to state their war aims and name their peace terms, if they knew them. But he had said in his note that the United States might undertake to guarantee a just peace, because "we as a nation are interested in the future protection and welfare of the small nations of Europe"—and this became the subject of impassioned debate. Senator Borah[3] wanted the Senate to reaffirm the doctrine of Washington, Jefferson and Monroe against meddling in Europe. William Howard Taft's private and very influential League to Enforce Peace ardently supported the President in that part of his position. Theodore Roosevelt violently attacked both the President as an appeaser and the idea of such a thing as a league to enforce peace, on the ground that under certain circumstances it might become wickedly absurd. George Haven Putnam,[4] one of the leaders of the war party, was advocating simply that the United States join with England and France to chain the Kaiser down on St. Helena Island. Neutrality was denounced as a moral debacle. Did the Administration "realize the damage to the American temperament and character attending the formation of the neutrality habit"?

Such was the state of feeling for and against war, and the national mind taut with excitement, when on January 22, 1917, President Wilson appeared before the Senate to announce the great idea of his life, which was "Peace without victory" and a League of Nations to enforce it. The Senate rostrum was his pulpit. He was talking to the world.

"I am proposing, as it were," he said, "that the nations should with one accord adopt the declaration of President Monroe as the doctrine of the world—that no nation should seek to extend its policy over any other nation or people, its own way of development, unhindered, unthreatened, unafraid, the little along with the great and powerful. . . When all unite to act in the same sense and with the same purpose, all are in the common interest and are free to live their own lives under a common protection. There is no entangling alliance in a concert of power." The foundations of peace among nations were going to be laid down; the American people were going to take part in that enterprise. It would have to be a just peace, of course, and then, how should it be made secure? Mere agreements would not do it. "It must be," he said, "a peace made secure by an organized major force of mankind. It will absolutely be necessary that a force be created as a guarantor of the permanency of the settlement so much greater than the force of any nation now engaged, any alliance hitherto formed or projected, that no nation, no probable combination of nations, could face or withstand it."

The Senate was dazed.

Senator LaFollette[5] said, "We have just passed through a very important hour in the history of the world."

Senator Warren[6] said, "The President thinks he is president of the world."

Another senator said, "It will make Don Quixote wish he hadn't died so soon."

The *New York World* said it was a message to mankind. The *New York Times* said that hunger, the spirit of aggression, the desire for national expansion were to be annihilated; and this, it thought, was the voice of the American people. Other editors treated it as either an oration on the millennium or as a colossal pro-American document.

Yet there was a terrific recoil from the idea of peace without victory. The British complained bitterly that this might have been expected of a President who had said there was such a thing as being too proud to fight. Generally, it was wishfully supposed that Germany was about to crack. Therefore, peace without victory would save her. And for that Mr. Wilson was called a cat's paw for Germany. At the next meeting of the Pilgrims in New York at the Bankers Club, James K. Beck said, "I do understand the temper of France and England—they will fight until they either conquer or are conquered. If the latter should come to pass, woe betide the United States. If the former should come to pass—as please God it will—then the most the Americans can hope is that the brave people of those nations who are fighting and bleeding and dying for ideals in which we have as vital a stake as they, may believe that Mr. Wilson's policy of peace without victory did not represent the views or reflect the sympathies of the American people."

What might have happened in place of what did does not belong to history. Germany had not lost the war. She was not about to crack. Nor was it inevitable that this country should go in. What did happen was that the Germans stupidly misunderstood the grim side of Mr. Wilson's character.

One week after he had proposed peace without victory, and the world still ringing with it, the German government announced the resumption of unlimited submarine warfare; it would sink any vessel, enemy or neutral, at sight and without warning, except only one American liner a week, provided it displayed marks and signals described by Germany. Thus the pledge to the President of the United States was broken. Three days later the German ambassador received his passports. Diplomatic relations were severed. Through the Austrian ambassador the German government made overtures to avoid war. The President said he was deaf to any word Germany might say, short of renewing its broken pledge. This it refused to do. Our next step was to begin arming American merchant ships. There was still some faint hope of averting war until, on March first, the American Government learned of the famous Zimmermann note inviting Mexico and Japan to join with Germany in war against the United States. On April second the President appeared before a joint session of

Congress and advised a declaration of war. The resolution declaring war was passed by a vote of 82 to 6 in the Senate and 373 to 50 in the House, and took effect on April sixth. But it was our war, our own quarrel with Germany. England and France were not our allies. On this point President Wilson was rigid. Formally the role of the United States was that of associate, not ally. Yet there had to be slogans in common. What were they? A War to End War. A War to Make the World Safe for Democracy.

The sequels have other anniversaries. There is one, however, that may have been forgotten. At St. Louis, in September 1919, President Wilson said, "The real reason that the war we have just finished took place was that Germany was afraid her commercial rivals were going to get the better of her, and the reason why some nations went into the war against Germany was that they thought Germany would get the commercial advantage of them. The seed of the jealousy, the seed of the deep-seated hatred was hot, successful commercial and industrial rivalry. . . It was not a political war."

And almost his last sad word of advice to his country was to forge for itself the longest and most dangerous sword of all, the form of it to be incomparably the greatest navy in the world.

Garrett's experience in World War I included a visit to Germany in December 1915, more than a year before America officially entered the war. In the New York Times *he wrote:*

"The conviction that the United States is not neutral pervades every class of German opinion. The charges are mainly these, that the United States furnishes ammunition to the enemy on a scale which cannot be reconciled with a neutral spirit, that its demands have rendered Germany's submarine warfare illusory, and that it has not in like temper insisted upon its neutral trade rights against the sea power of England."

What that meant was that the United States had insisted on being able to ship cargoes to Britain unmolested by

Germany, but had not insisted on a similar right to ship them to Germany unmolested by Britain. America was not minding its own business nor looking out strictly for its own interests.

Chapter seven notes

[1] George Wharton Pepper, 1867-1961, was chairman of the Pennsylvania Council of Defense during World War I, and later a senator from Pennsylvania. John Grier Hibben, 1861-1933, succeeded Woodrow Wilson as president of Princeton University in 1912. Billy Sunday, 1862-1935, was an evangelist and prohibitionist.

[2] Hall Caine, 1853-1931, wrote several best-selling novels, including *The Christian* (1897).

[3] William E. Borah, 1865-1940, "the lion of Idaho," Republican senator 1907-1940. Borah led the "irreconcilables" in the Senate against the Versailles Treaty and opposed U.S. entry into the League of Nations. He opposed military intervention in Latin America in the 1920s and fought a weakening of the Neutrality Act in 1939. A key isolationist.

[4] George Haven Putnam, 1844-1940, book publisher—one of G.P. Putnam's sons.

[5] Robert La Follette, 1855-1925, senator from Wisconsin 1906-1925. He opposed entry into World War I, conscription, the Espionage Act and the League of Nations. He broke with the Republicans in 1924 to run for president a Progressive, winning one-sixth of the vote. His son Robert La Follette Jr. was senator from Wisconsin 1926-1946, when he was defeated in the primary by Joseph McCarthy.

[6] Francis Warren, 1844-1929, Republican of Wyoming, was awarded the Congressional Medal of Honor during the Civil War and served in the Senate 1890-1893 and 1895-1929.

Chapter Eight
LAST STAND

In December 1940 Britain ran out of money. President Roosevelt appealed to the nation: If your neighbor's house was on fire, he said, wouldn't you lend him your garden hose? Would you quibble over cash? This idea became Lend-Lease, a bill, artfully numbered H.R. 1776, to aid any country "whose defense the President deems vital to the defense of the United States."

Not just Britain, but any country. It was a huge delegation of power. Senator Robert Taft, Republican of Ohio, said it gave the President "power to carry on a kind of undeclared war all over the world, in which America would do everything except actually put soldiers in the front line trenches." To Garrett, it was the real declaration of war. With Lend-Lease, he wrote years later, the anti-interventionists "were making their last stand."

Behold! The Brass Serpent, February 15, 1941

We date the words that are to follow. The moment is mid-January of the one hundred and fifty-second American year. We do this for the reason that by the time they are printed the debate may be closed, which would mean that freedom of expression could no longer be defended. On the other hand, we owe it to what we believe, and to the millions who have believed it with us, to hold our position at least until dark.

We speak here of neither war nor peace.

As we write, the news is running that the President has asked the Congress of the United States to abdicate. In the news it is worded softly. The headline in the *New York Times* reads: BILL GIVES PRESIDENT UNLIMITED POWER TO LEND WAR EQUIPMENT AND RESOURCES. A triumph of ingenious understatement. The formal title of the bill is softer still. It reads: A BILL FURTHER TO PROMOTE THE DEFENSE OF THE UNITED STATES, AND FOR OTHER PURPOSES.

Then we look at the bill. Remember, it is the President's own bill. It is what he wants. Therefore, it is the authentic revelation of his mind. Taking it from the bill, this is what he wants:

Power in his own discretion, on his own terms and as he may see fit, to conduct undeclared war anywhere in the world.

Power in his own discretion to make friends and enemies of other nations.

Power in his own discretion to employ the total resources of the country to such ends.

Power in his own discretion to make military alliances with other governments; and to lend, lease or give to other governments any of the military resources of the United States, nothing excepted save man power, and that only by not being specifically mentioned.

Power to make by edict such laws as he may deem necessary in order to carry out his intentions.

Power to command money in any amount.

Power himself to delegate any or all of that power to whom he likes.

Significantly, and the for the first time in the eight-year history of progressive acts of surrender on the part of Congress, there was in his bill no limit of time. It might be forever.

These are the standard powers of a dictator.

There is always the saying that what the Congress gives it can take back. This is to forget, first, that it is the nature of power to entrench and ramify itself; secondly, that the hook with which the executive principle draws tame Leviathan out has a barb. It is much easier for Congress to delegate power than to take it back. To delegate it requires but a bare majority. To get it back, if the President is unwilling to give it up, requires a two-thirds vote.

We do not suppose that the bill will be enacted in the original form. Undoubtedly, Congress will at least give it a time limit. But nothing that the Congress may write into it or out of it, reminiscent of its equal power, can erase the original writing or change its meaning.

In the last great temple of freedom the image of absolute government has been unveiled, and prepared multitudes have cried, Huzza! To be saved from the scourge of the totalitarian principle sinful democracy now must embrace the anointed likeness of it. As a brazen serpent it has been held out to the people by their leader; and among those who have said, "Behold, this will save us," are as many who only a little while before were afraid of this very thing, foreseeing that it might happen, and exhorted others to harden their minds against it.

History may say the people were carried away by one of the great leaders of modern times, one who knew how to play upon their fears and passions as upon strings. It is not so simple. They were a believing people. They believed words.

In his message to Congress on the state of the nation, January sixth, declaring it to be the policy of the American Government to defend freedom and democracy everywhere in the world, the President said: "In the recent national election there was no substantial difference between the two great political parties in respect to that policy. No issue was fought out on this line before the American electorate."

Why not? Because during the campaign both parties and both candidates held rigidly to the formula of aid to the democracies by "measures short of war." The people believed these words. Literally, they believed them.

Immediately after the election, the President jettisoned that formula for what it was—a slogan. Never after he had been re-elected did he use it again.

During the campaign these were the words of the President: "We will not participate in foreign wars and will not send our army, navy or air forces to fight in foreign lands outside of the Americas except in case of attack. . . The basic purpose of our foreign policy is to keep our country out of war."

Suppose he had said then: "If I am re-elected we are going to go all out for England. If I am re-elected I shall demand that Congress delegate me the power, in my own discretion, to conduct undeclared American war anywhere in the world in defense of the democracies, and to employ for that purpose any weapons, munitions, aircraft, vessels, commodities and facilities whatever; and power, moreover, in my own discretion to make such laws as may be necessary. And then, my friends, we need not waste your time and my time debating whether or not to repeal the Neutrality Law or the Johnson Act. Let Congress send them out to be framed and keep them."

If he had said these things—if he had told the people what he had meant to do—would there have been no issue on this line before the American electorate?

We did not believe it could be done to the American people; and we were wrong. We did not believe they could be moved by suggestion to involve their birthright in this contradiction. The President tells them that America must put its strength forth to save Great Britain, to save China, to defend democracy of all kinds, everywhere in the world, and to destroy out of it forever the principle of aggression, because, for one reason, "In times like these it is immature—and, incidentally, untrue—for anyone to brag that an unprepared America, single-handed and with one hand tied behind its back, can hold off the whole world." All in one speech.

The figure of a country with one hand tied behind its back is obviously a reference to the manner in which the parliamentary principle—namely, the Congress—handicaps a ruler. The dictator, with no Congress to worry about, has both hands free. And that is what the President wants.

Whither now, America?

To save yourself you must save the world. To this you have been persuaded. That road, whatever else you may make of it, is the totalitarian road, straight and fast at first, then more and more perilous to the end of the pavement. There is no way back but through futility, confusion and disaster. There is no going on but with the fantasy to become moral emperor of the whole world.

In "Rise of Empire" (1952), Garrett said the whole structure of America's foreign alliances and military commitments, which amounted to Empire, started here, with Lend-Lease. He wrote: "It was the most reckless delegation of power by the Congress to the President that had ever been made or imagined, amounting in fact to abdication."

Toward the Unknown, March 29, 1941

Looking back is to say farewell. Misgivings are forbidden, but let us not on that account be mistaken about what has happened. It is not a new chapter of American history that now opens. It is a new book with a new theme. The story that began with the Declaration of Independence is finished.

We have broken with our past. We have thrown away our New World, our splendid isolation, our geographical advantage of three to one against all aggressors, our separate political religion. There is no longer a New World, nor an Old World, but now one world in which the American people have been cast for a part they will have to learn as they go along.

There is no longer a Monroe Doctrine. In place of it there is an American Internationalism. We do not yet know what this means.

From now on for us there is no foreign war. Any war anywhere in the world is our war, provided only there is an aggressor to be destroyed, a democracy to be saved or an area of freedom to be defended.

Our ideas of aggressor, democracy and freedom are emotionally clear. Unfortunately, as we go forward in this crusade we shall encounter many moral and logical contradictions. These we must learn to resolve. Every Hitler we

159

must crush. That has been made definite. But every Stalin too? For practical and strategic reasons we have just now relieved Stalin of our moral disapproval. That does not necessarily mean that we have forgotten Finland; it does not mean that we shall not in time restore to her that which was her own. It does show how liable we are to be misunderstood and how easy it will be for the world to say that our moral indignation is selective.

It is too soon to be either critical or analytical. Hardly the first page of the new book has been written. What will follow we do not know. How could we? There was never in all human history a story like it. We began it unconsciously. That is to say, we did not know we were doing it. Indeed, we kept saying we were not. This fact, no doubt, will give the historian some trouble. It may restore him to his faith in a mysterious agency that moves people unawares; it may even wreck the wretched theory of pure economic determinism in human affairs.

In August last year, the British prime minister, speaking of the fifty destroyers he had got from the U.S. Navy, said to the House of Commons, "Undoubtedly this process means that these two great organizations of the English-speaking democracies, the British Empire and the United States, will have to be somewhat mixed up together in some of their affairs for mutual and general advantage. . .No one can stop it. Like the Mississippi, it just keeps rolling along."

The American people took this to be rhetoric. They did not know the British government was announcing American foreign policy.

In October, at Philadelphia, the President of the United States said, "I give to you and to the people of this country this most solemn assurance. There is no secret treaty, no secret obligation, no secret commitment, no secret understanding of any shape or form, direct or indirect, with any other government, or any other nation in any part of the world—no such secrecy that might or could, in any shape, involve this nation in any war or for any other purpose. Is that clear?"

160

He said, "The United States today is at peace and is going to remain at peace."

He said, one rainy day at New Haven, of the draft, "It is just for the same reason that you have got umbrellas up today, so as not to get wet."

And on October twenty-fourth he said, "I repeat again that I stand on the platform of our party: 'We will not participate in foreign wars.'"

On that platform he was elected to a third term. On Election Day the American people were writing the last line in the old book and did not know it.

Three months later the President announced, "We are committed to the proposition that principles of morality and consideration for our own security will never permit us to acquiesce in a peace dictated by aggressors and sponsored by appeasers."

"We" were the people, suddenly staring at the fact that we had assumed ultimate and unlimited liability—moral, physical and financial—for the outcome of war on three continents, for the survival of the British Empire, and for the utter destruction of Hitler. Anything less or else would be the first American defeat.

How had we arrived there?

Not by any act of conscious will on the part of the American people, but by will of government. If you say, therefore, the people have lost control of government and such is the end of the American system, that may or may not be true, but you are reading from the old book. Destiny is not legal.

How the people would have voted if the question of taking over war on three continents had been put to them will never be known. The question was not put to them.

We know what the people did vote for. They voted for a President who stood upon his platform saying, "We will not participate in foreign wars." But there again make sure to remember which book you are in. Words in the old book were simply understood. In the new book that cannot be so. Why it cannot be so belongs to another essay. Anyhow, what is a foreign war? In that instant when you say, or even think, "This is our war too," it is no longer a foreign war, no matter what you said it was yesterday.

We have said it. Standing in the middle of the world we are saying, "Here is the arsenal of all democracy," meaning by democracy any nation that will employ our weapons against Hitler. That makes the Battle of Britain our battle, too, and the battle of Greece our battle, and the battle of the Mediterranean our battle; and everywhere in the world it is the London-Washington Axis against the Berlin-Rome-Tokyo Axis. Where then, is foreign war, strictly speaking?

What if our axis should break? What if Great Britain should fail in spite of us? That could happen. We should then have Hitler on one side and his Japanese partner on another side, neither of whom has attacked us, both of whom we have challenged, one of them to mortal combat.

For perilous isolation on those terms we are unprepared. Yet we have accepted that risk. It was not a realistic thing to do. You would expect school boys fighting on a sand lot to know better statesmanship. But a crusade is above statesmanship. So is any great transaction of the human spirit. Essentially it is heedless of danger and romantically creating its own political realities. Everything about it is improbable.

But if we speak of the improbable, what could have been more improbable than the story in the first book? Was there ever a more reckless political deed than the Declaration of Independence? One outcome more unpredictable than that a few ragged, undisciplined farmers with muskets, and some solitary mountaineers with rifles, should expel the trained armies of Europe from this land in order to create what was not yet imagined and had not yet a name—the United States of America? Why no more can we imagine the end of what now is beginning, nor has it any name. We cannot see the shape of the world to come, not dimly. It is not permitted. We know for sure only that neither the world that was our own nor that world which is round will ever be the same again.

At the beginning of the blitzkrieg, with its revelation of the frightfulness of modern technology turned in full use to the business of killing and conquest, the *Post* said it was this country against Hitler—simply that, because no other country possessed the strength, the skill and the resources to create in defense of peace a weapon power equal to this new power of aggression in the hands of a war-loving people. We have never modified this conviction. We say it still.

Our quarrel with the interventionists has been upon other grounds.

Firstly, upon grounds of military and political sagacity, that by taking the war to Hitler we forfeit our natural geographical advantage, that the status of a nonfighting belligerent exists only in puerile delusion, that as we strip the American arsenals and put weapons in the hands of others we weaken our own defense, and that by all of this we involve our fate with cards of war that might at any moment be played out of our hands.

Secondly, we have quarreled with them on the ground that they stultify the American motive. They say the battle of Britain is our battle, and they say that to save ourselves we must save Great Britain, and then they said the by making America the arsenal we may ourselves avoid the battlefield, using the bodies of the British as a bulwark to save the body of every American mother's son. If we had ever believed that, or felt it, we should have been ashamed to say it. We never knew, on the other hand, a true isolationist who was not willing to fight and die for it.

And thirdly, we quarrel with the interventionists still, on the grounds that they conceal, or have not themselves the courage to face, what it means to this country, not merely to take over the war, but in doing that to assume a role in which it must either go on and on until it has gained moral hegemony of the whole world—or fail.

There is the truth; and there is a sense of grandeur in it. The battle of Britain becomes but a terrible episode. The London-Washington Axis is a platoon. This is our walk with destiny, toward an end we cannot see, and if we arrive we shall have walked most of the way alone, as England did before us.

The Lend-Lease bill was amended to say that nothing in it authorized convoying of merchant ships by the U.S. Navy. It was passed 260-165 in the House and 60-31 in the Senate, with most of the support from Democrats. President Roosevelt signed it into law March 11, 1941.

Now One War Aim, April 12, 1941

Having arrived at the war, the League of Many Names to Save America by Saving the World is in search of aims. It is saying: "Now that we are in—and for a fact we are in—let us take thought and think big and make up our minds what it is we are going to fight for. We have agreed that to save the American way of life we must save the British way, the Norwegian way, the Chinese way, and so on, but do we know what we mean? Do we know what we are going to save them for? Let us say now what kind of new world we want. Let us say what the shape of the peace shall be, write the specifications and get them initialed all around by those who are about to be saved."

We understand the crusader passion, even though we seldom share it, but when the crusader begins to think, we lose him entirely. He ought not to spoil it by thinking. By thinking, he may become as much a liability to the war he has helped bring us into as he was to the peace before.

Democracy is the beautiful damsel to be saved—democracy in the whole world. Having girded ourselves for that heroic errand, shall we pause to ask if she will mend her morals and submit them hereafter to American opinion? Under the circumstances, what would her promise be worth? Either she is worth saving as she is and was, or she is not worth saving at all. Moreover, nobody can possibly foretell, few can even imagine, what the state of the world will be when this is over, or what materials there will be to restore it with.

The time to have thought of war aims was before. Suppose the British should state their war aims and we liked them not; or suppose we should formulate ours and Britain declined to embrace them. On either account,

164

would it be possible for us to abandon democracy and retire within our hemisphere? And if that were possible, what becomes of the original defense thesis—namely, that on cold strategic grounds we could save ourselves only by saving Great Britain?

The reasons why people go to war are three only. They go to war to defend something, to destroy something or to take something. There is nothing we wish to take. Our reasons, therefore can be two only. They are, first, to defend our own; second, to destroy a monstrous and menacing principle of aggression. To be dreaming at the same time to be bringing to pass a near-perfect world may be a grand and necessary emotional release, but let us not be too much self-deceived.

We shall be lucky, indeed, to get back a world as good as the one we had, full of evil and trouble still, but with the balance of power in the hands of people who, on the whole, prefer peace over war, and such a world as it was when governments were loath to repudiate their bonds, dishonor their money and break the law of nations, or, when they did, had at least a sense of guilt about it.

How we got into the war we shall not know entirely until we read the history that now is hidden. We are in it. We are in it all together. Rightly we may say that we got into it and could have been got into it, only because a great majority of us want one thing, no matter how violently we may have disagreed about the way of getting it. We want a world ex-Hitler. Here we hold with Winston Churchill, the mighty realist, who is impatient with those who in the midst of a battle clamor for a statement of war aims, a charter, a covenant, a blueprint of the new order that is to come afterward. The one war aim is to destroy Hitler.

If we should fail to do that, it would be the first American defeat. And it would be a defeat for all of us alike—for those who believed in taking over the war instead of standing upon our own defense and for those who did not, for interventionists and isolationists, for reactionaries and liberals, for federal unionists and world savers.

After Lend-Lease, the next issue was convoys. On March 17 the Committee to Defend America by Aiding the Allies called for U.S. warships to escort merchant ships at sea—a measure that opponents said would lead directly to war. Antiwar legislators introduced measures in Congress that would forbid convoying. Roosevelt did not authorize convoying—but he did authorize "patrolling."

The Case for Unity, April 26, 1941

We have said that for us the debate was closed when Congress enacted the bill that nobody wrote, called the lease-lend bill, also called the aid-to-democracies bill, indexed as H.R. 1776, giving the President unlimited and uncontrolled power, in his own discretion, to conduct undeclared war anywhere in the world against the aggressors.

We were then in the war to defeat Hitler by name. How we were got into it, whether it was inevitable, and what the alternatives were, are questions we leave to be answered in the leisure of historic time. The less we think of them now, the sooner we make up our minds to forget them for the duration of the war, the better it will be all around. All together we are in it. How to get through it and out of it all together must become the one shape of our thoughts; and to do it will require all the mind and character we possess. Such is our contribution to unity. And it is now unity we speak of in a new way.

What is it, to begin with? Common consent is not unity, for there may be unwilling consent. Common obedience is not unity, for whereas you may command obedience, you cannot command unity. Nor is it the sound of many voices all saying one thing at the same time. True unity is that state of mind in which people are freely willing to sink their differences of feeling and conviction for the common end. It is and must be an act of free will. But there is a condition; and the condition is that in order to achieve this act of will, in order to arrive at true unity, people must have absolute faith in the integrity and wholeness of words. The dialectic word, the half-truth, the hypnotic phrase, the

166

wedgelike intention, the progressive revelation of policy—the art, in short, of backing the democratic mule across the bridge to war—may be defended on the realistic ground that democracy in this case had to be saved in spite of itself and could be moved only step by step to embrace the war in time. This we forbear to argue. We do say very earnestly to the war bringers that it now behooves them to cease and desist. Their work is finished, and they impair that unity which has become imperative by reminding the people of how they did it.

It was a mistake, we think, and a disservice to unity, for the Committee to Defend America by Aiding the Allies, immediately after the enactment of H.R. 1776, to issue a new statement of policy, calling for American warships to convoy shipments through Hitler's blockade to Great Britain, for more naval vessels to be transferred to Great Britain, and for a law to permit raising American volunteers to go overseas and fight.

Why was it a mistake? Because it reminds us that every statement of policy that has been made by the Committee to Defend America by Aiding the Allies has turned out to be a precise forecast of Government policy. But that is only what gives its statements news value. It reminds us further:

That immediately after the election last November the committee cast aside the worn-out formula that had done its work, the formula "measures short of war," and so likewise did the Government;

That the committee's next statement of policy called for protecting at any cost the British life line to America, which would mean to send in the flag as an act of war;

That this statement of policy by the committee exactly foreshadowed the President's "arsenal-of-democracy" message to Congress, which was followed at once by the bill H.R. 1776, which we have called "the bill that nobody wrote" because Congress was unable to trace its authorship, but in trying to do so heard the Secretary of State say three times that the Treasury Department wrote it, and the Secretary of the Treasury say he didn't think that was so, and the Secretary of War say that he, for one, had nothing to do with it;

That while this momentous law was in debate by Congress, with questions about convoying the aid with the American flag and transferring more naval vessels to the British being very anxiously discussed, the President said at a White House press conference that he had never considered using the American navy to convoy the shipments, and the Secretary of the Navy announced that he could not afford to transfer away any more naval vessels;

That a few hours after signing H.R. 1776, the President made his "bridge-of-ships" speech, at a dinner of the White House Correspondents Association, with not a word about defending the bridge, and

That the Committee to Defend America by Aiding the Allies then immediately issued its new statement of basic policy, calling for "supplying to the Allies of all possible merchant tonnage, transfer to the Allies of additional destroyers and other naval craft; permission to the Allies to organize convoys in American ports," and *"convoy of ships with American naval vessels if need be."* (italics mine)

To this point, which is war actually, the policy of the committee had been all the time steadily tending, and yet step by step it denied the truth; to the same point the foreign policy of the Government was tending in the same way, and yet step by step the Government denied it.

No reasonable person ever supposed that we should provide a bridge of ships to save democracy and then let Hitler destroy it—that we should provide it and then not defend it with all the force necessary. Not to defend it would be utterly stupid. That we should defend it does not follow as a matter of policy; it follows as B follows A. When the first German gun will be fired at an American target or the first American gun at a German target, nobody knows. But let the Committee to Defend America by Aiding the Allies restrain its impatience; and in the meanwhile we suggest that it be thinking of how to guard the cause of unity from the shock of another individual confession like that of its Herbert Agar, editor of the *Louisville Courier-*

Journal.

No member of the war party has been more forthright about it, and we say that to Mr. Agar's credit. Nevertheless even he comes forward with a trouble on his conscience. On receiving an honorary degree from Boston University he spoke on what journalism should be, and deeply regretted the evasions, and what he was privileged to call the lying, with which H.R. 1776 had been supported to its passage. As one who himself had ardently supported it because he was for war, he could say, when it was all over, that the bill was what Senator Wheeler[1] said it was—not a bill to keep America out of war, but a bill to enable the President to fight an undeclared war on Germany. "That," said Mr. Agar, according to the *New York Times,* "is precisely what it is, and if its defenders had defended it on those grounds we would have won two weeks sooner. Our side kept saying in the press and in the Senate that this lend-lease bill is a bill to keep America out of war. That is bunk. And I think a failure to say exactly what a thing means is an illustration of why our democratic world is being threatened now."

It took some moral courage to say it. Even so, our theme being unity—unity as an imperative—we recommend to Mr. Agar that he sleep with his conscience for the duration of the war, or bequeath it to history. The time to have said this was long before. To be saying it now changes nothing at all and can only bring painfully to mind what has happened to the integrity of words.

There is a faith to be restored, as the President must have felt when, at the dinner of the White House Correspondents Association, he appealed to people for that loyalty, much more than obedience, which "springs from the mind that is given the facts" by a Government pledged "to tell the truth to its citizens."

We must begin to build there, and we must begin to build there simply for the reason that there is no place else to begin; and Mr. Agar does not help by reminding us that until we got into the war by a false formula for staying out of it, we were bewildered by the fact that American foreign policy was what the British prime minister said it was, what the Committee to Defend America by Aiding the Allies said it ought to be, and what the Government said it was not.

The second lull in the European war ended. On March 31, 1941, General Erwin Rommel led the Afrika Korps against the British in Libya. On April 6 Germany invaded Yugoslavia and British-occupied Greece.

Also that month, Japan signed a neutrality pact with the Soviet Union.

The Peril, May 24, 1941

Before it was too late, the *Post* said what the enactment of the Lend-Lease Law would mean. We said it would mean that the Congress had surrendered to the President the power in his own discretion to make undeclared war anywhere in the world; power in his own discretion to make friends and enemies of other nations; power in his own discretion to employ the total resources of the country to such ends.

It would mean that the people had lost control of government. It would mean, we said, that the country had been persuaded to take a road in which, "There is no turning back but through futility, confusion and disaster. . . no going on but with the fantasy to become moral emperor of the whole world."

A few weeks later the law was passed.

Then, we said, in an editorial on March twenty-ninth, entitled Toward the Unknown, that for us the debate was closed. From the beginning we had been on the losing side of it. Not that the people were resolved to embrace the war. They were not. Walking straight toward it, they would not believe it. The directional signs were all reversed, reading, "This way to stay out of the war," and they believed the signs. Nothing was called by its right name, least of all the last thing, which was the Lend-Lease Law.

Everything we said on the losing side we still believe.

We could wish that much less of it had begun to come true. Yet we say none of it again, at least not now, for reasons which we trust will become clear as we go on.

Whether we were right or wrong no longer matters. What we now write is neither to defend an old position nor to prepare a new one. We had said all along what our present position would be. We said that if war came we should be found supporting the Government that got us into it. We could hardly suppose this would need to be clarified. Seemingly, however, it does, for we have received a great many letters from those who believed what we believed, and do still believe, asking us why we gave up the fight to keep the country out of the war.

Our answer is to say to them that a time comes when every American must somehow resolve one simple question:

If for anything you could do about it, your country nevertheless becomes involved in war, where are you going to stand?

Many keep saying that time has not come. The clock has not struck. The fatal words have not been uttered in the form of a resolution by Congress.

But do they see what the world reads on the American banner? We spell it out to them.

The American government has proclaimed that Hitler must be destroyed.

It has solemnly pledged itself before the world to employ its total resources to bring that result to pass.

It has proclaimed that there can be and shall be no peace with Hitler.

It has announced that a negotiated peace would be a defeat for democracy and freedom and the American way of life.

It has proclaimed that the American way of life cannot exist on the same planet with the German thing. One or the other must die.

For all these reasons the American Government is giving warships, merchant ships, planes, guns and ammunition to Hitler's enemies and has commanded American

171

industry to prepare for them an unlimited arsenal, to be called the arsenal of democracy.

Read it. Read what is written there on the American banner. The world has read it. Hitler knows it by heart and probably sees it in his anxiety dreams.

To speak of this as national defense is absurd. It is the American crusade.

Trying, therefore, to maintain the fiction that this country is not in the war against Hitler is like running from an earthquake or hiding in the nursery. Those who say there is still a last ditch, that until the shooting begins we are not really in, and that until then you can still do something about it by writing letters to the senators and representatives who passed the Lend-Lease Law and surrendered to the President the power to write the banner and then under it to conduct undeclared war for freedom anywhere in the world, are only confusing the truth.

For the truth is that the only way now to avoid the shooting, if it has not already begun, is to repudiate the Government.

Let them say that. But before they say it, or think it, let them realize what the consequences would be.

As we write, the President is saying that the people seem not to be aware of the peril their country is in, and exhorts the press, the columnists and the radio commentators to make their blood run cold.

It is true that the people are not fully awake to their country's peril. We wonder if the Government is. If so, when did it begin to be? Was it aware of it all the time it was telling the people that the one aim of American foreign policy was to keep the country out of war? We think the answer must be that it was not, and that it believed its own slogans, else it is convicted of having willfully disguised its intentions.

It is not necessary to doubt the word of the Government when it says that its foreign policy was never intended to involve the country in war. In that case, of course, it was bluffing. The beginning was the President's quarantine-the-aggressor speech in Chicago. The idea of being quarantined did not terrify the aggressor. He ignored it. Then the American Government produced the formula of measures short of war, but more to be feared than words. It seemed to think this threat would give the aggressor pause, and again it was disappointed. Since then every cast of American foreign policy has been made on bad guessing, wrong information and unlucky inspiration.

Firstly the Government absurdly underestimated the German power, taking for it the complacent word of Great Britain and France. Beginning then the American Government has been involved in every error and failure of British policy. It was betting so heavily on the Maginot Line that it could speak of it as the first line of American defense, and when, to its utter dismay, France was about to fold, it made the desperate fling of throwing the American arsenal open to the allies. That also was a bluff. There was not enough in the American arsenal to alter the event, what there was couldn't be put there in time, and, as we now know, the whole United States Navy could not have saved France.

The next cast was all aid to Great Britain, including the transfer of warships, the delivery of planes by air, where in the beginning they had been towed or pushed across the Canadian border to save the pretense of neutrality, and unlimited access to the country's industrial resources—all to save the British Empire in order, as the Government said, to keep this country out of the war.

Together with Great Britain, the American Government made a frantic bet on Jugoslavia and one on Greece, promising them unlimited aid if they would fight and hold on, and all the time there was a bet at long odds on the possibility that Stalin would seize a moment when Hitler was not looking to attack him in the back. And the two bets that kept piling higher and higher with each spin in the wheel, because they were irrevocable, were, first, that the power of the British fleet would be invincible, and, second, that Great Britain would be able sometime to reconquer Europe without our man power, if only we provided the weapons in great quantity.

Every guess has been wrong, every assumption has failed, every bet but one has been lost, and the chances in favor of it are not what they were. That Great Britain alone, with all the man power of the British Empire, can reconquer Europe is no longer imagined. That the British navy, no matter what else happens, will survive intact and stand on our side is no longer a premise on which you would stake the life of America.

We thus review American foreign policy for a limited purpose. We said what we thought of it as we saw it evolve. As we thought of it then we think of it still, and it is immaterial. We are obliged now all together to face the consequences.

What are the consequences? What is the total peril in which this country is involved?

We say we doubt if the Government itself has arrived at a realization of it. Certainly those do not see it who are saying, as we write this, that the people must make up their minds to go all in or stay all out, as if you could choose to call it a bad day and go home. To do that, as we have said, the people would have to repudiate the Government. But that is not here the point.

To see what the peril is, you have to imagine our saying now, "We never intended to go as far as the shooting, and when it comes to that, we retire upon our own defense."

What, then, should we do with the American banner our Government has raised in the name of civilization, promising to confer upon all deserving mankind the four precious freedoms?

We might bury it out of our own sight and forget it. Who will erase it from the mind of the world? We should be the people who, having launched a crusade with the mightiest words that were ever uttered, turned back in the Balkans at the sound of the first shot.

Now do you begin to see what the choice is? We shall have to make up our minds to go on and on at any cost, to reconquer Europe and destroy Hitler there, even with American man power—or turn back; and if we turn back we shall be remembered forever as the Falstaff nation of the world, boasting of a power it did not really possess, boasting of how it would put it forth against the aggressor, and then changing its mind when the night came.

But the peril we speak of does not lie in making the wrong choice. It is there whatever we choose to do. We cannot now escape.

Everyone must be aware of what it will mean to go on. Do we see what it will mean to go back? The peril in that case is no less, may even be greater.

In going on we face the possibility of defeat, whether we can imagine it or not. But to go back is to face the possibility of national death. Why? Because it is not probable that a Falstaff nation, so rich and so free, would be able to survive in one world with Hitler.

That is the reality as we see it; that is the reality we accept. It was not inevitable; that we admit and argue it no more. The alternative had been to create here on this hemisphere the impregnable asylum of freedom and let tyranny in Europe destroy itself, as tyranny always has done and is bound to do again.

In Defense of the People, May 31, 1941

The seeds of propaganda are like natural seeds. You cannot expect the seed of the touch-me-not to grow and bring forth a thorn tree. Nor was it reasonable to expect that—

"The United States today is at peace and it is going to remain at peace,"—implanted in the American mind October 30, 1940, or—

"Your President says this country is not going to war,"— implanted November 2, 1940, or—

"The first purpose of our foreign policy is to keep our country out of war,"—implanted November 2, 1940, all by the President, would in the spring of 1941 produce a unified passion for war.

The Lend-Lease Law was from a seed secretly planted in the garden of the Government's mind. The people knew nothing about it. Suddenly in the winter it was revealed to them full grown, and they were dazed. Yet even as they looked at it they were told it was not what it appeared to be. They were to trust their Government, not their senses. It was not a law to get the country into war; it was a law to keep it out of war.

While it was on passage through Congress under this false representation, the reporters at every White House press conference asked the President the question the Congress was asking in vain. What would he do with the extraordinary powers about to be conferred upon him? His replies were jaunty, evasive or sarcastic. They pointed out to him that within the powers of the Lend-Lease Law he could give away American warships. At least it was not prohibited. He replied that neither did the law prohibit the President of the United States from standing on his head in the middle of Pennsylvania Avenue; and was there anybody who supposed he was going to do that?

Very soon after the enactment of the law he transferred to Great Britain a fleet of Coast Guard cutters, and after that, such a thing as the transfer of a motor-torpedo-boat fleet was a piece of news that the newspapers could put on the inside page.

When it had its Lend-Lease Law safely in the drawer, the Government was ready to get into the war. The people were not. Each time the Institute of Public Opinion inserted its sampling instrument and drew it out, the temperature reading was low. Government by Gallup Poll has its embarrassments.

A trick of the gardener for getting something he did not plant is called grafting. It requires very deft procedure. So did grafting war upon the no-war tree. Let us therefore observe it.

On April eighth the New York chairman of the Committee to Defend America by Aiding the Allies announced a rally to be held in Madison Square Garden, New York, to "prepare the mind of America for the next step—if it should be made necessary, not by us but by Hitler—the convoying of our goods across the Atlantic." That was saying to send in the flag if necessary.

Knowing that this extraordinary committee had hither-to unerringly forecast "the next step," many people were still unbelieving. They remembered that the Secretary of the Navy, testifying for the Lend-Lease Law before the House Foreign Relations Committee, had said about con-voys under escort of American warships, "No, no; in my judgment that would be an act of war"; and especially they remembered that the President himself had said, "Convoys mean shooting and shooting means war."

On April fifteenth, the Secretary of War, testifying before a special committee of the Senate, said, "Our forces must be prepared for the possibilities of war in many and varied terrains, it being quite uncertain in what part of North or South or Central America, or even possibly other regions, it ultimately may be necessary to use them."

Other regions. That was startling. But after all, this was only the Secretary of War, and people remembered that on October thirtieth the President had said, "And while I am talking to you, mothers and fathers, I give you one more assurance. I have said this before, but I shall say it again, and again, and again. Your boys are not going to be sent into any foreign wars."

On April eighteenth, at a White House press conference, the President expressed deep anxiety over the fact that the American people were apparently not aware of the coun-try's peril. The reporters added that the President was very guarded in his exchanges with the correspondents on the subject of convoys.

On April nineteenth, by an act of fission, a group of the Committee to Defend America by Aiding the Allies resolved itself into a Fight for Freedom Committee, under a manifesto, saying that if Hitler did not sink America's aid to Great Britain, he was beaten; and if he did, we were beaten. "This means," he said, "accepting the fact that we are at war, whether declared or undeclared." Once we accept the fact that we are at war, it said, "we shall at last find peace within ourselves." Sen. Carter Glass, who had long before declared himself for war, accepted the chair-manship of the committee, and you would know, therefore, that its utterances would be candid and forthright. And this, we admit, was like an oasis of emotional and intellectual integrity.[2]

On April twentieth, however, the Gallup Poll showed still a low temperature reading—67 per cent of the people saying "no" to naval aid to Great Britain, for fear that would mean shooting.

Convoy!

That was still the dangerous question.

On April twenty-fifth the *New York Times* led its front-page summary of The International Situation with this paragraph: "Indications that the United States Government is preparing American opinion for the major step of convoying war materials to Great Britain emerged last night in the speeches delivered by Secretaries Hull and Knox."

The Secretary of State said, "Aid must reach its destination in the shortest of time and in the maximum quantity. So ways must be found to do this."

That could hardly mean less than convoy and escort, and to face the shooting. What else? And yet he did not quite say it.

The Secretary of the Navy, who, while the Lend-Lease Law was on passage, announced that he was against transferring any more of the Navy to Great Britain and then immediately changed his mind in his speech that same night said, "We have declared that the fight that England is making is our fight. We have likewise affirmed that the enemies she is fighting are our enemies. . . we are in the fight to stay. . . We have irrevocably committed ourselves. . . Having gone thus far, we can only go on." And he adopted the words of the Fight for Freedom Committee, saying, "Hitler cannot allow our war supplies and food to reach England—he will be defeated if they do. We cannot allow our goods to be sunk in the Atlantic—we shall be beaten if we do."

Before this the *Post* had said it was too late to talk about staying out of a war we were already in, and that we were already so far in that there could be no turning back but with humiliation and defeat. The people did not believe it. For saying it we received a great many letters of grieved and indignant protest. Well, here was the Secretary of the Navy saying it for the Government, and that was a shock. If we turned back, we were beaten; therefore, we could only go on. And yet he, too, avoided the fatal word—convoy.

The next day, at a White House press conference, the reporters questioned the President on these two speeches, one by his Secretary of State and one by his Secretary of the Navy. The President said he believed they spoke for a majority of the American people. But did they speak for him? To that he replied, "Yes, yes."

Was it then to be inferred, the reporters asked, that the Government had made up its mind to adopt the convoy system under escort of American warships? No. The Government, said the President, was not thinking of convoys. It had thought of another word—patrol. The "American neutrality patrol" would be extended. How far? He was pleased somebody had asked that question—how far? It would be extended as far as was necessary, even beyond the Atlantic into the seven seas. On the difference between patrol and convoy, he said U.S. warships on neutrality patrol would be like the scouts that went ahead of the wagon trains in pioneer days on the plains to watch for savages. He was asked what the scouting warship would do if it sighted the savage on the high sea. He supposed it would relay the information back to the wagon trains.

After the words of the Secretary of the Navy the night before—words endorsed by the President—imagine an American neutrality patrol.

There we leave the record. It is a record of the Government treating the American people as if they were children.

More than that, it reveals a Government not sure of itself and afraid of the people, blaming them for a confusion in which they did not involve themselves, impatient with them for believing so many things that were not so that when the time came they could hardly believe they were in a war their Government was pledged to keep them out of.

Never did the Government tell the people they were in the war until it could say to them that it was too late to turn back, or that to turn back would mean national defeat. In defense of the people, we say, let the blame for disunity lie where it belongs. And yet the people are somewhat to blame. Knowing better, they believed a campaign book.

On May 27, 1941, the Royal Navy trapped and sunk the battleship Bismarck, killing more than 2,100 Germans. The victory avenged similar losses from Bismarck's sinking of the battleship Hood and was a huge boost to British morale. A key role in the British victory was played by the United States. Bismarck had given the Royal Navy the slip, and was about to reach sanctuary in occupied France when it was found again by a Royal Air Force Catalina flying boat, made in the U.S.A. The copilot was British but the pilot was Ensign Leonard B. Smith, U.S. Naval Reserve.

Chapter eight notes

1   Burton K. Wheeler, 1882-1975, Democrat of Montana. As a young U.S. attorney, Wheeler refused to prosecute sedition cases during World War I. He was elected to the Senate in 1922 and ran for vice-president under the Progressive Party ticket in 1924, with Sen. Robert LaFollette, R-Wis. Wheeler was a free-trade, wet, pro-silver progressive. He supported the anti-big-business parts of the New Deal such as the utility holding-company bill, but he led the fight against Roosevelt's court-packing plan in 1937. Wheeler was leader of the isolations in 1940 and 1941, and lost the renomination in 1946 because he strayed too far from the Democratic Party.

2   In *Roosevelt and the Isolationists*, 1932-1945, Wayne S. Cole writes: "The Fight for Freedom Committee and its leaders were much more aggressive and vicious in their attacks on the America First Committee and on isolationist leaders such as Lindbergh, Wheeler and Nye. By comparison the Committee to Defend America seemed almost bland."

Chapter Nine
GLOBAL DREAM

Here is an idea that has been out of sight for decades, but raised its head in 1940 and 1941: a political union of the democracies. Garrett hated it.

The Bitter Question, March 8, 1941

There is already a London-Washington Axis, and there is in effect an Anglo-American military alliance against the aggressor in which we assume unlimited liabilities with no conditions, terms or stipulations beforehand; but before going forth to war in Europe, actually, the American spirit demands above all a crusading theme. Defense is not a crusade. The thought alone of crushing Hitler is not enough. What would come after that? There might be another Hitler. The British are saying that when the victory is won they will state their war aims and entertain designs for a new world. But the British are not temperamentally crusaders; they are a practical, unromantic people.

Happily for the relief of this peculiar psychic necessity in the American people, and happily, too, for the crusade makers, the object of the first American crusade in Europe was not attained. Just as the hand of mankind was about to touch the grail of universal peace, it vanished. Now it has to be imagined all over again. Not this time a League of Nations for wicked and bungling statesmen to play with. But now a United States of the World, one sovereign government for all free and righteous nations, with a constitution like the American Constitution, and under this a common citizenship, one kind of money, uniform wage standards, unlimited free trade—and one political ideal.

Such is the theme of Federal Union, and Federal Union is a modification of Union Now. When the Union Now cult began to spread its propaganda it was possible to speak of the North Atlantic democracies. Since then the Germans have conquered Europe, and now the democracies that might at first unite are seven—namely, the United States, Canada, the United Kingdom, Ireland, the Union of South Africa, Australia and New Zealand—or, to begin with, English-speaking people only.

We are looking at the papers that were read at the Federal Union dinner in New York a few weeks ago. We are interested particularly in the one by Clare Boothe,[1] not only that it is the most brilliant exposition of the theme, but because also she had the wit to state the case of millions of noninterventionists for not doing it. These, she fairly said, are the "twice-bitten patriots," people with "more knowledge of the past than instinct for the future," who "generally give three sound reasons for their non-interventionism." She recites their three reasons:

"First, they dread, not the military consequences of the war, but the political and economic consequences of the peace. They have long, bitter memories about the outcome of the last war to make the world safe for democracy. They remember quite vividly that all the thanks America got for the role we played in that struggle were the ugly names of Scrooge and Shylock. They saw our former allies one by one repudiate their honorable debts. They are keenly aware that our own depression was the backwash of our European adventure. They feel that Europe's motto is, 'When bigger and better bags are made, America will hold them.'

"Secondly, American noninterventionists dread a repetition of the diplomatic blunders of the last peace. They saw the unholy mess the politicians of Europe and America made of the Versailles Treaty. They know that victory is

not a peace plan. . . They even remember the names of yesterday's dimwitted British and French statesmen, some of
them still in high office, whose diplomatic butchery has led
so inexorably to today's military butchery. In those blunders we had no part, though we are being called upon to
help extricate Europe from them.

"And thirdly, they dread the temporary, perhaps permanent loss of our own democratic way of life if we embark
on a long, exhausting war to defend it. They ask, as cynical
but patriotic Americans, 'Why would it be any different
this time?'"

This, she says, is all one bitter question, and those who
ask it must be answered "before their sons are sent to
death in another futile European war, before their grand-
children are saddled with the gigantic cost of the conflict,
before they are called upon to sacrifice for two years,
maybe four, maybe forever, their own peace and liberty."

The answer, she says, is Federal Union—a United
States of the World, a federation of nations patterned upon
the union of American states. And her peroration is to say,
"And please remember this: *There is no other peace plan,* or
war aim, being presented *anywhere,* by anyone, or any
group of statesmen, or any nation, but this!"

You make take it, as we so, that Clare Boothe is an authentic voice of Federal Union. The speech from which we
quote now belongs to the organized propaganda of that
movement. And there is implicit in it a very awkward
truth.

She begins by saying that morally we are in the war
now. "We have named our enemy. We have chosen our
allies. We are sending in the material of warfare to their
distant fields of battle to kill our named enemy. All talk of
nonbelligerency, of technical neutrality, of loan-leasing, is
so much congressional persiflage, which, however obtuse
the Germans may be, certainly does not deceive them."

Then at the end she says there is no war aim or peace
plan anywhere but this one she expounds—this idea of
Federal Union. What she is saying, therefore, is that we
are already involved in a world war—too far involved now

to turn back—without a plan or an aim that would justify a sacrifice. Federal Union is neither a plan nor an aim. It has no official status either here or in Great Britain. For the sincere it is a theme only—a theme invented by the crusading American spirit *after the fact!* The theme might fall, and yet the war would go on and we should be involved in it just as we are.

The American passion to act upon the evils of the world is a moral and political fact unique in human history—a fact greatly to be reckoned with. And yet we wonder if it is always what we think it is. It is easier to imagine a United States of the World working perfectly than to say how the United States of America shall be made to work better.

Hear the opposite words of Robert M. Hutchins,[2] president of the University of Chicago. "We have no plan," he says. "We are drifting into suicide. . . The path to war is a false path to freedom. A true moral order for America is a true path to freedom. . . We are turning aside from the true path because it is easier to blame Hitler for our troubles than to fight for democracy at home. If Hitler made the Jews his scapegoat, so we are making Hitler ours. In the long run we can beat what Hitler stands for only by beating the materialism and paganism that produced him. We must show the world a nation clear in purpose, united in action and sacrificial in spirit. The influence of that example upon suffering humanity everywhere would be more powerful than the combined armies of the Axis."

That World Feeling, July 19, 1941

*F**ederal Union World,* the organ of Union Now With Britain, prints at the top of its June editorial the uncompromising statement by Harold J. Laski[3] about what will happen to national sovereignty in the new world government of the democracies.

The Laski quotation is this: "There can be no peace without international organization which abrogates the sovereignty of individual states."

Federal Union World does this for the edification of the

Saturday Evening Post. We had said the evangelists for Union Now had not been forthright on this point; that they had been speaking softly of the fate indicated for American independence and national sovereignty.

So now it says: "Challenge accepted, S.E.P. There is your Laski quotation. . . We have been telling Americans for over two years, in fifty-seven different ways, that Union Now demands a limitation of national sovereignty and independence."

To print the Laski statement on a dare is not the same thing as to embrace it. Laski has embraced Union Now. Do the American evangelists for Union Now accept his logic? He is saying that no such scheme will work unless it abrogates the sovereignty of individual states. *Federal Union World* goes no further than "a limitation of national sovereignty and independence." Abrogation means to cancel, annul, do away with quite.

Federal Union World goes on: "Neither from the *Post* nor from any of our other hecklers has come the slightest glimmer of a realization that almost if not quite all of their arguments against Union Now and Union Now With Britain have been anachronistic echoes of the catcalls which greeted the United States Constitution at its first appearance."

Always they come to this. It is the very core of their argument. Their world federation of democracies will be like the federation of American states. If it worked on the scale of the American scheme, why won't it work on a world scale?

In this perfect and isolate environment, with a people self-selected for it, there had to be a civil war to hold the American scheme of dual Federal and state sovereignty together beyond the second generation. In the fifth generation it has culminated in the New Deal, with central government triumphant and all-powerful, as Jefferson feared, and state sovereignty reduced to a specter of its once noble and arrogant self. Laski is right.

Whose America? October 25, 1941

It passes in the news, almost without comment, that the American ambassador to His Majesty's Government in Great Britain made this public utterance: "What many of us now have come to want is world citizenship."

An ambassador is not a private person. He speaks for his Government. If he misrepresents it, he is subject to rebuke and disavowal. Therefore we ask: What does Mr. Winant[4] represent? Does he speak for the American Government, for the movement to share America, or for both?

The United States does not belong to the American Government. It belongs to the American people. They have not been asked about sharing it. They know very well what Mr. Winant is saying. It is in the air. In the book of international propaganda it is the first theme. What they want to know is where the American Government stands; they want to know whether it, too, is for that world to which the American ambassador longs to transfer his citizenship and his allegiance.

What is that world? It is the world simply imagined by Mrs. Roosevelt when she says: "I think the union of all free democracies, whether English-speaking or not, is much to be desired in the future. Without it, I see no prospect of eliminating war."

It is a world-to-be of the elect and righteous, called democracies all alike, who shall rid themselves of war by the simple act of surrendering the sovereign right to make war. To whom shall this right be surrendered? To a supreme or union government. This supreme government alone shall have the right to make war and peace for all, and the power of that right, because it will have all the weapons; these, too, having been surrendered to it, along with the baubles of national sovereignty.

It is to be a world of wonderful individual freedom in exchange for the loss of national freedom. National sovereignty will be abolished. The American Declaration of Independence will not be needed any more. It will be superseded by a declaration of interdependence.

It will be an Anglo-Saxon world, naturally; but an Anglo-Saxon world based upon the principles of federal union.

How shall it be governed—this world?

By a constitution, of course, and a congress; but there must also be a president, a world executive.

How shall he be chosen? The cult of Union Now with Britain, which has made the only distinct outline there is, comes to face that problem, and solves it, at least for the time being, by proposing two equal presidents, or chairmen—one Franklin D. Roosevelt and one Winston Churchill, like the two equal consuls of the Roman Republic.

"Who doubts," asks Clarence K. Streit,[5] in *Union Now With Britain,* page 42, "that the citizens of the Union would welcome Chairman Roosevelt enthusiastically when the Union Clipper set him down in London to confer with Chairman Churchill? Who can imagine their welcome to Chairman Churchill when he came here to the Union capital to meet with Chairman Roosevelt and report to the provisional Union Congress, as he now reports to the British Parliament?"

Well, but it is also the fabulous world of Lend-Lease as the British see it—the world of Winston Churchill's "we," in the Declaration of the Atlantic, with no commitment on the part of His Majesty's Government beyond coming to the aid of the United States if it should have to defend Britain's Singapore and the Burma Road; it is his world of "united we can save and guide the world."

It is the world Col. Josiah Wedgwood,[6] member of the British Parliament, maladroitly spoke of when he came lecturing here to make sentiment for any kind of union or any kind of Anglo-American alliance. He said: "From the war in which accounts between Britain and America are now getting somewhat mixed, the step forward to a common army, navy and air force—and taxation to pay for them—is not far distant. We have in Great Britain all to gain by a union, and the invitation must come from

America."

For that the embarrassed British Government called him home. Common taxation by a supreme government, which would be laid on, of course, according to the ability of each nation to pay, is something you would not dress in the hearing of the richest country, especially not just before a meeting of the President of the United States and the British prime minister at sea, in the course of which the British prime minister hoped to get the signature of the President of the United States to an Anglo-American alliance for the duration of the war to destroy Hitler.[7]

Says Mr. Streit, naively, in *Union Now With Britain:* "Prime Minister Churchill's offer to form a Federal Union overnight with France has shown how ready the British are to accept such an offer from Washington."

We could have believed it on slighter evidence; or we would be willing to take it on the word of Leslie Hore-Belisha, formerly secretary for war in the British Cabinet, who hopes the Declaration of the Atlantic will turn out to be the prelude to a common citizenship with America. "Mr. Churchill," he says, "had the imaginative idea of offering France a common citizenship. There is far more reason for a common citizenship with America. If we can replace the Declaration of Independence with a declaration of interdependence, it should lay the firmest foundation for permanent world peace."

So then, we should save Europe again, this time by self-renunciation, surrender our national sovereignty, and marriage.

The savior complex is the grand and costly American emotion. We cannot expect other people to understand it, since we do not understand it in ourselves, nor can we rightly blame other people for exploiting it. It is our own business. These zealots for a government of mankind are Americans. The world they imagine is a world that cannot be proved, a world that has no historical probability, a world that we think does not exist beyond the beautiful mists of political hallucination. The intensity of their propaganda provokes violent resistance and divides people, not on lines of reason but on lines of deep feeling.

You cannot reason about the happening that takes place in the heart of one who says and thinks and feels, "I am an American citizen." You would have to show this American your perfect world, and even then he might not wish it. That goes for us.

On the opposite hand, we have learned that you cannot reason with one who has embraced the denationalized thought of world citizenship and allegiance to an all-wise, all-powerful government of mankind. To such a one, national sovereignty is a fetish and the Declaration of Independence is but a scrap of honorable paper.

Therefore, we say, this propaganda is bad for the cause of unity, dividing hearts and minds at a time when the Government's principal anxiety is the state of public morale for the war against Hitler.

Chapter nine notes

1 Clare Boothe Luce, 1903-1987, was wife of *Time* publisher Henry Luce, war correspondent, House member (R-Connecticut) 1943-1947, and ambassador to Italy, 1953-1957.

2 Robert Hutchins, 1899-1977, president of University of Chicago 1929-1945, advocated the study at university of great writing, logic, rhetoric and mathematics rather than the learning of practical applications.

3 Harold Laski, 1893-1950, was a socialist intellectual, a professor at the London School of Economics; co-founder of the Left Book Club and chairman of British Labour Party, 1945.

4 John G. Winant, 1889-1947, former governor of New Hampshire and chairman of the Social Security Board. A pro-intervention Republican, he was U.S. ambassador to Britain 1941-1946.

5 Streit was a prophet of the "Atlantic Union Movement" for years, and edited its magazine, *Freedom and Union.*

6 Col. Josiah Wedgwood, 1872-1943, was a British Liberal politician before World War I, when he was wounded at Gallipoli; a member of Independent Labour Party after WWI and devotee of Henry George's single tax.

7 This refers to the Declaration of the Atlantic, covered in chapter 13, "Maneuvers."

Chapter Ten
COUNTRY

To Garrett, nothing was more important in a war than knowing what it is for—the political objectives, first, but also the motivation for the soldier to fight.

But Let That Dream Return, June 14, 1941

There are many like the young man who writes a piece in a magazine, saying, in effect, "We dreamed the dream of Soviet democracy and it failed us. But where is another? Give us a dream"; and then the elders who take up such a thing in a spirit of self-reproach, saying, "This is the voice of our youth. Our democracy has failed also in this—to provide a dream."

In the cloisters of learning, rare minds are revolving the curious thought that in a world of clashing ideologies American democracy has no ideology to call its own; and it concerns them how now to invent one before it is too late.

Speak Up For Democracy, by Edward L. Bernays,[1] a book addressed to all lovers and defenders, is a manual on how to sell it, how to write and speak for it, how to meet its enemies in debate and overcome them, how to use the telegraph and telephone, buttons, stickers, all the arts of propaganda and publicity; and to sell it well, he believes, is very important for the national morale.

Doctor Hutchins, president of the University of Chicago, asks, "Is Democracy a good form of government? Is it worth dying for? Is the United States a democracy?"

It is a democracy and it is worth dying for, he says, because it is the only form of government that can combine three characteristics—namely, law, equality and justice; whereas a totalitarian state has none of these and hence is the worst of all possible states.

But there is then Dorothy Thompson,[2] on being crowned for valiancy by Winston Churchill, saying the democracy we should be willing to fight and die for must be one of a new order; at least as we go to war for democracy in the whole world we must be at the same time thinking up a way to make it work better, especially here, because "the democracies are endangered not only because they have not got enough guns but because they have been bracing themselves against the yearnings of all human beings to achieve what they have not achieved and to be what they are not." This must be democracy in the abstract, a thing in itself, outside of people. Are democracies that resist the yearnings of human beings democracies? Or do people resist themselves? It may be, of course, that the trouble with democracy is people.

We agree with Doctor Hutchins that what he calls the three characteristics of democracy are worth fighting for. But that it his democracy. There is in his school no student of history who does not know that something calling itself democracy may possess none of these characteristics, but in place of them the one characteristic of tyranny. That, of course, would not be what either we or Doctor Hutchins would call a democracy; it would be what someone else had called a democracy.

Such words as freedom, justice and equality have souls; and it is only for words with souls that men are willing to fight and die. If the word democracy has a soul left, it "dies of its own too much."[3] It is an omnibus word, an unregulated common carrier, a common depot for political and social ideas. Meaning so many different things to so many different people, it means precisely nothing.

Therefore, whether the United States is a democracy or not, we do not know, speaking for ourselves alone. It was once a republic. That we do know. We have thought the difference was important. To elucidate it we have written many small essays on the science of government, and on the age-old and still-unsolved problem of how to reconcile government with liberty; the natural tendency being, as Jefferson said, for government to gain and people to give way—for government to extend its authority and for the people to surrender to it their responsibilities and liberties.

Yet now, as we face the question that Doctor Hutchins asks, we discover that those differences and values we could be so dogmatic about, even perhaps right about, begin to recede.

What are we willing to fight and die for?

Certainly, for no such thing as a form of government. There are many forms and none is fixed. There may be good government under bad forms and bad government under good forms. Anyhow, we can change them.

But there was a dream; and when it comes back to us, all else will seem unreal. Democracy was not the dream; neither was a scientific republican form of government the dream. Ideas of equal freedom, equal justice, equal opportunity, did inhabit it, they were implicit in it; yet these were very old ideas and the dream was new. What was it?

The dream itself was America.

Well, you cannot define America either, but that is no difficulty, because you either know what it is or you don't. It is everything good and bad, ugly and beautiful, sublime and absurd, rude and gracious, and all belonging. It is a scrap of paper enshrined in the Congressional Library, a cracked bell, Molly Pitcher's Well marked by a board in the New Jersey pine barrens,[4] Valley Forge and what our forefathers were fighting for then, which was not a democracy, not a republic, not any form of government, but the right to set up whatever kind of government they liked and govern themselves.

It is what one hundred and eighty-seven died for in the Alamo, and if you had asked one of them then what it was, he would have said, "Why, hell, can't you see? This is Texas."

It is Carpenters' Hall in Philadelphia, and then, as you

193

face away, it is what the triumph of the gold standard over free silver did to commercial architecture in Chestnut Street. It is a June morning in Concord. It is the Capitol at night with the floodlights on it, the flag at Gettysburg, the second inaugural address, a battleship on the sea. It is Harvard University and Tuskegee. It is Baltimore, the Shenandoah Valley, the smell of ham frying in the hill cabins of Tennessee, and then such a democratic happening in nature, a little above St. Louis, as when the muddy, turbulent Missouri River makes His Majesty, the Mississippi, move over.

It is Bernays' truck driver, saying, "I don't have to vote if I don't want to; it's a free country." It is Westbrook Pegler and Harold Ickes, and old Iron Pants, who was the Blue Eagle dictator, now mending his idols and breaking them again.[5] It is the Roosevelt clan with its passion to govern, and Fred Perkins, of New York, who would sooner see the Government seize his little battery business and sell it on the auction block than to pay a social-security tax he doesn't believe in. It is Frank Hague's political machine and Kelly's Chicago. It is Miami Beach and Hollywood and Secaucus, the pig town on the Hackensack Meadows.

It is the sky line of New York against the dawn, and the way the sun sets 3000 miles west in Monterey Bay. It is Wall Street and Snake Alley. It is John L. Lewis and Tom Girdler.[6] It is the Erie Railroad, the Dust Bowl, the Corn Belt, and Kansas when it is a sea of billowing gold. It is the ballad of a magnificent city, leveled by earthquake and fire, singing, "The Damndest Finest Ruins!" while sitting on them, and now in the miragelike beauty of San Francisco as it comes suddenly into view from the Golden Gate Bridge.

On the east it is a rock and on the west a sea lion, and the hasting sun is three hours going between them; glacial streams in the north, and on the south everglades, palm trees and subtropical waters. It is that perfect segment of the earth's surface that had been long reserved. Here we made a new and unlike world, our own entirely. Here people were free as people never had been free before; and

194

although the design of it was borrowed by others, nowhere else did it work like this. Here the standards of common living, of material well-being, of comfort and creature enjoyment, were raised to levels never before attained by human exertion in the history of the human race. We became very rich. But although the rich were richer, the poor were less poor than in any competitive country.

Come judgment or revolution, where would you sooner be? Where, for all its faults, was a better order? Where is there a people who would not exchange their order for this one?

There is no end to this dream that is America. None that we yet know. It can go on and on.

Then what happened to it? Why does the young man say, "Give us a dream"?

We can think of several reasons. So can Doctor Hutchins, and Doctor Conant, of Harvard, who has spoken of the creeping paralysis of disaffection in youth. But the principal reason, we believe, is that the youth of our generation had the misfortune to be born at a bad time, with not enough of anything that could be taken for granted and yet too little of anything really to fight for. It has been taught to be skeptical, dialectic and critical of what it found.

Now democracy is being sold to it. But the dream has not been imparted. Who will do that? Give it the dream and it will be ready enough to fight and die, not for any political ideology, but for America.

There was a part of America special to Garrett: the factory floor, where man met machine and the watchwords were precision and efficiency.

Many Planes, July 26, 1941

Hardly more than a year ago, only people who did not know any better said we could make planes as we make motorcars, on a moving line, with uniform parts and subassemblies arriving by tributary lines at the sound of

195

an automatic gong, so that the hand, the thing and the place exactly meet in time. One of those who did not know any better was Henry Ford, who said it could be done; he said a plane was no more mysterious than an automobile and could be made by the same method.

Well, now it is happening. You can see it in the big aircraft plants. Swinging to an overhead track by roller-bearing wheels, the plane begins to move as a center wing section and engine nacelle, and as it moves, not continuously but by periodic impulse, everything else is added to it, until at last the engine is mounted and your finished bomber is ready to roll out. Body and wing sections, engines, landing gear, hundreds of big and little subassemblies, are manufactured by industry all over the country and shipped to the aircraft plant, where the grand assembly takes place.

As you watch it, you know what you are looking at. It is the application of the motorcar industry's method of mass production to planes. It represents a degree of collaboration between the aircraft industry and the automotive industry such as, a year ago, seemed very far off, if not quite improbable—with the machine-tool industry, of course, actively assisting both of them.

What you may not realize is that you are looking at beginnings—that is to say, at an aircraft industry which, as such, is where the motorcar industry was twenty-five years ago. Once the idea of mass production is released there is no telling how far it may go. There is no definite limit. The motorcar industry has never found a limit. The ingenuity of machine craft is now working away beyond old limits with a kind of free ecstasy, producing week by week a series of minor technical feats the cumulative sum of which will be enormous. Only a few weeks ago, counterboring 280 holes in the crankcase of an airplane engine required nearly seven hours of a machinist's time. Now the job takes a little more than one hour. In another case it took seven machines to drill fourteen holes in the cylinder; now three machines do it in three minutes. The time for machining the grooves in an engine exhaust valve has been reduced from half an hour to half a minute, and for one four-engine bomber you multiply this saving of time by seventy-two, because there are seventy-two exhaust valves. A troublesome pump liner that was produced at the rate of three an hour, now is produced at the rate of thirteen an hour. And what of precision at this speed? The precision is within three one-thousandths of an inch.

As we were the first and only people to make many automobiles, so we shall be the first and only people in the world to make many, many planes. There begins an epic.

In June 1940, the month France fell, Congress passed the Smith Act, which made it a crime to advocate the violent overthrow of the government or to join any organization that did. The Post *supported it; in the August 3, 1940, issue it said: "Every political organization subject to foreign influence should be outlawed. Any American citizen belonging to one, knowing it to be such, should be charged with treason. These are simple political decisions. The Congress is competent to make them. If the law is inadequate it should be amended. That many Nazi and Communist organizations do exist and flourish is a brazen fact. That the Communist Party, owing its allegiance to Moscow, should have a place on the American ballot is a perversion of liberty and in all sanity intolerable. But first of all the Administration must rid itself of the Communist stench and wipe its own hands."*

Here is what Garrett wrote a year later, just before Hitler turned on Stalin and all loyal Communists suddenly became supporters of the war:

Harvest Notes, July 26, 1941

The Government now wishes organized labor to purge itself of Communist Party elements because they are subversive and purposely foment strife to obstruct the national defense; and if labor is unable or unwilling to do it, then in serious cases troops will be sent to put down the sabotage.

But this is the same Government that had been saying

for eight years that American capitalism was controlled by brigands of the skyscrapers and economic royalists who exploited labor, knowing as it said these things that the Communists followed in that furrow.

It is the same Government that warned labor at the beginning of the defense emergency to beware of the pincers movement by which the wicked employer would seek to destroy its social gains.

It is the same Government that took Communists, fellow travelers and intellectual revolutionaries to its bureaucratic bosom and has not yet purged them entirely away.

It is the same Government that made it an unfair labor practice, and punishable, for an employer to tell employees that their new leaders were Communists and Reds, even if it was true, because that tended to discredit unionism and frustrate organization. (See *Third Annual Report of the National Labor Relations Board*, p. 59.)

It is the same Government that obliged employers to reinstate employees who were believed to be Communists and had been discharged for that reason. A notable case of this kind involved a confidential secretary in the *New York Times* organization, who, having been discharged for alleged participation in the activities of a Communist Party unit, was ordered to be reinstated, on the ground that her denial that she was a Communist was more trustworthy than the word of the *New York Times* on why it discharged her, and this notwithstanding the fact that one member of the board thought she was lying. (Reference 26 NLRB, No. 122, decided August 24, 1940.)

It is the same Government that favored the CIO over the AFL when John L. Lewis was putting it together, though it knew what he did. He made no secret of it. He employed Communist organizers because they were the best organizers he could find, and he was in haste; he kept saying that when the time came, he would get rid of them.

Now the harvest. Who can change the harvest? Tares come from the seed of tares in a natural way. The ground does not select the seed nor does the sickle taste what it reaps.

Chapter ten notes

1 Edward Bernays, 1891-1995, was called "the father of public relations," and also "the father of spin." He wrote *Propaganda* (1928) and edited *The Engineering of Consent* (1955).

2 Dorothy Thompson, 1894-1961, was the first U.S. correspondent in Nazi Germany ejected on orders of Hitler, 1934; a columnist for N.Y. *Herald Tribune* and syndicate, 1936-1958; was ranked by *Time* as the second most popular woman after Eleanor Roosevelt; married to novelist Sinclair Lewis, 1928-1942; and correspondent of Rose Wilder Lane, 1921-1960.

3 From *Hamlet*, in which King Claudius said: "There lives within the very flame of love a kind of wick or snuff that will abate it, and nothing is at a like goodness still; for goodness, growing to a plurisy, dies in his own too much."

4 "Molly Pitcher" was the name George Washington's men gave to a woman who brought them water at the Battle of Monmouth on June 28, 1778, in fierce fighting and 100-degree heat.

5 Westbrook Pegler, 1894-1969, was a newspaper columnist, called the "angry man of the press." Old Iron Pants was Gen. Hugh S. Johnson, 1882-1942, draft administrator in World War I and in the early New Deal boss of the National Recovery Administration, symbolized by the Blue Eagle. Johnson later became one of Roosevelt's many enemies.

6 Tom Girdler was the boss of Republic Steel who fought against the union drive of the Congress of Industrial Organizations, headed by John L. Lewis. Writing to Rose Wilder Lane, Garrett called Girdler "a small bull in a very big field, with only one sound, which is no."

Chapter Eleven
COMRADES

On June 22, 1941, Hitler turned on Stalin, throwing 148 divisions into a front a thousand miles long. World War II was now a land war between Germany and Russia—two totalitarian powers. In a statement June 23, the America First Committee said, "The war party can hardly ask the people of America to take up arms behind the red flag of Stalin." The attack on Russia also meant the pressure was off Britain. Hitler had his hands full. Years later Garrett wrote, "If Hitler and Stalin had been left to fight each other down to the knees, history now might be telling a very different story."

But it was not to be. Though Stalin had conspired with Hitler to carve up Poland in 1939, and though he had attacked Finland and seized the Baltic states, the New Dealers had never included him in their list of enemies. And now, Stalin was fighting Hitler, which meant he was to be welcomed as an Ally.

Garrett could hardly believe it.

The Foreign Malady, August 2, 1941

One effect of Hitler's murderous assault upon his Russian partner in aggressor crime was to make vivid in this country certain extreme and ugly symptoms of the foreign malady. We think no American could ponder what was thereby revealed without a sense of foreboding and sickness of heart.

The news broke on Saturday night, after the Sunday newspapers had gone to press, and for many hours radio was the only means of dissemination.

Two thoughts were immediately present.

The first was to ask whether the Soviet government, with its hands still foul from the rape of Finland on its own account and the cynical murder of Poland in joint account with Hitler, would now be received among the defenders of freedom and have access to the arsenal of democracy.

The second was satirical. Now the sabotage strikes in American defense industries would cease, by a new Communist Party line.

The question that came first was answered Sunday afternoon, not by the American Government but by the British government. Winston Churchill came on the radio, saying any hand against Hitler was welcome, even the hand of Stalin, although, as he himself had often said and would not unsay, this was the hideous hand of a slayer of freedom. "It follows," he said, "that we will give whatever help we can to Russia and the Russian people. . . It is not for me to speak of the action of the United States, but this I will say: If Hitler imagines that his attack on Soviet Russia will cause the slightest division of aims or slackening of effort in the great democracies, who are resolved upon his doom, he is woefully mistaken."

This was the British government pledging to the Soviet government indirect access to the American arsenal of democracy. And why not? It may do what it likes with the weapons and munitions it receives from that arsenal under the Lend-Lease Law; it may use them itself or lend them to others.

After the Churchill broadcast, which of course was directed at the American people, there could be no intelligent doubt about the policy of the American Government. Promptly on Monday the State Department restated the Churchill statement and presented it as its own to a "realistic America."

And the satirical thought—that, too, was very soon confirmed. On Sunday afternoon, from the office of the

Communist *Daily Worker*, that had gone to press Saturday night praying for the Stalin-Hitler pact and breathing sabotage against the American armament program, the Communist Party issued a manifesto, saying the Soviet government was fighting not for itself alone but for the freedom of all people, including the American people—the American farmer, the American worker, the American Negro, and then, for good measure, even the hated middle class. Therefore, down with Hitler! All out for the American effort to destroy him—and save the Soviet Union!

Then something happened in the honorable stomach of the Committee to Defend America by Aiding the Allies. The New York chapter changed its name. We understand that.

One of the sinister effects of the foreign malady is to make Americans suspect one another and impugn one another's patriotism. Many Americans were moved by both reason and deep feeling to say the Battle of Britain was our battle too. But to the voices of these were added alien voices saying the same thing in the same words: and their evangel for war was supported by an organized alien propaganda that could not have been thinking, and should not have been thinking, of America first.

Many more Americans—a great majority, we think— were equally moved by reason and feeling to say this country should jealously mind its own defense and stay out of the war, let Europe commit suicide if it would. That is the side we were on. But on that side, too, were alien voices saying the same thing in the same words. After a year it had become a habit, on opening the editorial mail to glance first at the opening sentence of a letter, and it if was with us against going to war, to look then at the signature; and if it was a German name or any name we knew bearing the taint of Communism, we shuddered. Our answer was to wish those who might agree with us for the wrong reasons to hold their peace.

The America First Committee made the same rejection; nevertheless, alien voices continued to embarrass its meetings, and Americans on the other side, together with their alien friends, made smear matter of it. Now the problem is theirs—how to repudiate the unwelcome support of the Communist.

Exercises in realistic thinking, now recommended by the American Government, were novel for a people who had just been brought to a crusade for the four freedoms in the wide world. Owing partly to the novelty, they were exciting and jammed all the channels of the air, alien voices intervening helpfully; but they were not easy, after all.

The Government was going to hit Hitler in the back with everything we had, by sending it faster and faster to Great Britain, and at the same time it was going to aid Stalin with everything that was left over after we had sent everything to Great Britain; and if that was not clear, you had not yet learned to think in a realistic manner.

In the *New York Times,* Arthur Krock cynically resolved the difficulty of treating the Stalin dictatorship as a democracy for purposes of aid under the Lend-Lease Law by calling attention to the fact that Greece was not a democracy, nor China, except in a way of speaking.

In the House of Representatives, a member rose to ask why he should vote for a law forbidding any of the money Congress was then appropriating to be used by the Government to pay the salaries of Communists employed in its various executive bureaus, some of them mentioned by name. What was the point?

We have produced this view of the formless national behavior only to prepare a question. Where in that view, or in any view you may construct for yourself out of the current material, do you see America itself, or any true symbol of it.

In all this confusion of thought and feeling and idea, where is the American core?

Russian Communism is an international snake treacherous even to itself, knowing only venomous and deadly enmity to any other kind of social organism. Nevertheless, the New Deal nested it. The White House made a fashion of petting it. Then just when the horrible awakening from this singular ophiolatry seemed about to take place—

204

troops having been sent to dislodge the coil that had been trying to strangle the aircraft industry—a violent turn of events in Europe brings the Soviet government under the American tent of the four freedoms, and the short-wave listeners in a New York studio hear the Moscow radio playing, "Columbia, the Gem of the Ocean" and other patriotic American and Scottish songs.

Nazism is a similar reptile. Happily, now the Government is killing that one; and yet, even as in this well-doing, our satisfaction must be offset by the reflection that as the American Government puts down one kind of foreign propaganda it favors another kind, and does now itself collaborate with a foreign government in ways of acting upon mass opinion in the United States. And this, we suppose, is so far the extreme phase of the foreign malady among us, all the more critical because it is so little resented.

For more than one hundred years this American republic was the world fountain of political innovation, giving forth ideas to whoever could use them and could make them work as they worked for us. Now we export arms and import ideas.

For more than one hundred years there was something we knew for sure about ourselves without thinking of it, which was fixed, and to which all alien isms and all problems of foreign relationships were instinctively referred—an American ethos, that is to say, a characteristic spirit of the nation.

There was an American ideology, though we did not know it and had not that word for it. That baneful word was taken out of the Communist book of dialectics, along with the proletarian man, a lot of other political jargon, and all the slogans of class struggle. The class consciousness of American labor was cultivated here by liberals and in intellectuals, from foreign seed. Marxian anticapitalism was imported in the same way by those who could not distinguish between the feudal capitalism of the Old World and American capitalism.

Every important idea of the New Deal was borrowed

from Europe, out of Harold J. Laski's exquisitely revolutionary mind, or from J. Maynard Keynes' brilliantly insolvent economics, and all of that beautifully printed literature of an aristocratically decadent British radicalism—foremostly of all, the idea of deficit government spending as a way to redistribute the national wealth without pain of vulgar revolution.

What have we been debating with rising fever during the last few years in this country? Foreign ideologies and how they might be adapted and suited to us; or why we should take the side of one to destroy another, lest the other should come and devour us.

Among the principal political ideas now in controversy among us, we an think of but one that could lay even doubtful claim to American origin. That one is the idea of a Federal Union World, called also Union Now and Union Now with Britain, and its proposal to surrender American sovereignty to a world government and denationalize the United States of America.

Where is this United States of America that would sacrifice its birthright for the sake of the world and give its substance to be spread for an international feast? It is a strange land, and if it is ours we are strangers in it. But we disbelieve in its existence. Nor do we believe the national totem is extinct. It is only sick.

In July 1941, Roosevelt had sent confidant Harry Hopkins, the former head of the Works Progress Administration, to Moscow, to see what aid Stalin wanted. On September 18, Roosevelt asked Congress for aid for Russia. There was some opposition: Representative Hamilton Fish, Republican of New York, called it "Lenin Lease." But aid for Soviet Russia was passed 323-67 in the House and 59-13 in the Senate. Through September 1946, the United States gave $11,297,883,000 in Lend-Lease aid, about one-third the amount it gave to Britain.

Playing the Red, November 8, 1941

A war partnership need be neither holy nor unholy. Mortal enemies may strike hands against a common foe and still keep their own quarrel. Such is the way of the world we live in. We are exhorted, therefore, to take a realistic view of the wrong-font hyphen that now links Communism with Capitalism, presumably for the duration of the war only. If Soviet Russia could love Christian and capitalistic countries, it would be no longer Soviet Russia; or, if the United States and Great Britain could embrace Communism, they would be no longer Christian and capitalistic. But why speak of that? Hitler has first to be destroyed.

"Shall I ask the brave soldier who fights by my side in the cause of mankind if our creeds agree?"[1]

Unhappily, first, the cause of mankind is not everywhere clear; in the second place, if what the war represents is a deadly conflict of two ideas—two utterly irreconcilable ways of life—then creed is the fighting matter.

It may be that too much has been said about the ideologies. We think so. Nevertheless, by what has been said and believed, emotions on both sides are conditioned. Until Hitler attacked Russia, the ideologies of Communism and Nazism, equally anti-democratic and equally anti-religious, were equally hateful in the Christian democracies. Now to be arming one against the other, purely as a matter of war strategy, may be realism of a very high order. None the less for that, it involves Christians, especially Catholics, in a dilemma of conscience; it involves both the United States and Great Britain in shocking political insincerities; and to the possibility that it may involve the world in further tragedy nearly all who take now the line of expediency are willfully purblind.

The extreme form of the dilemma of conscience is reserved for the Catholic, as he reads the encyclical of Pope Pius XI on Atheistic Communism, saying: "Communism is intrinsically wrong and no one who would save Christian civilization may collaborate with it in any undertaking whatsoever."

Does aid to Soviet Russia against Hitler come under the head of collaboration with Communism? That is a very serious question.

"The Church," says *America,* the able Catholic review, "as yet has raised no specifically religious issue out of the problem of collaboration with the U.S.S.R."

That leaves it open to debate, and Catholic opinion appears to be deeply torn. "If the announcement of aid to Russia," says *America,* "releases a state of Communist Party enthusiasm in this country, Nazi propaganda is by no means slow to take advantage of an anti-Communist panic."

Realism has no place in the conscience. It belongs to the sphere of politics. How fares it there? Not so well there, either, because the realistic conclusion must somehow be squared with feeling.

When, on the Sunday after Hitler's invasion of Russia, the British prime minister went on the air to say that Britain would support Russia, he could not say it in a bald manner. He was obliged to perceive a distinction between Soviet Russia as such and the Russian people per se; and for the sake of the Russian people, defending their soil and their homes against their treacherous ally, he was willing to seize the hand of Stalin, although never would he unsay the unforgivable things he had said about the blood upon that hand and what it had done to Finland by itself and to Poland in guilty collaboration with Hitler. The British could not bring themselves to add the Communists' revolutionary hymn to the medley of national airs playing in London. That was July. In September there was an unveiling of British tanks for Russia, the tanks were named for Marx, Lenin and other revolutionary heroes, and the British workers sang the revolutionary hymn, including the line, "The International Soviet shall be the human race."

When the President and the British prime minister met in the Atlantic to evolve, among other things, the strategy of aid to Russia, they made the outline of a free, eight-point postwar world and omitted from it any mention of freedom of speech and freedom of religion. To the suggestion that these freedoms had been left out as a matter of delicacy, for fear of offending the sensibilities of Stalin, the dictator, the President retorted that all four of his freedoms were included; the missing two were implicit in the others. Religious feeling continuing in spite of that to express itself with doubt and misgiving, the President began at his White House press conferences to advise the reporters to read the constitution of Soviet Russia, especially Article 124. Then one day he came out broadly with it. In the matter of religious freedom the constitution of Soviet Russia was not so different from our own, merely saying it in another way.

The reaction to this was bad. Two days later, the White House issued a statement saying that wasn't what the President meant. A certain thing had happened. Some Poles, weighing their hatreds, and finding that their hatred of Germany was heavier and more urgent than their hatred of Russia, were taking up arms with the Russians against Hitler, and Stalin in return had been gracious enough to grant them the special privilege of religious freedom. And what the President meant was that this might turn out to be the entering wedge for religious freedom in Russia.

If Soviet Russia could be called a land of religious freedom, so it could be called a democracy. But if it were called a democracy, it would be entitled to access to the American arsenal of democracy under the Lend-Lease policy, whereas in the beginning the American Government had announced that Soviet Russia would have to pay for aid, cash down. That was discrimination, to be sure, only tempered by the generosity of Jesse Jones, who began at once to lend Stalin the cash out of his inexhaustible RFC till.[2]

There are many, like Doctor Conant, of Harvard, who see the political and social dangers, who utter words of anxiety and warning, and yet hold for arming one totalitarian power against another, on the reasoned ground that we are obliged to choose between lesser and greater evil. They may be concealing from themselves what they do not say. They are for aid to Soviet Russia and yet they do not want Russia to win.

Few have been so callous as to carry the logic of this position to its base extreme, as in the words of a New York newspaper editorial, reprinted in the *Congressional Record* by request of Senator Hill, of Alabama,[3] saying: "Keep your selfish and cold-blooded approach—and what do we care what the Communists think and stand for if they are willing to die to stop the Fascists? Who are we to complain about who does the dying for us?. . . Regardless of his motive, we know that for every Communist who has the guts to stand up and fight and go down shooting at the Germans, that's just one less life of our own we're going to have to jeopardize to save our own country."

If that were an American voice, or if by any possibility it could be so mistaken, almost we should be persuaded to go Communist. For the Communist by contrast is admirable. He does at least believe what he believes, holds it above life, and is willing to die for it. That is why he is dangerous and brave.

It seems to occur to nobody to wonder what Stalin may be thinking—with what added cynicism he may be viewing the mores and manners of his despised democracies. They do not deceive him. He knows perfectly well that they do not want him to win. They want him only to kill Germans. The partnership, therefore, is morally and politically false. How could it be otherwise?

It is not necessary to speculate on what the problem would be if Soviet Russia should win. Imagine a much less impossible thing. Imagine that between Hitler and Stalin it should come to a stalemate with a powerful Russian army still in being and beyond reach, and that then, in time, Germany should collapse, not in the face of an Anglo-American army but from internal strain and attrition. Soviet Russia, in that case, would be the paramount land power of Europe.

What should we do about that? Having saved the world from Nazism, should we not be morally obligated to go on and save it from Bolshevism? To ask the revelationists—

such as Secretary Knox with his vision of one tenth of a millennium for an Anglo-American world, and Mr. Justice Jackson[4] with his international order of the Golden Rule that shall come to pass when America has outstripped, as he says she must, all "the rest of the world's naval, air and perhaps military forces"—we ask them, what will they do with 180,000,000 Russians who may no more want our world order that we want theirs or Hitler's?

Chapter eleven notes

[1] Quotation from Irish poet Thomas Moore, 1779-1852.

[2] The RFC was the Reconstruction Finance Corporation, started by President Hoover to lend money to railroads and other failing businesses in the Depression. It reached its height of power under Jones during World War II.

[3] Lister Hill, 1894-1984, Democrat of Alabama, was senator 1938-1969. Hill served in the Army infantry in World War I.

[4] Robert H. Jackson, 1892-1954, was general counsel to the IRS, 1934-1936; assistant attorney general, 1936-1938; solicitor general, 1938-1939; and attorney general, 1940-1941. A fervent New Dealer, he supported Roosevelt's court-packing plan, and Roosevelt appointed him to the Supreme Court in 1941. In 1942 Jackson wrote the majority opinion in Wickard v. Filburn, the case that said the federal government might tell a farmer how much grain to grow for his own chickens. However, Jackson balked at the spread of federal power in the second Korematsu case in 1944, arguing in dissent that the internment of Japanese Americans violated their constitutional rights. And in 1952 Jackson joined the majority in declaring President Truman's seizure of the steel mills unconstitutional.

Chapter Twelve
CONFIDENCE

In the summer of 1941, as the German tanks rolled across the Ukraine, many Americans saw Germany as the sure winner. "The myth of the German superman had affected the wits of all the military experts," Garrett wrote in The American Story, "and they agreed that Russia could last only a few weeks."

This Hitler Myth, August 9, 1941

It will be written down as the strangest instance of psychic blindness in all history that even after the German blitzkrieg machine had been tried out in Poland, the finest military minds of England and France were unable to see it. Looking straight at it they could not believe it. Six months after the demonstration in Poland, the Germans meanwhile perfecting their frightful apparatus by what they had learned, and taking their time about it, the world was asking, "Where is the war?" British generals were saying complacently that Hitler had missed the bus. French generals, sipping their *apéritifs,* were politely waiting for him to come and break his mechanical weapons against their impassable Maginot Line.

Well, but now there is a Hitler myth. His diplomacy is diabolic; there is no match for his skill in perfidy. His strategy is invincible; at least there is no answer to it yet. He does not need sea power; he will march around all the oceans. This is a war in a new dimension. And those to whom it was inconceivable that he could conquer France in contempt of British power and then in turn beat Great Britain but for the aid of the United States, now are fearful of total world conquest and can give you the complete pattern of it.

Here, we suggest, is blindness of the extreme opposite kind, known to the psychiatrist as hysterical amblyopia— that is, a loss of vision induced by fear. Hitler might well know what that is, for it is credibly said that his own medical war record, now erased, contained an entry for hospitalization for hysterical blindness.

This myth of invincibility has become a powerful German weapon. It has the singular efficacy of acting twice. First Hitler's propaganda ministry hurls it; then those on whom it has acted, especially in this country, seize it and employ it against others on whom it failed to act, or did not act enough; and they do this, as they believe, to awaken in others a sense of their extreme danger, thinking thereby to create unity through fear.

But let us examine it as an old Roman weapon. It will not explode in our hands. It is intangible, made of psychic stuff, and therefore subject to analysis of reason. Will it bear analysis?

The trick, we believe, is kaleidoscopic. Battles one after another are presented to view, with marginal glimpses of superhuman precision and efficiency, and as you add them up the effect it terrifying. You are bound to concede that in battle the Germans have outthought and outfought the defenders, save only in the air battle over Britain, and that is not finished. But remember, you are looking at battles and not at the war. The strategy of battles in relation to the strategy of war is as the strategy of means to the strategy of ends. What are battles for?

If you look away from the battles and at the war itself, you will see a startling thing, not visible through the kaleidoscope tube. You will see that for all his dazzling and scientific Geopolitik, Hitler's grand strategy, or, as you may say, his design for war, has utterly collapsed. Take it in the largest possible outline. What do you see? Leave out the

Italians, who are a liability, and the Japanese, who are staggering and elusive, and some little boughten people who do not count, and you have—what? Eighty million Germans against the world. It is a picture. Less than one-twentieth part of the human race separately hated and feared and subject to vengeance.

Hitler never dreamed of finding himself in that situation. In his *Mein Kampf* his most bitter denunciation of the regime that lost the other war was that it made the wrong alliances. He wrote that to escape the fate of extermination in Europe, the German people would have to remember and take care never again to "make enemies of everybody in the world." He would not make that mistake. He would make strong alliances. In order to be able to do that, Germany herself had to be made strong. That was the first thing.

Then, as he looked about, he could see only two possible allies in Europe. They were England and Italy. He reasoned it. He said it with exclamation points, with italics, and at last in blackface type. Then, has he weighed these two, one against the other, Italy went out.

It was England above all, England only, because there was no longer "a necessary English interest in crushing Germany." He could dream of dividing the world with England; he could not imagine fighting her. The "catastrophic self-deception" of the German regime in 1914, he insisted, was to underestimate British power and mistake the English fighting character.

Then he made the same blunder. He had to take Italy, after all. The jackal was no substitute for the lion. Facing the lion, as he never meant to do, with only the jackal behind him, he made his pact with Stalin. But of Russia he believed and had written in his book, firstly, that it was ruled by criminals who could not be trusted to keep a pact, and secondly, the prophecy that any treaty with Russia would mean a war the outcome of which was bound to be "the end of Germany." And mark, that would be a war in which Russia was Germany's ally, not an enemy.

Therefore, it was against his convictions and feelings

215

both, that he made his pact with Stalin. He did it of necessity. Less than two years later he says he was right about the Russians; he ought never to have made a pact with them. Breaking that pact himself, on pretext that the Russians were going to break it, he turns to fight them, which leaves his back to the lion.

So much for the grand war design and the ruin of it, by reason of something he left out—something about the British first and then something about the moral sense of most of mankind.

What is left is the sheer fighting power of the German war machine. Hitler himself never imagined that alone could conquer the world. Yet that is that it must now do, or perish.

We know, concerning this power, that it is not continuous, ceaselessly flowing from a source. It has to gather itself and coil in order to strike. Then it strikes terrifically and with prodigal manifestations, as if it had means to waste; but that is a phase of strategy.

It takes time for it to gather and coil. Consider not the battles, but the interludes. After six years of preparation and then a campaign of twenty-seven days in Poland, it took six months to gather and coil again. The second campaign, beginning with the invasion of Norway and ending with the fall of France, was one of less than ninety days— from April 9 to June 24, 1940. To coil a third time for the Balkan campaign took nine months. That campaign began with the invasion of Jugoslavia in April and ended with the British disaster in Crete less than sixty days later.

But for the fourth campaign, against Russia, there was no time to take. Why not? An unpredictable necessity was acting. This, says Hitler, was the necessity to turn immediately and strike Russia because his Moscow partner was about to stab him in the back. If that is true, then for the first time he was unable to control the interlude. He was obliged to strike with no time to gather and coil. But it is probable that from now on nothing he can say about his reasons will be more than rationalization, less and less convincing, because there will be one thing he cannot say.

In January he was telling the German people he could come to a decision with Great Britain within the year. In May he was in the Balkans for a campaign that he says he did not want but was obliged to accept because the British plan was to occupy him there until Stalin was readier and more aid from the American arsenal had arrived. In June he was deep in Russia, although the most he could win there would be a very costly means toward a long war, whereas a long war was the last thing he wanted. None of this quite makes sense.

The one thing he cannot tell the German people, and dare not tell himself, is that he is caught in his own power. Above every other necessity is the necessity to strike, becoming more and more urgent. He cannot stop. In that fact lies his fatal weakness. If he stops, both his war machine and his economic system will crash. Peace is beyond him. He has saved no word for peace that any nation would be willing to hear. And one defensive gesture might well be the beginning of the end.

The perfect parable was produced by the Germans themselves. It was a nature film of a battle between the cobra and the mongoose. For the cobra there was no retreat, and no defense but to go on striking until its power was spent, and in that condition it was obliged to accept the death struggle.

The False Fear Theme, September 6, 1941

If Hitler wins— "I tell the American people solemnly that the United States will never survive as a happy and fertile oasis of liberty surrounded by a cruel desert of dictatorship." These were the President's words on Independence Day.

If Hitler wins— "Our standard of living and our concept of human life will be placed in jeopardy," says Col. Wm. J. Donovan,[1] who was sent to Europe to see with his own eyes what would happen and now is editor in chief of Government information.

If Hitler wins, that will be the end of the American way

of life, says Mr. Willkie. American agriculture will be ruined, American labor will be enslaved, American freedom will become a memory.

If Hitler wins, we shall face a Frankenstein monster in a Nazi helmet, with unseeing white holes for eyes, one foot in the burning ruins of Soviet Russia and the other already in Alaska. In his right hand is a flaming torch; in his left arm is a mortuary tub filled with a skull named Dakar, and attached to the tub is a tag, reading, "Threats to America." Dakar is a mean little seaport on the west coast of Africa, opposite the great bulge of Brazil. You are supposed to know that when Hitler has conquered Asia he is going to build a railroad across Africa to Dakar in order to be able to jump from there to the swamps of Brazil. By that time he will have course moved across Siberia to the Bering Sea, almost within sight of Alaska. Then he will have the American way of life within his pincers where he wants it, one jaw of the pincers bearing down from the Arctic Circle, the other up from the Equator. This is from the "Shoot First Shoot Now" poster of the Fight For Freedom Committee—Sen. Carter Glass, honorary chairman; The Right Reverend Doctor Hobson, chairman; Mrs. Calvin Coolidge and Mrs. Dwight Davis, vice chairmen.

If Hitler wins, our gold will be worthless. If Hitler wins, we cannot sell our wheat and cotton. If Hitler wins, we shall be unable to trade anywhere in the world but on terms dictated in Berlin.

What a theme for America! We can imagine Hitler, on a dull evening when his ego is low, calling to his propaganda minister, saying, "Bring me the file on the American fear. I need some new ideas."

There are two war themes.

The crusader theme—America going forth to destroy the aggressor, liberate the world and establish a millennium of the four freedoms—produces its effects principally in the higher brackets of emotion. The crusader finds that he must reach also the lower brackets. He consults the book of propaganda and it tells him that it is not enough for people to hate what they are going to destroy; they must be made

218

to fear it too. So the crusaders, who of course are fearless, believing that people for their own good must be made afraid, become themselves the fear bringers. When emotion in the lower brackets does not respond as they expect it to do, they return to the book. It tells them not to be discouraged; if they go on saying it over and over, people will begin to believe it, but they must lay it on, which they do. Nevertheless, they have their bad moments, near to despair, when they may be heard saying: "We call fate to be our witness. We have cast the truth upon them. What is wrong with people that they do not believe it?"

But do they believe it themselves?

On this great segment of the most favored continent, called now an oasis, are one hundred and thirty million Americans, possessing fabulous natural resources, a body of science and technology inferior to none, and the paramount machine power of the world.

Who might be going to surround this oasis in a fatal manner? Who might be going to enslave these one hundred and thirty million Americans? Does anyone really believe that ninety million Germans are going to do that, whether Hitler wins or not?

If these one hundred and thirty million Americans cannot keep their own world, and keep it as they want it; if they cannot trade with whom they will and on terms they like; if they cannot survive as a free people against ninety million Germans, then the American way of life is what Hitler thinks it is and not what we have thought it was.

This fear theme, we say, is false and contemptible; and if it were possible for Hitler to win, it would be a grave moral and psychic liability. For suppose people had believed it and then after all Hitler should win?

Happily for the outcome, people have not believed it. They have in fact resisted it, not from lethargy or indifference but by a reaction of good American common sense. If they had to choose they would prefer, we think, the crusader theme, for however romantic and unreal that may be, ignoble it is not. What they would greatly prefer, however, is no theme at all intended to manipulate their emotions, but a statement of simple integrity concerning what we are going to do and why we are going to do it.

We are not fighting Nazism for fear it will devour us. Not really. We are not fighting it because we have to choose between "dying on our feet and living on our knees." We are going to destroy it because it is intolerable. We could live in the same world with it; we could compete with it and beat it on any field, even the economic field. But we don't want that kind of world and we possess the power to prevent its coming to pass.

We are resolved to destroy it because it is cheaper now to do that, no matter what the immediate cost may be, than to live with it.

And why is Nazism intolerable? Not for any way of life it may evolve, nor for its political and social ideologies, but because it prefers and glorifies the solutions of force.

An event of incomparable meaning is taking place. The stupendous American omen is beginning to assume a certain form. We did not ourselves foresee it, nor could it have been foretold. We may be still unable to define it clearly, and yet we already know what it is. Never before in the long story of the human race has it happened that the ultimate power of war lay in the hands of people who morally and temperamentally abhor war and would willingly renounce it as an instrument of national policy.

Germany, representing the extreme opposite principle, is under a declining sign. And what a just and terrible design now begins to appear! The one kind of warfare it was certain suicide for Germany to release in the world was mechanized warfare—the war of technology and machines. That was bound to call forth American power in the aspect of its most formidable supremacy. We are the machine people. America is Machine Street. The only thing that could possibly defeat us is fear.

Chapter twelve notes

[1] William "Wild Bill" Donovan, 1883-1959, in 1942 founded the Organization of Strategic Services, America's first foreign spy agency, which later became the Central Intelligence Agency. He was a major general in World War I and was awarded the Medal of Honor.

Chapter Thirteen
Maneuvers

On May 21, 1941, the Germans sank their first U.S.-flag merchantman, the Robin Moor, *which was carrying steel rails and trucks to South Africa. The Committee to Defend America by Aiding the Allies said it was time for the Atlantic to be policed by the U.S. Navy.*

On May 27, President Roosevelt warned the nation that Hitler's goal was world domination. Again Roosevelt rejected a negotiated peace and proclaimed an unlimited national emergency. This, Garrett wrote, "gave him what were in effect wartime powers over management, property and labor relations."

On July 7, U.S. Marines occupied Iceland.

Historical Fragment, August 16, 1941

Through all that devious pattern of getting into the war by staying out of it there were certain constant thoughts, like threads that appeared and vanished and came suddenly to view again, running always against the supposed design, no matter what the weavers said they were thinking or thought they were doing. Trace backward the one that was leading all the time to the first American expeditionary force—that is, to Iceland, where the armed forces of the United States now stand side by side with the British and where the United States Navy and His Majesty's Navy are acting together against the aggressor.

At any time last year, and especially during the campaign, anyone who asked who was going to reconquer Europe, or who suggested that Great Britain would be unable to put Hitler back without American man power, was called a defeatist, a fifth columnist or a pro-Nazi. Did not Winston Churchill say Great Britain wanted from us only the tools to do the job, not our man power? You might suppose he had political and strategic reasons for saying that. But if you had any doubt you could take the word of the President for it. During the campaign, Oct. 23, 1940, the President said: "We are arming ourselves not for any purpose of conquest or intervention in foreign disputes. . . We will not participate in foreign wars, and we will not send our Army, naval or air forces to fight in foreign lands, except in case of attack."

The thread is there. But you would have needed a cynical glass to see it. Almost no one did see it. The entire country understood the words, "except in case of attack," to mean except in case of attack upon American territory, or, by the widest interpretation, upon this hemisphere. Congress so understood it and wrote it into the Draft Law, saying the army it was about to raise was not to be sent out of this hemisphere.

The next appearance of the thread was on April twenty-fifth, this year, when the Secretary of War, appearing before a special committee of the United States Senate, said: "Our forces must be prepared for the possibilities of war in many and varied terrains, it being quite uncertain in what part of North or South or Central America, or even possibly other regions, it may ultimately be necessary to use them." That was but a glimpse of it in two words— "other regions."

Meanwhile the Congress had passed the Lend-Lease Law. Its anxieties and misgivings were quieted by the most solemn assurances that the Administration's one aim was to push the war farther away. Those who said it was a law that released the President to conduct undeclared war against Hitler and would lead to an expeditionary force were confronted with the pledges that had been made to the contrary and then overwhelmed with a question. Did they doubt the word of their own Government?

On May twenty-seventh the President delivered the fireside chat in which he proclaimed an unlimited emergency. The constant thread now makes a startling reappearance, and you can see how it was there all the time. In this fireside chat the President said: "I have said on many occasions that the United States is mustering its men and its resources only for purposes of defense—only to repel attack. But, we must be realistic when we use the word 'attack'; we have to relate it to the lightning speed of modern warfare. . . We. . . will decide for ourselves whether and when and where our interests are attacked." That was the speech in which he spoke of Greenland, Iceland, the Azores, the Cape Verde Islands and the cost of West Africa as points that might have to be regarded as outposts of American defense.

From this point on, there is a very shapely arrangement of events with dates.

JUNE 10. The President makes his first ninety-day report of the operations of the Lend-Lease Law. This thirty-nine-page document is a formal statement of the American Government's participation in the war. The President says: "Allied ships are being repaired by us. . . and are being armed by us. . . Naval vessels of Great Britain are being repaired by us so that they can return quickly to their naval tasks. . . We will help Britain to outstrip the Axis in munitions of war, and we will see to it that these munitions get to places where they can be effectively used to weaken and defeat the aggressors."

JUNE 11-28. Senator Wheeler, the America First Committee and all last-ditchers continue to support the fiction that the country is not in the war and cannot be until Congress declares war. . . *Rumors of expeditionary forces preparing.*

JUNE 27. Senator George,[1] chairman of the Senate Foreign Relations Committee, says: "The way to national unity is to give our people assurances that when we are called upon to move into the actual range of fire and send our men there, whether on board naval vessels or aircraft,

225

the American people themselves will have some opportunity to pass upon the question, in other words, that they will have the ultimate decision." *By a secret understanding with the British government the first American expeditionary force is then about to set forth.*

JUNE 30. The Secretary of the Navy, speaking in Boston, declares the time has come to send in the Navy and rid the Atlantic of Germans. *The first American expeditionary force is then on its way.*

JULY 1. At his press conference the President declines to comment on the declaration made by the Secretary of the Navy. He tells the reporters he still hopes the country can avoid fighting, but he cannot be very confident about it. He derides private polls showing public opinion to be against war. Of course people are against war; but that, he says, is like being against sin.

JULY 3. The War Department makes public a report from the Chief of Staff, saying the military arm is hamstrung by the law which forbids sending the new Draft Army off this hemisphere; he urgently recommends that it be repealed. Senator Wheeler says that he hears that an expeditionary force is going to Iceland.

JULY 4. In Cairo, Gen. Sir Archibald P. Wavell, the retiring British Commander in Chief in the Middle East, gives an interview in which he says the outcome will have to be decided in Europe by man power and that the war cannot be won without American man power.

JULY 7. The President notifies Congress that the first expeditionary force has arrived in Iceland to take over from the British; also that he has ordered the Navy to clear the Atlantic Ocean between the United States and Iceland. . . In Cairo, Gen. Sir Claude Auchinleck, succeeding Wavell as British Commander in Chief in the Middle East, gives an interview saying the war will have to be won in Europe and that it will take American man power to do it.

JULY 8. At a White House press conference the President tells reporters the lines of the Western Hemisphere are geographically dim. Anyhow, the Government will act beyond them when and if necessary.

He declines to comment on the report of the Chief of Staff.
. . The military critic of the *New York Times* says the occupation of Iceland means that the Government intends to
help Britain with military means and the beginning of our
definite participation in a shooting war.

JULY 9. Winston Churchill says that instead of the
American forces taking over in Iceland, as the President
told Congress, the American and British forces and the two
navies will act together there, "with the same object in
view." . . . At his press conference the Secretary of the Navy
is asked if the United States Navy will shoot if necessary
to keep the North Atlantic clear, and he answers that the
reporters ought to be able to answer that one for themselves.

JULY 10. Congress receives from the War Department
the draft of two bills—one to extend all enlistments for the
duration of the emergency, the other to authorize the
President to send the Army anywhere, "within or beyond
the limits of the Western Hemisphere, as he shall deem
necessary in the interests of national defense." . . . the
Senate Committee on Naval Affairs resolves to have the
Secretary of the Navy before it to ask him if the United
States Navy has done any shooting.

We believe this marks the point in time when the
weavers themselves had lost, or were about to lose, control
of their own design. They had released the forces of defense
by aggression in the new fashion of the world. You may say
their thread was spun on the wheel of fate. That may be.
Nevertheless, though it could tow a hemisphere, it could
not tie us to the British Empire nor drag American man
power in until one end had been made fast in the European
war zone. Fate itself could not have done that. It was an act
of will.

*In August 1941, Congress debated extending military
conscription—a measure the House passed by one vote.
Garrett supported it, but he worried that in many more cases
the Roosevelt administration was asking for consent only
after a thing was done, or ignoring Congress altogether.*

Government by Consent, September 20, 1941

The change that has taken place in the character of American government—a change within the form—may be studied in the behavior of the parliamentary principle, which was designed by the Constitution to be the creative, lawmaking power. Observe it in action. Observe particularly that eccentric movement of congressional debate, as if it was revolving off center. The explanation of this bewildering phenomenon is that the immediate matter of debate is not the axis upon which the debate turns. Always there is something else, something that is not there—and what that is, asserted on one side and denied on the other, can be neither proved nor disproved for the time being.

For example, the ostensible subject may be a matter called A. The vote will be upon that. But what the debate really turns upon is whether A is simple or compound. Does it involve saying B later, and if so, why is B not there?

It is as if the executive principle were spelling out a word. The consent of the parliamentary principle is necessary in order to preserve the form. The parliamentary principle is Congress. But Congress does not know what the word is. Only the executive principle knows that. If Congress knew, it might not consent. Therefore, what the executive principle does is submit one letter at a time.

This was perfectly illustrated in the debate on the bill to extend the period of involuntary military service beyond the one year for which the draft army was first called up. Granted that all the arguments advanced by the President as commander in chief and by his chief of staff for extending the period were valid; yet why had they not been foreseen when Congress was asked to consent to the original draft act in 1940? Why was it not told then that a term of twelve months was too short, that an army could not be trained in that time, and that to begin releasing the draftees serially at the end of their one year's service would be not only disruptive and wasteful but, in the words of the President, a tragic error, and in the words of the chief of staff, a fundamental and tragic error, bound to weaken the country's prestige abroad and thereby invite war? Why had none of this been foretold? Had the General Staff foreseen it and said nothing about it?

The Senate Committee on Military Affairs sent for the chief of staff and asked him why, if he knew better, he had approved the one-year draft in the first place. He reminded the committee that, in the first place, he had asked for a period of eighteen months, and continued: "I said I would compromise on fifteen, but certainly we must have at least twelve. I admit that is a peculiar way to put it, but I was trying to get the Selective Service Act passed."

The meaning of that naive admission is perfectly clear. The original draft act with the one-year limitation was the letter A. Letter B, the extension, was bound to follow. The General Staff knew that. If the General Staff knew it, the President knew it. But they were afraid that A and B together would be too much. The Congress might not consent.

So then the immediate matter of the debate was B. Ostensibly it was B—this one question of extending the period of service, and on that there should be aye and no. But what everyone was thinking of was C, which was not there. For an interesting reason it was not there. It was visible for a moment, everybody saw it, and then it was suppressed, leaving B to stand alone.

B and C arrived at the Capitol together and were to have been presented together. B was the bill to extend the period of involuntary military service; C was a bill to repeal the provision of the original draft act which said that the army thereby created should not be sent off this hemisphere. B meant an army extended in time; C meant an army to be free in space, one that the commander in chief could send anywhere in the world in his own discretion, with no further benefit of congressional opinion. What happened was that the reaction to C was instantly hostile—so hostile that it was immediately withdrawn. Why? Because it was evident that Congress would not consent to B and C together.

In the debate, Senator Vandenberg[2] referred to C, saying, "It was a sinister request. It was an ominous request. I fear it was a prophetic request." Yet C was not there to be either debated or voted upon. It had been withdrawn for the sake of obtaining consent to B alone. Whether C would follow B as B followed A, nobody knew. So the Congress voted upon B alone.

We speak here not of the merits of A, B or C. We speak of what is happening to government.

You cannot say when it was that Congress ceased to determine public policy. It relinquished that prerogative little by little and unawares, until it had passed to the executive principle—to the President, that is. During the first phase of this change the significance of it was obscured by the happy fact that the executive principle was not yet autocratic. It held fast to the tradition. It submitted its policies to Congress. That was collaboration. But it was not likely to continue forever. It discontinued suddenly with the advent of a President who had neither the reverence for the tradition nor a fear of power.

Since then, great matters of national policy, foreign policy especially, have been submitted to Congress never as a whole, but as parts of a rebus, A by itself, B by itself, until the word was spelled out. And since then every important act of Congress has been an act of consent, not an act of will.

You may say, even so, that the power to give or withhold consent is the ultimate power. But this is a veto power, uncreative in itself, able to act only upon what is presented to it.

Read Article I, Section I, of the Constitution: "All legislative powers herein granted shall be vested in a Congress of the United States." Imagine it to read: "Such policies as the President may from time to time determine and that laws that may be necessary to carry them into execution shall receive the consent of the Congress of the United States."

In a fine essay on Democratic Discipline, Dr. C.R. Mann[3] says: "In practicing self-discipline the American citizen is generally confused by no less a pillar of democracy than the Declaration of Independence. . . Near the beginning it says: 'That to secure these rights, governments are instituted among men, deriving their just powers from the consent of the governed.' This Declaration was issued some thirteen years before the Constitution and few seem to have noticed the misleading implications of the phrase, 'consent of the governed.' Yet mere consent generally is a passive or negative action, not strictly comparable with the positive action called for by 'We, the people. . . ordain and establish this Constitution.' Had the Declaration said, 'governments are instituted among men, deriving their just powers by delegation from the people,' would not the two have been more compatible, since both would call for positive action by the people?"

The form survives; but now for the first time we have government by consent of the people, not government by will of the people. For better or worse, that is the change.

On July 24, 1941, Japan seized Indochina from the Vichy French forces. That day, Roosevelt froze Japanese assets in the United States and embargoed shipments of oil to Japan, offering to relent only if Japan withdrew from Indochina and China, which Japan was not about to do. This was the seed of the attack on Pearl Harbor.

From August 9 to 11, Roosevelt and Churchill met secretly off the coast of Newfoundland. Afterward they produced an eight-point declaration of their aims after the "final destruction of the Nazi tyranny," which would include no "aggrandizement, territorial or other;" no changes in borders except as approved by the people concerned; national self-determination; "access, on equal terms, to the trade and to the raw materials of the world;" freedom of the seas, and an "abandonment of the use of force." This was an accord between allies—which Churchill was more forthright about, afterward, than Roosevelt was.

231

Declaration of the Atlantic, September 27, 1941

When the memoirs come to be written, especially the second memoirs of Mr. Churchill, we may find out what happened to the millennium at the meeting of the President of the United States and the British Prime Minister, somewhere in the Atlantic.

We have learned to know a good deal about Mr. Roosevelt's tenacity of idea and purpose. Therefore we cannot doubt that he took with him his four freedoms. They were, if you remember—

First: "Freedom of speech and expression—everywhere in the world."

Second: "Freedom of every person to worship God in his own way—everywhere in the world."

Third: "Freedom from want—everywhere in the world."

Fourth: "Freedom from fear—anywhere in the world."

In his famous message to Congress last January he set them out very carefully in that order of value—and this was no vision of a far-distant time, he said, but "a definite basis for a kind of world attainable in our own time and generation."

He must have taken with him also the State Department's annunciation, by Mr. Welles, of the two essential conditions for bringing that world to pass. The conditions were, first, to abolish offensive armament under some power of international control, and, second, to establish "fully and adequately the natural rights of all people to equal economic enjoyment," because, "so long as any one people or any one government possesses a monopoly over natural resources or raw materials which are needed by all people, there can be no basis for a world order based on justice and peace."

We have never been able to make sense of such words as the "natural rights of all people to equal economic enjoyment." Suppose the Japanese should insist, as they once did, that for their equal economic enjoyment they must be permitted to settle in California. Certainly the words do not mean that. Then do they become rhetorical and mean only equal access for all people to natural resources? Among our natural resources we count the fertility of Iowa land, and water power at Boulder Dam and Grand Coulee. Shall all people in the world have equal access to these resources? If so, how? Do they mean, perhaps, only raw materials?

In time of peace there is a world market for all raw materials at world prices. How well do our Southern farmers know there is a world price for cotton, even though they had a monopoly of it. When they tried to get more than the world price, they lost their monopoly. To whom in time of peace are raw materials denied at the world price? For her war machine Germany bought rubber and copper in London, right up to the outbreak of war, and essential raw materials all over the world.

The doctrine of underprivileged nations that must be appeased for the sake of the world, belongs to a fantasy of international Socialism; moreover, it partly concedes the Hitler thesis that because the natural wealth of the world was not equally distributed by the Creator, he is justified to redivide it in favor of Germany by force. Nevertheless, it is idealistic and Mr. Roosevelt believes it ardently, thinking of it, perhaps, as a New Deal for the whole world; and, as we say, he undoubtedly took it with him to the rendezvous, along with the four freedoms.

What did he bring back?

Only two of these freedoms—the lesser two. Only freedom from want and freedom from fear were written into the Declaration of the Atlantic, and these not as a definite basis for a kind of world attainable in our own time, but as a desirable feature of peace which "the President of the United States and the Prime Minister, representing His Majesty's Government in the United Kingdom," say they "hope to see established" after the final destruction of the Nazi tyranny.

Freedom of speech and freedom of religion were left out. Were they omitted, perhaps, in deference to the sensibilities of the Russian dictator, to whom both freedom of speech and freedom of religion are anathema? If so, we would impute it to Mr. Churchill's magnificent and somewhat impish sense of political realism. He would embrace Satan to save England. Yet Mr. Roosevelt appears to have been somewhat conscious about it, afterward. When he sent the Declaration of the Atlantic to Congress, for its "information" and "for the record," he said: "It is also unnecessary for me to point out that the declaration of principles includes of necessity the world need for freedom of religion and freedom of information." A slight change there. Not his own "freedom of speech and expression—everywhere in the world," but "freedom of information." We don't know quite what that is.

Nor was that all.

The "natural rights of all people to equal economic enjoyment," to be fully and adequately established, fared badly in the sea air, and came home like this: "They"—again the President of the United States and the Prime Minister, representing his Majesty's Government in the United Kingdom, announcing certain common principles in the national policies of their respective governments—"will endeavor, with due respect for their existing obligations, to further the enjoyment of all States, great or small, victor or vanquished, of access, on equal terms, to the trade and raw materials of the world which are needed for their economic prosperity."

The principal "existing obligations" of His Majesty's Government are those of the British Empire to its economic self—and, we say, very rightly and properly so.

As he left the deck of the Augusta, U.S.N., Mr. Churchill's person must have bulged with the trifles he got away with. Not the millennium. That was nothing. He probably dropped it overboard. Those Americans! What else had he got?

He had got a formal, irrevocable declaration of purposes in common: first, a purpose to destroy Hitler; second, a purpose to disarm Germany forever; and, third, a purpose to restore the overturned sovereignties of Europe.

He had got his Anglo-American alliance for the duration

of the war, in writing.

He had got the signature of the United States of America, by its President, to an unlimited undertaking to save the British Empire.

And what did he give for what he got? To what did he pledge His Majesty's Government? Only to forgo the thought of aggrandizement, territorial or other, and to share with the United States the job of policing and minding an Anglo-American postwar world.

On his way home Mr. Churchill passed the largest convoy of American aid that had yet been seen. We wonder what he was thinking. Maybe of what he will do with Joseph Stalin at the peace conference and of the old hat he gave to Harry Hopkins, the Lend-Lease Administrator.

On September 4 the Navy announced that the destroyer U.S.S. Greer had been attacked by a submarine off of Iceland. In a radio speech September 11, Roosevelt called this "piracy, legally and morally." He said, "I tell you the blunt fact that the German submarine fired first. . .without warning, and with deliberate design to sink her." He denounced the "Nazi design to abolish freedom of the seas, and to acquire absolute control and domination of these seas," and said that henceforth, U.S. warships would shoot on sight. General Robert E. Wood, head of the America First Committee, retorted that Roosevelt had started "an undeclared war, in plain violation of the Constitution."

On October 11, Admiral Harold Stark, Chief of Naval Operations, told the Senate that the Greer had tracked the U-boat for three and a half hours, radioing its location to a British plane that dropped depth charges on it; and that the submarine and the destroyer had attacked each other, in turn, twice.

The Drift, October 11, 1941

It was strange and an ominous sign, that for six months after the enactment of the Lend-Lease Law the American people should have debated the question: Are we in the war? Stranger still is the fact that before that debate was ended another one began on the question: When did the United States enter the war against Germany?

In a recent one of his scholarly current essays, Felix Morley[4] suggested that the second question might never been answered precisely. "Lacking," he said, "the congressional sanction, which seemingly will not be requested, it is going to be difficult for future historians to name the date on which the present Administration drifted across the line which separates peace from war. But it is apparent from the President's Labor Day address that he regards the decision as having, somehow or other, already been made."

And what will the historian do with these lines by Doctor Morley? They were true in both the premise stated and the premise implied. The United States was then at war with Germany, without having declared war. And the premise implied was that the President alone could take the country to war, without the sanction of Congress.

Beyond the line Doctor Morley speaks of—the one that runs between peace and war—the historian will see another, across which we have drifted in the same way; and that other one is the line that divides limited, representative, constitutional government from a kind of unlimited government for which there is yet no American name.

Two years ago Doctor Morley's words could have referred only to a foreign country. One year ago it was still unimaginable that this country could become involved in another world war unless or until the Congress declared war in the name of the American people. Yet that has happened.

When did it happen?

For us it happened with the passage of the Lend-Lease Law, which the Administration represented as a measure to put the war further away, but which was, as we said, a law under which the President, in his own discretion, could conduct undeclared war against Hitler. After that we were unable to support the fiction that the country was not in the war. We said so. And we were not surprised when the President's first report to Congress on the operations of the

Lend-Lease Law turned out to be an official statement of the Government's participation in the war.

For Hanson W. Baldwin, the military critic,[5] it happened with the dispatch of an expeditionary force to Iceland. That meant, he said, that the Government had plunged for military aid; it meant the beginning of a shooting war.

For the *New York Times* it happened in retrospect. On September third, after the President's Labor Day battle speech, in an editorial entitled We Are in the Battle, the *Times* said: "The United States is no longer a neutral in this war. It is no longer on the side lines. It has made its choice. It is a belligerent today. . . The definitive action was the passage of the Lend-Lease Act."

When it happened for Doctor Morley we do not know. It is probable that, like many others, he does not know.

And all the time a majority of the American people, more or less—a very large majority, we think it was—simply would not believe it could happen. They believed words to the contrary. They trusted the words of the Constitution and trusted the Government to keep them.

The words are: "The Congress shall have the power to declare war."

This power was one the Congress had not surrendered or delegated, they said; it was the one power it would defend with fierce jealousy, because if it lost that one there would be almost nothing left of the parliamentary principle to save.

Yet on the Greer episode, which was the first of the shooting, it was a member of the United States Senate who said, "I don't think the incident will lead to a declaration of war. We don't need such a declaration because we already have said that we are going to deliver the goods and the German Chancellor has said that if ships come under his guns they will be attacked. . . When they shoot, we will shoot back."

The idea of undeclared war not only was foreign to the American way of thinking; it was repugnant morally. Was not that one of the aggressor's sins? But it was an idea the

Administration began to entertain a good while ago. Last year the Secretary of War, who has often uttered the pilot thought, began to say declarations of war had gone out of world style.

Then last May sixteenth, at a White House press conference, the President began to recite early American history. There had been two undeclared wars, he said; one was against the Barbary pirates in the Mediterranean 1803-04, and another, a few years later, was to clear the waters of the West Indies. Reporting this on May seventeenth, the *New York Times* in its news columns said: "When a reporter asked indirectly what his remarks meant, the President said he should use his head."

Never from the beginning was there a forthright statement about going to war. For all his gifts of expression, never did the President make a speech on his foreign policy that had not revolving doors through which people could pass in opposite directions without touching; never one that did not open the international question: What does he really mean?

The art of equivocation reached its peak in the enactment of the Lend-Lease Law, concerning which Herbert Agar, one of the Committee to Defend America by Aiding the Allies, who supported it ardently, made afterward this confession: "Our side kept saying in the press and in the Senate that it was a bill to keep America out of the war. That is bunk. And I think this failure to say exactly what a thing means is an illustration of why our democratic world is being threatened now."

In many ways the American mind was the most naive in the world. Its political cynicism was reserved for civic machines and local corruptions; its faith in the word of the Federal Government was simple and unlimited. If Uncle Sam said it, then it was so. The oblique word has been encountered only in specific cases and the stigma was personal. Never before had it been employed as a method of government. That was the new experience, and the people were not prepared for it.

One result is a canker of the spirit, defined by the

Government as a problem of public morale.

Now, if one says that the deep cause of disunity is not the war, but the fact that the question of peace or war was submitted neither to the will of the people nor to the sanction of Congress, or, with Senator Taft, that it is owing to the fact that the President's policies and methods have been so "secretive and dictatorial" that "his own followers disagree as to what his intentions are" and 130,000,000 Americans did not know where they were going, one is smeared as a partisan, or as a disaffectionist seeking to promote discord in a time of national crisis.

But if one holds with Ralph Barton Perry, professor of philosophy and Chairman of the American Defense Harvard Group,[6] that what public morale needs is more good propaganda from a central Government agency, meaning a propaganda ministry, in order that the President may be better able "to carry into effect policy which has already been adopted, whether by congressional or by executive action," one is going with the drift.

That is easy. Too easy. No ship of state adrift ever yet has drifted back.

On October 17, the Navy said the destroyer U.S.S. Kearny *had been torpedoed in the North Atlantic while coming to the aid of a convoy. The Kearny wasn't sunk, but eleven Americans were killed, becoming the first American casualties on a U.S. ship.*

On October 27, President Roosevelt said of the incident, "America has been attacked." Journalist Arthur Krock recalled the promise in the Democratic platform of 1940 to keep out of war "except in case of attack." Here was the attack. Actually the sub had attacked an unarmed merchant ship, the Kearny *attacked the sub, and the sub put a torpedo into the* Kearny.

On October 31, a U-boat torpedoed the destroyer U.S.S. Reuben James, *killing 100 men on board and sinking the first American warship of World War II. Leftist balladeer Woody Guthrie wrote a song about it, "The Sinking of the Reuben James."*

On November 7, the Senate voted 50-37 to permit the arming of merchant ships and to permit their entry into combat zones.

On November 13, the House voted 212-194 to open up the combat zones. On November 17 Roosevelt signed the measure arming merchantmen and opening combat zones.

Chapter thirteen notes

1 Walter George, 1878-1957, Democrat of Georgia, senator 1922-1957. In 1940-41 he was chairman of the Foreign Relations Committee and shepherded the Lend-Lease bill through the Senate on behalf of President Roosevelt.

2 Arthur Vandenberg, 1884-1951, Republican of Michigan, Senator 1928-1951. An enemy of the New Deal during the 1930s and an isolationist before the war, Vandenberg joined the internationalist camp in 1945. As chairman of the Foreign Relations Committee 1947-1949, Vandenberg was a key supporter of the North Atlantic Treaty Organization.

3 Charles Riborg Mann, 1869-1942, editor of the journal of the American Council of Education, 1923-1934.

4 Felix Morley, libertarian journalist, editor of the *Washington Post* 1933-1940, winner of the Pulitzer Prize for editorial writing, author of *Freedom and Federalism*.

5 Of *The New York Times*. Baldwin wrote *The Caissons Roll: A Military Survey of Europe* (1938), *United We Stand: Defense of the West* (1941) and *The Crucial Years 1939-1941: The World at War* (1966).

6 Ralph Barton Perry, 1876-1957, taught philosophy at Harvard 1902-1946 and won the Pulitzer Prize in biography for *The Thought and Character of William James* (1935). The American Defense-Harvard Group is chiefly known for identifying and locating artworks in the war zone.

Chapter Fourteen
ELEVENTH HOUR

On November 6, 1941, Roosevelt was advised by Ernest Lawrence, Robert Oppenheimer, Vannevar Bush and others that they believed they could develop "a fission bomb of superlatively destructive power" from Uranium 235. On December 6, Bush told the scientists that Roosevelt had given the go-ahead.

On November 25, 1941, the new Tojo government in Tokyo, which had taken power Oct. 16, decided to attack the United States at Pearl Harbor without a previous declaration of war.

The Meaning of Total, December 6, 1941

That there could be a physical limit to the American undertaking has not been imagined. The only problem, we have thought, was to get our sights raised high enough.

For defense and defense aid, the appropriations already made amount to more than twice the cost of the American part in the World War before—and it is not enough. The appropriations already made under the Lend-Lease Act amount to more than the total of our loans to Great Britain and France in that first war to make the world safe for democracy—and it is only the beginning. At this rate, say the OPM's[1] sight raisers, we might have to go on for ten years to beat Hitler. Suddenly, therefore, the sights are raised to aim at a Victory Program of one hundred billion dollars in two years. Everything we are going to do will be doubled.

This is an enterprise beyond anything that has been measured. In order to perform it, we shall have to change, not only our ways of living but our ways of thinking about many things, especially money.

The forms and rituals of a money economy may continue to be observed, but we shall be passing, in fact, to a much older kind of economy—something like the economy that built the pyramids. What the Pharaohs needed to build the pyramids was not money, but command of labor and materials.

Those who spend the one hundred billions will use dollars as the engineer uses inches and feet, only to measure with; they will not be thinking of the dollars as money.

Appearing before the House Committee on Appropriations for the second Lend-Lease bill, and speaking in favor of making everything as general as possible, the Under Secretary of War called attention to the advantages of the totalitarian method, that of Germany in particular, where all anyone has to think of is production in terms of time and quantity; the money—the financing of it—is a minor matter. They take that for granted. No one has to worry about it. "The more we can bring our attention to bear on production," he said, "and the less time we have to spend on some shortage of financing, I think, the better."

The committee was sympathetic to that point of view. One member wanted to know why larger appropriations were not requested, since it was just as easy to vote eleven billions as six and took no more time.

Congress has already ceased to think of billions as money. Just when it did, you cannot say; it could not itself say when. At one billion most of us fall out. Men like Jesse Jones, the Federal Loan Administrator, can go up to perhaps ten billions and still be thinking of money. The Treasury experts, by holding hands, may be able to last up to forty or fifty.

But nobody can think of one hundred billions as money. There is no such sum. It is a statistical concept. The only reality it can have is one of ratio. For example, it approximates one-third of our entire national wealth at normal valuation—that is to say, all the ponderable wealth of every kind that has been accumulated since the Pilgrims landed. And we are going to spend it, or the equivalent of it, in two years!

It is easy to say that we ought to be willing, if necessary, to give one-third of all we possess to destroy Hitlerism. Unfortunately, it is not so simple. How can we give it? More than half of it is in the form of real estate. You cannot fight Hitler with real estate. Nor can you convert real estate into planes and tanks and ships until you liquidate it, and you cannot liquidate it unless somebody buys it, which leaves you nowhere.

How are we going to raise one hundred billions in two years? So far, the nearest approach to a calculation takes the form of premise and conclusion. If Great Britain can manage to spend one-half of her national income for war, and if Germany can do even more, up to three-fifths, then certainly we can do as much, if not better. But the premise is open to qualifications.

Firstly, as to Great Britain, she had very large investment assets that could be pawned or sold. Where? In the United States. She had credit and could borrow. Where? In the United States. Great Britain's borrowing in this country, under the Lend-Lease Act, will soon amount, roughly, to one half of her own total war expenditures. But where could the United States pawn or sell its assets? Where could it borrow anything?

Secondly, as to Germany, nobody can say what her national income is; therefore, the ratio of her war expenditures to her income can only be guessed at. In the first phase of preparation, she had all the billions that a stupid, believing world put there on loan and lost. To this you add the confiscated wealth of the Jews, plus the extortionate profits during several years from a system of barter trade with her neighbors, plus now the loot of conquest. Lastly, in such a totalitarian regime as Hitler's, there is no financial grammar.

In a money economy the government has three

resources. It can levy taxes, it can borrow from the people on its bonds and it can inflate the currency. Usually, in the extreme emergency, it does all three of these things in combination. But within the rules of a money economy it is hardly conceivable that by any combination of these means we could raise one hundred billions in two years, thinking of it still as money.

To speak first of currency inflation, which means simply to print the money, that is out. There will be inflation, of course, but as a consequence, not as a means. Bubble money on any such scale as that would burst too soon.

So we look at the possibilities of taxation and borrowing. What people pay in taxes and what they lend to the Government when they buy its bonds must all come out of the national income, meaning by national income the total annual amount of wages, profits, earnings, interest and rent, which will correspond, of course, to the total national product of all goods and services whatever.

The peak hitherto of national income was touched in 1929 at approximately eighty billions; it has touched since then a low of forty-five billions in 1933. Owing to the enormous defense expenditures it is supposed now to be running toward ninety billions, and may next year go higher still.

Take it to be one hundred billions. Then the question is: Out of a total national income of one hundred billions, is it possible for the Government, by taxation and borrowing, to raise fifty?

The first difficulty is that one third of the total national income goes to people whose living begins at what we are accustomed to think as the minimum standard of social decency, and ranges from there downward. If that one third is to be spared you have left only sixty-six and two thirds billions. Is it possible for the Government, by taxation and borrowing, to take fifty billions from sixty-six and two thirds billions?

The highest point of voluntary lending was touched in the World War before, when the Government borrowed on its bonds in one year nine billions and in another year thirteen billions.

In the World War before, the largest amount the Government took in one year by taxation was a little more than four billions. It is taking this year thirteen billions, which is, so far, the extreme high point for taxation in our history.

So the most that was ever raised in one year by the Government, by taxation and borrowing both, was seventeen billions; and that was roughly one-quarter of the national income at that time. The one-hundred-billion-dollar Victory Program calls for fifty billions a year, which is one-half of the total national income.

Can it be done?

It is possible. Moreover, if we mean to destroy Hitlerism out of the world, it is the thing to do. No matter what it costs, the swiftest way will be the cheapest in the end.

But let us not be deceived. It will hurt. The disturbances already beginning to be complained of are, as yet, nothing. We cannot give one-half of our total income to it and keep our present standard of living. There is no such margin. Taxes will have to be increased until the beet is white, and borrowing may have to be carried to the point of compulsory lending, as in Great Britain; but when the money that can be raised by these means is not enough—and it will not be enough—then it will be necessary for the Government to command labor and materials by further means, and the test of further means will not be whether they are sound according to the rules of money, but only whether they are effective.

In a money economy, when the laws of supply and demand and price are freely acting, it is money that divides among the people the total annual product of goods and services. That function of money will have to be more and more dispensed with, and, if necessary, suspended. Why? Because when the Government has created a condition of scarcity by taking half the total product for itself, it cannot in fairness leave the remainder to be divided by money— that is to say, by auction in the market place—but it must then go on to administer the distribution of the other half

245

among the people, according to some idea of social equity, and do it by a system of priorities, quotas, allocations, rationing and price control, touching all the transactions of everyday life.

There is no other way. The pattern is well known. We see it working in Europe. Much more than the necessity to embrace it, we hate the one word that defines it. Nevertheless, the sooner we make up our minds to accept it and the sooner the Government decides to go all the way, just so much sooner we shall come to the end of an ugly job.

The spending went up as much as Garrett imagined, and more. From 1940 to 1945, defense spending, in billions, zoomed from $1.9 to $14.2, $52.4, $85.2, $90.9 and $59.8. In 1945, federal outlays totaled 42 percent of gross domestic product. Federal debt, which had been 51 percent of GDP in 1940, jumped to 123 percent in 1945.

Garrett hated the debt. In 1935 he had written, "All the things needful to conduct a war exist at the time. . . Why a fiction of borrowing them from the future? Why create a debt to represent them? The reason in both cases is the wish to postpone and avoid payment. Let others pay. Let tomorrow pay. Let the next generation pay. A war that was charged wholly to its own time, one paid for in full by taxation, would be a very unpopular war. But it would be a solvent war."[1]

Total Taxation, December 11, 1941

We have said that such a sum as one hundred billions for the war against Hitler is not money, that it cannot be raised by taxation or borrowing within the conventions of a money economy, and that neither can it be raised by inflating the currency, because a money bubble of that size would burst too soon.

What does that mean? If meant that the Government will be obliged to take what it needs. It means that when the Government takes a very large proportion of the total national product of things, up to one half or more, there is

246

not enough left to satisfy the ordinary demands of civilian life, with the result, in the first place, that the income from profits, earnings and wages upon which money taxes are levied tends in many directions to fall, and in the second place, that priorities, allocations, quotas and rationing become forms and aspects of taxation beyond any let or hindrance of finance.

Consider how that works.

A very simple illustration would be that of a young man who has found himself a good livelihood making reproductions of early-American hardware and decorative objects of wrought iron. His gross income, let us say, was five thousand a year. Now, if the Government should say to him, "For the defense of your country you are required to contribute your entire gross income for one year," that would be 100 per cent taxation in terms of money. But that would not work. Why not?

Because what the Government wants is not money; it wants iron. If it waited until this young blacksmith had earned his five thousand and then took it from him as money, it would not have the iron. He would have used the iron. And it is the iron the Government needs. So what it does is to say to him, "For purposes of defense, your country needs all the iron there is. Your use of it is not essential. Therefore, you cannot have any more iron. No maker of iron will be permitted to sell to you." Cutting him off from his iron cuts him off from his livelihood. It is 100 per cent taxation. Yet the tax is not levied in terms of money. Indeed, since it has denied him the iron, the Government will be unable to get any money from him at all. He will not have any income to be taxed. But the Government will have the iron.

Multiply this illustration by many, many thousands and you will get some idea of how it will work and what is going to happen.

The next piece, despite its publication date, was written before the attack on Pearl Harbor—but as if Garrett knew that something like it was imminent. It shows that he had

not given up his position that the war was "not our war."
And though he concedes that the anti-interventionists have
lost the debate, he says, "they were never confused."

Review, December 20, 1941

It was fitting that the *New York Times* should speak the last words at the obsequies of that fatal and inglorious formula—measures short of war. "The President has hoped, Congress has hoped, we have all hoped"—these are the words—"that aid short of war would suffice; that the transfer of destroyers, the occupation of advanced Atlantic bases and the Lend-Lease Act would make a shooting war unnecessary."

But what happened? The Nazis "made war on us in the Atlantic," and we "are making war in return," and "Congress could not vote these facts down."

Of course it couldn't. What could the Congress do, facing the fact of an undeclared war? It could amend the Neutrality Act!

The formula, therefore, was what the nonintervention-ists said it was, and did what they said it would do. As an emotional device it was extremely effective, but effective in reverse. As the expression of a powerful, high-spirited people, it was bound in time to become morally repugnant, only then it would be too late to turn back, too late to reexamine the question of war or peace.

The crisis—that is to say, the shooting—might have been postponed, says the *Times,* by a policy of "scuttle and run"; we could have "twiddled our thumbs in a state of technical peace"; we could have "waited in shame and cowardice while Fascist elements in this country took courage and lovers of freedom were jeered at and silenced." This for the isolationists.

Well, if it is to speak of waiting, what were they waiting for who supported the policy of measures short of war? We ask the *Times* because its voice was high on that side. Intoning each day the formula for defending freedom without fighting for it, the *Times* presented the argument that our "bulwark"—a bulwark protecting "our young men from the danger of battle," giving us "such security as we now enjoy," was—what? It was "the bodies of British civilians exposed at their own free choice to mutilation and death" because they would sooner die than yield. What were the measures-short-of-war people waiting for then? To see if that bulwark would hold?

Whether the noninterventionists were right or wrong is now a question that belongs to history. Their cause is lost. But they were never confused, never involved in a moral dilemma. It was not our war. That is what they believed. They did not believe the British were our mercenaries—as the saying was in Washington—to do our fighting for us if only we provided the weapons. The thought of using the bodies of British civilians to protect America's young men from the danger of battle was revolting. They did not believe the fate of American freedom was bound up with the fate of the British navy. The place to defend American freedom was here, not in Europe, Asia and Africa. The only security they could imagine was the security that 130,000,000 Americans, willing to fight and die for their own world, were able to provide for themselves. So, in all that sense, they were isolationists.

Their assumptions and premises ought to have been debated in a dispassionate manner, on grounds of grand strategy. Could we stand upon our own hemisphere and defend it against all aggressors, or are we obliged by military necessity to take the war to Hitler?

We suppose there is today no competent military authority who believes that Hitler or any combination of Hitlers could invade the American hemisphere against the defensive power we should be able to exert on the sea and in the air; nor one who does not think that, with an outlay of at most one third of what it is going to cost us to defeat Hitler in Europe, we should have been able, entirely within our own resources, to create for this hemisphere an impregnable defense.

But the question was not debated in that manner. It was debated in terms of an idea that must have been all the time taking shape in the President's mind and now appears fully clothed in these magnificent words: "The American people have made an unlimited commitment that there shall be a free world. And against that commitment no individual and no group shall prevail." A war to make the whole world free—and for that, says the President, "the shooting has started."

Let us hope that what was wanting in the noninterventionists was grandeur of vision; let us hope also, for the sake of the whole, that they were in every rational way wrong. But let it not be said that they were cowardly or mean-spirited or have anything to remember with shame. They were willing to fight for what they believed. They were no more pro-German than they were pro-British. Among them, we should suppose, about the same majority as in the population as a whole—an overwhelming majority—was anti-Nazi. Nor did they believe in waiting to see if the aggressor would come.

We know what we are saying because we were on that side. Now, as we look back at the line to which we were hewing, we see, of course, many chips from awkward strokes, and yet a fairly true line. We were bitterly opposed to intervention. By word, the Administration, too, was against becoming involved, or it was so for at least a year; and we were indignantly denounced for doubting its word. We doubted its word because its steps were not going in the path of its sayings.

Nevertheless, for all that we said and felt against intervention, we said also that the rise of Hitlerism imposed upon this country a task of heroic proportions. No other people would be able to create a power of defense equal to this monstrous new power of aggression, and so restore a kind of balance in the world. That was our part. In that sense it was America against Germany. But this was defense we were thinking of—an invincible defense for a citadel of human freedom.

From the beginning we were far ahead of the Administration's ideas of defense, saying that the first appropriations requested by the President were absurdly inadequate and that either the Administration did not comprehend the nature of the crisis or it was treating the people as if they were children. That was true. We were for a two-ocean Navy before it was part of the defense program. We supported the Selective Service Act.

From the beginning we have advocated and continue to advocate much heavier taxation, on the ground that the more we pay now the greater may be the hope that we shall come through with any considerable part of our capital intact. The Administration postponed taxation. Why?

From the beginning we have advocated drastic measures to prevent inflation. We said at the first, that we should have to work harder, produce more and consume less, and said it while the Administration was telling the people that their lives were not going to be upset. Never have we uttered the faintest thought of meeting the aggressor by appeasement. "They are defeatists," we said, "who could wish their country to buy its peace with the aggressor either with things of its own or the things of other people."

The fight for nonintervention was lost on March 11, 1941. On that day the Lend-Lease Act, which Mr. Churchill says is the "most unsordid act in the whole of recorded history," became a law. After that it seemed to us to be a disservice to understanding and a confusion of truth to go on making believe the country was not in the war. We accepted the fact and, having accepted it, we said we had resolved for ourselves that question which every American would have to face. The question was: When your country becomes involved in war, for anything you could do to stop it, where are you going to stand?

For a while we received a great many letters from people asking us why we gave up the fight. These have all been answered by now. We acknowledged them; the President has answered them. But we continue to get letters from the other side, asking why we continue to criticize the Administration, after having said it was the duty of all Americans to support their Government in war, whether they had been for it or against it before the fact.

To these we say, in the first place, that the Administration is not the Government—not yet. For all we know, the American Government may still be at war when this Administration is gone. We say to them, secondly, that loyalty to one's Government in war is an American duty, and freedom to criticize one's Government, even in war, is an American right.

We have not surrendered that right—the right to criticize the Administration's conduct of the war, the right to tell the truth as we believe it about the war, which is, after all, the people's war because they will have to fight and pay for it; nor the right to say what we think about what is happening at the same time to the principles of free, representative, constitutional government, not necessarily on account of the war.

If we have not that right, if every American citizen has not that right, what are we fighting for? Shall we take the four freedoms to the far corners of the earth, confer them upon other people, by force if necessary, and forget that they belonged first to us?

Chapter fourteen notes

[1]Office of Production Management, a federal agency.

Chapter Fifteen
UNITY

On December 7, 1941, Japan attacked Pearl Harbor. On Dec. 8, it began landings in Malaya and Dec. 10 in the Philippines. Germany, whose troops were being pushed back from the frozen gates of Moscow, declared war on the United States, and America was officially in the war.

The America First Committee said, "Our principles were right. Had they been followed, war could have been avoided." But it was too late, and the group voted to disband.

Fate and War, January 3, 1942

There is one destiny that no nation, possessing as we do the paramount physical power in the earth, can for long avoid. The book of human history has been thrust into our hands. We will write there what we believe. If it is true, it will endure; and a thousand years hence a sane and better world will remember us as we remember those from whom we inherit for liberty and justice a greater love than the love of life.

Let us say this once and think of it no more—not until the victory. For, meanwhile, there is total work to do.

To those who think that total means a statistical zebra called quantity we recommend the words of a correspondent who looks at what he sees and does not look away.

"No," he says, replying to something we had said to him in a letter. "I do not see that we are aiming at a victory effort of one hundred billions. I had thought it was to be total, and that no man could gauge the caliber of a total effort in this hemisphere. The American people have never had to face a total effort. Valley Forge was a single glorious spark and not an outpouring of Colonial conviction. Château-Thierry was a rather amateurish rehearsal. This one may still be the prelude. I would not wish to be the figure at which a total American effort is directed."

Then he adds: "My great-uncles returned to South Carolina to find the wind gone. Their immediate concern was not the amount of the public debt which the carpetbagger administration in that state was to load them, but where to find a fairly sound mule and a few seeds. South Carolina still permits two great rivers to course through her forests and plans to meet at Charleston and form the Atlantic Ocean."

The meaning of total is heroic. What it requires is that by a free and unqualified act of mind people shall first consecrate themselves and their entire means to an end they would sooner die for than lose. Until they have done this, they will never know what their utmost is.

We did not come to the business of destroying Hitlerism out of the world in a heroic mood. We put quantity first. Quantity would do it. And were we not the quantity people of the earth? All that we had to do, therefore, was to increase our production in a prodigious manner. Thus, we were going to save freedom without fighting for it—by measures short of war. We were going to defend America by aiding the Allies. With our billions we would buy the war to stay away.

We know now that we were looking away.

When these statements of valiant delusion began to break down, other word situations were invented. The country had become involved, yes; but indirectly so. It was in the war, in a way of speaking, but not at war; or it was virtually at war, but not actually. It was the nonbelligerent enemy of the aggressor, providing only the arsenal. Little by little the word "victory" superseded the word "defense"; even so, it might be victory without a shooting war.

Then the President announced what everybody knew.

The shooting had started. He proclaimed at the same time that the American Government had assumed an "unlimited commitment" to destroy Hitler and make the whole world free.

The Reuben James was lost in battle. The first casualty list appeared. Yet the President declared that the situation had not changed; and the Congress, to facilitate the conduct of an undeclared war, was willing to disembowel the Neutrality Law, but unwilling to repeal it.

Was it unwilling or afraid? In either case, it was looking away.

Sunk with the Reuben James was the idea of a vicarious war—a war in which others should do all the fighting. But in place of it appeared at once the idea of a war in which we should not have to do much fighting—a naval war, a war of sea and air battles, an expeditionary force of small specialized units sent off the hemisphere for shrewd strategic reasons only, a war of limited casualties.

And still we were looking away.

But fate works with strange formulas. When the Yellow Serpent struck on our Western side, there were released in the veins of liberty the terrible compounds of an avenging wrath. It is a wrath that will destroy not only Japan, as an aggressive power in the world; it will destroy Hitler as the Serpent's mentor, and Hitlerism as a principle of evil.

There is no more looking away. Fate has willed it to be our war. From now until victory, fate and war are the total words.

To fight out a war, said Justice Oliver Wendell Holmes, you must believe something and want something greatly. Then the course is there. It is long and hard, and you cannot foresee the end of it. But having taken it, then what is required of you "is that you should go somewhither as hard as ever you can. The rest belongs to fate."

Garrett's editorial on censorship was one of the last before he was forced out by the owners of the Saturday Evening Post. *It is not in any sense a protest against being silenced. First, his dismissal was the action of an owner*

255

exercising a private right, and not, strictly speaking, cen-
sorship. Second, he acknowledged the need for censorship
during war. But he clearly did not like the odor of it.

Censorship, January 24, 1942

It says much for the powers of self-discipline in a free and willful people that liberty of the press very willingly submits to put itself in a straitjacket for the duration of the war. Everyone uncomplainingly takes it for granted that communications will be censored and that news will be controlled at the source, and that this will be done not as the law says it may be but as military judgment says it shall be. Censorship on those terms requires a pledge of unlimited confidence to be exchanged between the Government and the people; and so, happily, it begins. But we shall do well at the same time not to underestimate the difficulties.

The Government lays down what appears to be a very legible rule to govern the release of news. The conditions are two. First, the facts must be fully verified; second, publication of them is forbidden if they tend in any way, direct or indirect, to give aid and comfort to the enemy. But you could not invent a general rule that would leave more to arbitrary discretion in its application to a particular case.

News is of two kinds—good and bad. Any bad news at all tends to give aid and comfort to the enemy. Then what will you do with it? Withhold it from the people until it is certain that the enemy already has it?

Take the communiqué. In its daily report to the people the Government cannot tell everything that has happened, and the more critical the situation is the more this will be true. Why? Because the enemy is reading it too. You cannot have two reports—one for the people and one for the enemy.

In the business of bombing, for example, the enemy's only firsthand knowledge of his hits is from his own pilots, who tend naturally to exaggerate what they think they have done and are liable in any case to be mistaken. The

256

enemy, therefore, anxiously watches the news on the other side in order to check the claims of his own pilots; and one of his artful tricks is to put forth fantastic claims in his own communiqué with intent to provoke on the other side a denial, on the chance that the denial will be informing. Thus, it was very important for the Japanese to know whether or not they had got an aircraft carrier at Pearl Harbor, as their own pilots said they had.

The communiqué, indeed, is now one of the weapons of strategy. The Russians in theirs were most despondent just on the eve of the unexpected counteroffensive that forced the German war machine suddenly into reverse. The purpose was probably twofold. One part of it was to deceive the Germans; the other part was to hasten American and British aid.

On the free, Anglo-American side there is no likelihood of bad military news being suppressed or long withheld for fear the people cannot take it. The British are extremely the other way. They are nourished by bad news. "It must be remembered," said Mr. Churchill, in a recent review of the war before the House of Commons, "that here at Westminster and in Fleet Street"—newspaper row—"it has been sought to establish the rule that nothing must be said about the war that is altogether discouraging. Although I must admit the British people seem to like their food cooked that way, a military spokesman addressing a large army might do more harm than good if he always put things at their worst, and never allowed buoyancy, hope, confidence and resolve to infect his declarations." He was defending the military spokesman at Cairo, whose reports on the North African campaign, the English people thought, had been disgustingly optimistic, and they were complaining of him on that ground.

But there is another kind of bad news which, although it is not strictly military in character, does tend nonetheless to give aid and comfort to the enemy; and the question about it is not whether the people can take it but whether the Government can, because it is news of the Government, its own blunders and failures and mistakes of political judgment. What will the censor do with facts of that order? What ought he to do with them?

This is the kind of news that free criticism tends to reveal; and here it is that censorship faces what is perhaps its most unruly problem. For all the aid and comfort it may afford the enemy, shall criticism be free? In England it is. Mr. Churchill has at times complained of it, yet very mildly and with grim understanding. Suppression of criticism would be incomprehensible in England. So it would be here. Free criticism is troublesome. It does present a problem. Nevertheless, it is one that will solve itself if left alone. A government in the popular principle, being trusted by the people to control their news at the source and censor their communications for military reasons, must in turn trust criticism to censor itself. And this it does much more than can be realized by those who know only when it errs and have no idea how many times it makes the right answer when it asks itself this question: All things considered, will the saying of this truth do more good than harm? And if, in a given case, it comes too often to a wrong answer, then people themselves by their extreme disapproval will extinguish it, with no aid from the censor.

Good news, you might suppose, offers the censor no problem at all. Nevertheless, good news can be a liability. People may make too much of it. Bad news moves them to greater exertion, whereas good news may tempt them to relax. In his very fine sermon on "most" to the representatives of labor and management just before they sat down to work out a truce for the duration of the war, President Roosevelt said: "Don't believe everything you read in the newspapers. . .I was reading a paper this morning which was telling how inevitable. . . a victory would be. I want to see what we can do."

To be on the safe side, we must expect a long hard war. News tending to belittle the resources of the enemy or to make us complacent about our own must be discounted. How? Not by suppression and certainly not by distortion, but by mixing bad news with good, by emphasis, by keeping the facts in perspective. Thus you come to censorship policy, touching the handling, timing and spacing of the news, for its effect upon public morale.

The poet said, "Let me write the ballads of the people and I care not who may write their laws." This was paraphrased by a New York managing editor who said: "Let me write the headlines and anyone who likes may write the ballads." He would not touch a word of the news to alter it, nor would he write a false headline. He would produce his effects entirely by selective emphasis. If there could be anything like that power of propaganda in mere headlines, and truthful headlines at that, imagine what lies in the hands of a censor, a national managing editor, acting upon news at the source not to change any of the facts, but to time the release of them, to counterweight good ones with bad ones, and so control the perspective. Whose perspective? Not his own. The censor has no policy of his own. He executes the government's policy, and when he fails to do that, there is a new censor.

Censorship is unavoidable. Although it may be authorized by wartime statute and is in that sense lawful, it cannot be administered by any rule of law. You may read in the Constitution that the Congress shall pass no law to abridge freedom of speech or freedom of the press; but when drums beat, the law flies away, says the proverb. Moreover, censorship entirely innocent of propaganda belongs to some faraway realm of the ideal. The subtle power of propaganda that is implicit in control of the news is bound to be exercised, because first, a government is human, and for the reason besides that every government is obliged to believe that it knows what is best for the total good.

This is our second experience. In the war before it was the Committee on Public Information. Now it is the Office of Censorship, which has a more honest and more severe sound and, we suppose, a more severe intention. Even so, there will be, we think, forbearing to almost any point, no want of cooperation and no unfair criticism, so long as the Government holds free of hurt and trespass the confidence with which people, both the believing and the unbelieving, have suddenly overwhelmed it.

AFTERWORD

Garrett left the *Saturday Evening Post* on March 12, 1942. His views were not wanted. In a note to Herbert Hoover, he said, "You are perhaps aware that the Satevepost has lifted up her garments to the New Deal. Stout has walked out and so have I. Ditto Miss Neall. The chance of policy begins at once." Stout was the editor-in-chief; Neall his assistant.

All the time Garrett was denouncing the drift to war he said that if his country got in it, he would fight on the side of his country. He was sixty-four; there was no way he could join the armed forces. But in a letter written February 6, 1942, to Donald Nelson, chairman of the War Production Board, he said:

"Is there any way for me to be helpful to you—for the duration?

"I have stopped writing for the editorial page of the *Saturday Evening Post,* and if I could find a way to make a direct contribution to the war effort I would stop writing entirely because I don't think writing now is important.

"Do you need eyes?

"I am first of all a reporter. I know industry from having been looking at it and writing about it for many years; and I mean looking at it on the ground.

"Do you need a mine sweeper, perhaps?

"I am, secondly, an editor. Therefore I know something about public reactions and how they are caused.

"I am not thinking of anything in Washington. I should

be wrong there. Nor am I thinking of a job with pay.

"If you care to ask anyone about me personally, I refer you to three such unlike men as Baruch, Hoover and Henderson.[1]

"Anyhow, I very anxiously wish you luck."[2]

Later in 1942 Garrett wrote to the U.S. Civil Service Commission, offering his services, saying "I am entirely at the disposal of the government, for anything it may wish me to do, for the duration of the war." But there were no takers. "What I want more than anything else is to get into the war," Garrett complained to a correspondent. "Washington is out. Even if I could work there I am not wanted because of my anti-New Deal history."

In October 1942, he wrote to Baruch, "None of the writing I might want to be doing on my own account would be likely to help win the war. So therefore, unless something unexpected happens, next Monday yours truly will be in overalls at work in a local ship yard, building Army freight boats, ten hours a day, six days a week. . . You didn't know I was a ship's carpenter, did you? Well, I'm good enough and I'm taking my own tools."

The shipyard job was too tough for him. In a letter to Baruch, November 16, 1942, Garrett said he was spending the weekend in bed. "The shipyard job is out in the open weather and seems to be getting me down," he wrote. "I am expecting to be transferred to a machine shop job, inside. Just to be doing something with my hands gives me a sense of relief. I can listen to the news with more fortitude." He signed it with the salutation, "Damn Hitler."

Baruch wrote back the next day, "I think it is silly of you to be doing the kind of work you are doing now."

Garrett went back to writing, but he was rejected by *Harper's, Colliers* and a column syndicate. He thought up a series of pamphlets on political ideas. In a memo to backers, he wrote, "There are ten or fifteen writers who now find themselves marked, as if they were on a black list. Some of them compromise by avoiding the subjects on which they cannot write as they believe; others, we understand, have resorted to the use of fictitious names in order to relieve the editors of a sense of liability—meaning the liability that now attaches itself to the name of a writer whose history is anti-New Deal."

Garrett worked with supporters on the pamphlet idea, but gave it up. In a letter he expressed the worry that "there would adhere to us, as to the America First Committee, a lot of company not to our liking, going along for wrong reasons, and no way to get rid of it." He wrote, "I begin to think that such a thing, if done at all, had better be done by individual initiative, with unlimited personal responsibility, probably in book form. . ."

In 1943 he wrote an essay, reprinted here, for Colonel Robert McCormick's *Chicago Tribune* arguing that "isolationist" was a propaganda word, and that the proper word was "nationalist." Garrett was pleased at the play the *Tribune* gave it, but wrote Hoover that there might be "some liability in going too far with McCormick," and did not write another. Instead, he went back to book projects. There he could speak with his own voice, which was less and less merely conservative. In the 1942 memo to pamphlet backers, he had said that in the atmosphere of the time, "the conservative now becomes the radical."

In 1944 he found a publisher in Idaho—The Caxton Printers—for his 1938 monograph, "The Revolution Was," a bitter, polemical essay that analyzed the New Deal as a coup d'etat. This was his radical voice, which posthumously became his trademark.

From 1944 to 1950, Garrett edited *American Affairs,* a publication of the National Industrial Conference Board. In October 1950, at the end of his tenure there, he reflected on the wartime economic controls. After World War I, he wrote, "the whole wartime bureaucracy collapsed, as it was expected to do. . . In a little while the economy was as free, or almost as free, as it was before." But after World War II, in the halls of government "there was no thought of taking the harness off." Parts of it did come off, but not enough to restore the freewheeling economy of a generation before.

Controls had been necessary. "Neither total war nor total mobilization can be managed within the framework of a free economy. . . [nor] can it be bought within the limitations of peacetime finance," he wrote. "The will to survive must in the end overthrow all conventions."

What is required is a people who cherish their freedom enough to demand *all* of it back when the crisis has passed. After World War II, the people were less demanding.

American Affairs' last issue was October 1950. With an $11,000-per-year grant from the William Volker Fund, Garrett went back to writing on his own. His next two monographs, "Ex America" (1951) and "Rise of Empire" (1952), were in the radical voice of "The Revolution Was." These addressed the last great debate on American foreign policy, in which the isolationist remnant, led by Sen. Robert Taft, R-Ohio, went down to defeat over the formation of NATO, the Marshall Plan, the Korean War and, finally, in 1954, the Bricker Amendment, which would have made treaties subordinate to the Constitution.

Caxton combined Garrett's three essays in *The People's Pottage* (1953). Garrett finished two more books, among his best, *The Wild Wheel* (1954), a history of Henry Ford and the world of laissez-faire; and *The American Story* (1955), an interpretation of American history. *The American Story* was published posthumously. Garrett died in 1954. His third wife, Dorothy, survived him for a short time. He had no children.

By the mid-1950s, a new generation of tories had begun to rally around *National Review*. Their crusade was against communism, at home and abroad. They were not isolationists. Just the opposite. If foreign military bases and alliances were useful in hemming in the Soviet threat, they supported them, just as they would support the undeclared war in Vietnam.

Garrett left two legacies. The first was an uncompromising denunciation of the New Deal such as no Republican has dared to utter in a generation. Garrett would not have amended Roosevelt's program; he would have repealed it. The second was an uncompromising denunciation of Empire. That was last such voice by a major spokesman of the Right for almost fifty years, until the Gulf War was denounced by Patrick Buchanan.   —*Bruce Ramsey*

Afterword

Chapter notes

1 Bernard Baruch was the financier who had run the equivalent of the War Production Board in World War I. He befriended Garrett early in the century and became a life-long Garrett correspondent. Herbert Hoover, the former president, was also a Garrett correspondent for more than twenty years, and had asked Garrett to read and comment on the manuscript of one of his books. Leon Henderson was the New Dealer who headed the Office of Price Administration, which set federal price controls during World War II.

2 In another letter, Garrett mentions that he wrote the letter to Nelson but never sent it.

The Mortification of History

From the Chicago Tribune, *September 19, 1943*

If you say, "I am first of all an American," you have to be careful. It may be misunderstood. You might have said, "I am for America first." And the American who says that will be denounced in his own country and by his own government. That is not enough. He will be denounced also in Great Britain, Russia and China, all accusing him of one thing.

His is an isolationist.

But what is that? An isolationist is one who is said to have sinned against the peace and well-being of the whole world. He is held responsible for the necessity now to mortify American history by rewriting it to a theme of guilt and atonement. According to that theme he is:

One who would crawl back into the shell America lived in for so long (a favorite figure, that of an American crawling back);

One who would have America put a Chinese wall around itself and cut the world off;

One who thinks America can go on living all to itself, declining to cooperate with the rest of the world;

One who, having believed this and having persuaded others to believe it with him, is now to blame for the fact that after winning the first World War we lost the peace, and so brought the second World War to pass; or

One who after the first World War, according to Mr. Wallace, belonged to the thing that "came out of its cave and. . . made certain that we would adopt international policies which would make World War II almost inevitable." The name of that cave-dwelling thing was isolationism.[1]

What nation during 150 years has done most to alter the ancient weights and measures in the world and the ways of thinking and living of all the people in it? What nation during that time has been the principal factor in world history?

Do you ask? The answer is not what you think. The answer will be: "That's just it. The more we did the more we were not there."

Nonsense may create a kind of reality. The Mad Hatter lives, although he never existed. So there might be an elephant that lived as a mole and suffered from megalomania. The story of a people who lived in a shell and changed the whole world is nonsense. Nevertheless it creates an image that becomes in itself an important political fact.

Isolationism, according to this story, was from the beginning, and not a great sin at first, because we received it as doctrine from the founders, especially from Washington, who pronounced it in the Farewell Address, and afterward from Jefferson. Thus the distortion began.

Neither Washington nor Jefferson was an isolationist, nor were any of the founders. They were Americans. They were Americans first. They were sick of the uproar and dissensions raised in the new American household by pro-European factions, first the pro-French always wanting the new republic to make war on England and then the pro-British wanting it to fight France. Washington well knew the weakness of his countrymen for such foreign infatuations, and it filled his mind with foreboding. That is why he so earnestly exhorted them forever to avoid embroilment in the quarrels and intrigues of Europe. There had been already one entangling alliance—the first, and the last until now. That was the alliance with France during our struggle for independence, and before we could buy our- selves off from that it had almost got us into another war with England.

Everybody knew at that time what Washington meant. Before 1776 the American colonists had been dragged through four European wars. On the frontiers they knew the war whoop of Indians armed and incited alternately by France, Spain and England, who in their struggle for con- trol of the North American continent thought nothing of setting the red savage to kill white pioneers.

Who could imagine there was such a thing as friendship among nations? Certainly this new republic in a new world was not only without a friend, even France having turned against it, but every monarch in the world was its natural enemy. The only sound foreign policy, therefore, was one of strict and jealous neutrality.

But if Washington or any one of the founders had pro- posed a policy of isolationism nobody would have under- stood that at all, for never had there been a people more joyously minded to go forth in the world, to trade and com- pete in it, to demand their rights, and to make known their dissatisfactions.

Freedom of the seas could not have been the idea of a people thinking isolation. Yet that was the first article of American foreign policy. We were willing to fight for it and did fight for it more than once. The Yankee skipper was the first in seafaring history to keep his sails up all night. His fast clipper ships, with the best-paid sailors and the high- est freight rates, carried tea from Canton to Liverpool, beating the slow British ships in their own China trade. This was to prove the American maxim that time is money.

The Mediterranean then was the private sea of the Barbary pirates, who dwelt on the north coast of Africa and levied tribute on merchant ships. America said to Europe, "Let's go together and abolish this nuisance." Europe declined, saying it was cheaper to pay tribute, and, besides, it was an old-world custom. So at last the little American fleet did it alone. On this page of the old book there is a curious footnote. Benjamin Franklin said:

"I think it not improbable that these rovers may be privately encouraged by the English to fall upon us and to prevent our interference in the carrying trade; for I have in London heard it is a maxim among the merchants that if there was no Algiers it would be worth England's while to build one."

A favorite distortion of the new theme makers is to say that during the first 100 years of its happy, isolated life, America went strutting around in a protective garment not of its own making, namely, the Monroe Doctrine, which had been a British idea to begin with, and then, calling itself American policy, owed its success entirely to the power of the British navy. That is not so.

After the downfall of Napoleon the reactionary monarchs of the old world set up what they called the Holy Alliance and conceived the idea of saving Spanish America for Europe. This boded no good for England. In the year 1823, therefore, the British government proposed to the government of the United States a joint undertaking to defend the new Latin American republics against the Holy Alliance. President Monroe discussed the proposal with Jefferson and Madison, and the three of them inclined to it, because the Holy Alliance, once established in Latin America, would be a perpetual menace to free government on this hemisphere. But John Quincy Adams, who was secretary of state, said: "Only 10 years ago they contemptuously burned our capitol. Now they are asking us to join them as an equal in a perilous enterprise. It is very flattering. But let us look to pitfalls."

The pitfalls were three. One, the United States would thereby become an ally of Great Britain against the Holy Alliance; two, the door would be left open to British colonization on any scale; and, three, the United States would itself be bound not to acquire any Spanish American territory. And although nobody had yet imagined it, we were

270

going to want Texas and California for our own territorial completion.

The founders were shrewd statesmen. The sequel was not what Great Britain expected or wanted. In his next message to Congress, President Monroe announced the doctrine that has ever since borne his name. It meant simply, America for Americans. Any attempt to extend the European system to this hemisphere would be regarded as an act unfriendly to the United States; the Americas, both north and south, were no longer open to colonization. That went for Russia, for everybody in the Holy Alliance, and for Great Britain, too.

Those who say that in any case the British navy did stand between us and the Holy Alliance, and that the American fathers had the astuteness to count upon it without the grace to acknowledge it, cannot know what would have happened if then or afterward the Holy Alliance had moved against this hemisphere. We do know that the British navy did not interfere when during the Civil War Napoleon III invaded Mexico and set up an emperor there, and that in 1895 in the Venezuelan boundary dispute Great Britain herself was the European power to whom an American president was saying in a peremptory manner, "Hands off!"

Before the end of our great maritime chapter, and while the clipper ship was the queen of the sea, Commodore Perry, for better or worse, went knocking on the door of Japan with cannon. He had a message from the president of the United States, saying: "Nobody can stay shut up like this, quite out of the world. Come forth and trade with the rest of us. It will make you rich and powerful!"

We lost our seafaring eminence during the Civil War. Just then the iron steamship began to supersede the sailing ship, and although the first iron steamship to cross the Atlantic had been an American vessel out of Savannah, still, when the war was over and we looked again at the sea, that view was less exciting than the vision of an empire to the west. The way to San Francisco was no longer by Cape Horn but by rail.

During the next 30 years the foundations were laid for the tower that was to be the one impregnable citadel of freedom in the whole world. That was something the builders did not know. They worked as if time were measured and running out, and it was, but they did not know that either. The only motive they were conscious of was the illusion of profit. Came then the war with Spain, over freedom for Cuba; and although Cuba was made free, the unintended sequel for us was a lurch toward imperialism when the flag went up in the Philippines. But even this was under a promise of ultimate independence for the Filipinos, which we never drew back.

Our next foreign adventure was to assist in putting down the fanatical Boxer uprising against all foreigners in China. Whereupon, facing Europe as a friend of Asia, we announced that America stood for the territorial integrity of China. Then Theodore Roosevelt, walking softly in the world with a big stick, tweaking the Kaiser's nose, stepping on the neck of a European war flame in Morocco, digging the Panama canal with one hand, inserting the peace between Japan and Russia, rattling the Monroe Doctrine, building a navy only second to Great Britain. After him was Taft.

By this time the tower was rising very fast. It was visible from every corner of the world. As an industrial power and in the international exchange of wealth, called foreign trade, we had arrived at first place, although never since the clipper ship had we possessed another great merchant marine. We had let that go. Our foreign trade was carried in foreign bottoms. Under Taft there evolved the idea—and a very naive idea it may seem to us now—that our surplus of industrial products could be loaned away in the form of foreign investments under a policy designed to promote international well being and to enable the backward peoples of the world to advance much faster. This was called dollar diplomacy, sneeringly, and Taft was its last prophet. But much more it will be remembered that he earnestly supported and afterward led the American evangel for a league of nations to keep and enforce the peace of the world. After Taft came Woodrow Wilson and then the slogan under which 2,000,000 soldiers went to Europe— "A war to end war."

For all of this, those who now are writing the theme of guilt and atonement say that the spirit of isolationism was always there, latent or manifest. They say it was not until after the First World War, however, that it took possession of our acts.

To say this, no one has agitated so much paper and ink as Mr. Willkie. In *One World,* he writes: "If our withdrawal from world affairs after the last war was a contributing factor to the present war and to the economic instability of the last 20 years—and it seems plain that it was—a withdrawal from the problems and responsibilities of the world after this war would be sheer disaster."[2]

The guilt theme stated.

Then he says that after the First World War "We entered into an era of strictest detachment from world affairs. . . We shut ourselves away from world trade by excessive tariff barriers. We washed our hands of the continent of Europe and displayed no interest in its fate while Germany rearmed."

One may allow for the fact that as Mr. Willkie discovered geography by flying around the world and seeing with his own eyes that "continents and oceans are plainly only parts of a whole, seen as I have seen them," so also he discovered American history and has the same naive impulse to impart his sensations. It is still too much to believe that he could be entirely ignorant of what happened during those 20 years of "strictest detachment from world affairs." You could as easily suppose he had missed the Pacific.

During those 20 years an event took place that stands unique and alone in the waste behind us, like a shaft of light, only now forgotten. Immediately after the First World War a new and ruinous armament race began. Even President Wilson, bitterly disillusioned, was for an American navy to be incomparably the most powerful in the world. Nevertheless we did believe in disarmament and preached it earnestly, only to receive back the echo of our own words. The armament race continued. Then one day the American government invited the principal naval powers to a Washington conference, and when they were assembled there the secretary of state said:

"The United States is forging the longest sword of all. No matter how much longer you make yours we can make a longer one still. Yet we do not want it. When we talk of disarmament, we mean it. To prove to you that we mean it, we offer now to break our sword to the exact length of the next longest sword in the world, on condition that we stop this mad armament race. Do you accept?"

The nation that was saying this—the one that was offering to limit its weapon power—was the richest in the world, possessing absolute industrial supremacy. Such a thing had never happened before. The delegates were stunned. However, they signed the famous 5-5-3 arms limitation treaty; they signed also the famous Nine Power Pact, which was to keep the peace in the Pacific, to maintain the American principle of the open door in Asia and to guarantee the independence and territorial integrity of China. While we were sinking our ships, the other parties were sinking the spirit of the treaty. It had limited the number of capital ships only; they began to build unforbidden ships of new design, and the race was on again, except that we hopefully continued to believe in disarmament and waited too long, with the result that the American navy fell to third place.

During those 20 years the American government persuaded the whole world in solemn writing to renounce war as an instrument of foreign policy. That was the Kellogg-Briand Pact, so called because Briand had first suggested such a treaty between France and the United States only, whereas Mr. Kellogg, the secretary of state, conceived the idea of making it world-wide.

During those 20 years we poured billions into Europe to finance reconstruction, to build new works, to restore her trade and credit—direct loans to France, Italy, Poland and the Balkan countries, besides enormous loans to Germany, which enabled her to pay all the reparations she ever did pay to Great Britain and France. And we did this while Great Britain at the same time was leading a movement to repudiate her own and all Allied war debts to the United States Treasury. All of those billions we lost.

During those 20 years Americans sat everywhere in Europe as advisers and administrators. An American administered the reparations commission in Berlin. An American was at the head of the Bank for International Settlements in Basel. The Dawes plan was American. The Young plan was American.[3]

During those 20 years the American government was untiring in its efforts to persuade the world to disarm in the land and on the sea. The Washington naval conference was in the time of Harding. The universal pact renouncing war as an instrument of foreign policy was in the time of Coolidge. One of Hoover's proposals was to abolish all weapons of aggression. At this the world scoffed. How could the weapons of aggression be distinguished?

All of that happened in the 20 years defined by Mr. Willkie as "an era of strictest detachment from world affairs."

We did not join the League of Nations. For this Mr. Willkie does not blame the people. He cannot, of course, blame the people for anything. "They were betrayed," he says, "by leaders without convictions who were thinking of group vote catching and partisan advantage." How strange! Much stranger really than the discovery that continents and oceans are all in one world when you see it from an airplane. The people wanted to join the League of Nations but their conscienceless leaders defeated that wish in order to catch their votes!

Neither in Mr. Willkie's writing of the guilt theme nor in any other will you find that Europe may have been to blame for the fact that the United States at last declined to adhere to the League of Nations. It is probably true that the American people did at first intend to join. Then they changed their minds. Why they did that may be debated to

any length, but certainly one reason was the disillusion-
ment that took place in the time that elapsed between
President Wilson's return with the document and the vote
of the Senate on ratification. In that interval of time, Mr.
Wilson had angrily rejected the British scheme for an all-
round cancellation of war debts at the sole expense of the
United States; he rejected it on the ground that it meant
charging German reparations to us. Thus we were already
cast for the role of Shylock whether we joined the League
or not. In that interval of time it became painfully evident
that Europe was Europe, and that European intentions
toward the United States had not changed since Canning,[4]
who, having accepted the Monroe Doctrine in place of the
Anglo-American alliance he wanted, made this curious
boast: "I have called the new world into existence to redress
the bounds of the old." Mr. Churchill supported the scheme
that Mr. Wilson denounced—the European scheme to
make America pay German reparations; he was saying
then what he said recently again: "I am after all a
European."

Now where in all that history is the Chinese wall, the
broken shell, the Wallace cave? And where is the meaning
of isolationism?

If you say of this history that its intense character has
been nationalistic, consistently so from the beginning until
now, that is true. Therefore, the word in place of isolationism that would make sense is nationalism. Why is the right
word avoided?

The explanation must be that the wrong one, for what it
is intended to do, is the perfect political word. Since isolationism cannot be defined, those who attack it are not
obliged to define themselves. What are they? Anti-isola-
tionists? But if you cannot say what isolationism is, neither
can you say what anti-isolationism is, whereas nationalism, being definite, has a positive antithesis. One who
attacks nationalism is an internationalist.

The use of the obscurity created by the false word is to
conceal something. The thing to be concealed is the identi-

ty of what is speaking. Internationalism is speaking.

It has a right to speak, as itself and for itself; but that right entails a moral obligation to say what it means and to use true words. If one says, "I hold with Mr. Justice Roberts[5] that for the sake of world peace we must be willing to surrender our national sovereignty," or, as the Federal Unionist says, "I would be a citizen of the world first, and secondly an American citizen," you know what that means. You know where that one stands. But what is concealed in the obscurities speaks warily. There is something it cannot say—not yet.

This is notably true of Mr. Willkie's book. He says of those 20 years, "We shut ourselves away from world trade by excessive tariff barriers." Sumner Welles, the undersecretary of state, in his "Blueprint for Peace,"[6] says: "After the last war, when other countries were looking to us for help in their stupendous task of economic reconstruction, the United States. . . struck heavy blows at their war-weakened, debt-burdened structures. Our high tariff policy reached out to virtually every corner of the earth and brought poverty and despair to innumerable communities." The vice president says that by high tariffs after the last war we "sowed the wind" and "could not avoid reaping the whirlwind."

You might be tempted to skip all this, pausing only to wonder a little that into a mighty discourse on the world to come they should have introduced a bit of the old debate, entitled protectionism versus free trade. But that is not what it is. This is not the old debate. It is the international point of view.

They do not go all the way. They are too careful. Mr. Willkie says that of course if all tariff barriers were cast down at once there would be trouble. Nevertheless what they mean, saying it so guardedly, is that we shall make our tariff laws hereafter not in benefit of ourselves alone but with international welfare in view, not as hitherto to protect the American standard of living only, but with the thought in mind that we are under a moral obligation to lift other people's standards, too. The shoemaker in New

England shall share his job with the shoemaker in Czecho-Slovakia, not in order that shoes may be cheaper here, as the old argument was, but in order that the shoemaker in Czecho-Slovakia may be able to sell shoes in the American market, for unless he can do that, he cannot raise his standard of living.

Formerly, says Mr. Wallace, the "high tariff prevented the exchange of our surplus for goods. (Other people's goods, he means.) And so we exchanged our surplus for bonds of very doubtful value." But what shall we do with our still greater surplus at the end of this war? "We can be decently human," he says, "and really hard-headed if we exchange our postwar surplus for goods, for peace, and for improving the standard of living of so-called backward people."

Goods so far as goods go. After that, what? So many dollars' worth of goods for so many dollars' worth of peace? Peace no doubt would be a bargain at any price in goods. Yet how shall peace be priced in goods? Anyhow, it shall be, as Mr. Wallace says, "the greatest adventure in sharing." He says: "Bread cast upon the waters does return." And Mr. Willkie says: "To raise the standard of living of any man anywhere in the world is to raise the standard of living by some slight degree of every man everywhere." If that is true, and it probably is, then it follows that by raising the standard of living here to the highest plane of all we have at the same time been improving other people's standards everywhere. But we were not thinking of that. We were thinking of ourselves, and that was selfish.

It is not yet inevitable that we shall have to buy the peace of the world with our standard of living; nor is it so resolved in the American mind. A terrific struggle for decision is bound to take place. When it comes the characters will be revealed, both to one another and to themselves, and many no doubt will change sides, seeing clearly for the first time where they were going. The isolationist will be an image cast aside and forgotten. The bitter conflict at last must be one between the nationalist and internationalist. And the longer this painful fact is concealed in a field of

278

engineered emotion, the worse it will be.

Nationalism as an American characteristic now is powerfully, perhaps dangerously, repressed. This is owing partly to intimidation and partly to censorship, but even more to self-imposed limitations upon the freedom of speech, from the feeling every patriotic person has that for the duration of the war and for the sake of unity among the Allied nations there are many things one ought not to say out loud.

Thus internationalism is released to pursue its own ideologic offensive over very wide and undefended spaces behind a screen of sanctioned propaganda. Its most effective propaganda is aimed unerringly at a singular weakness in the national character. Deep in the American heart lies a longing for the heroic errand—the errand of the plumed knight, clothed in the armor of right, bearing the sword of justice, going forth to perform feats of crusade, rescue and deliverance, at any sacrifice whatever. But we are not like that in fact. We love the fantasy and sometimes indulge it to the point of ecstasy. Then just in time we remember that we do live in this world. If ever we had forgotten that, there would be nothing here now to Lend-Lease away.

So it may turn out at last that the apparent success of the international evangel is somewhat deceptive. At least, the internationalist cannot be sure. And moreover he has trouble of another kind.

American nationalism may be for the time being repressed. It may continue to be successfully repressed to the end of the war. All elsewhere in the world, however, nationalism is rising, becoming more and more vocal, powerful and assertive, even in Russia. If this continues, and there is no sign that it will not, an astonishing sequel may begin to appear. The proposed great American adventure in world-wide sharing may assume a solitary aspect; internationalism at last may become isolated in America.

Chapter notes

[1] Henry Wallace, 1888-1965, vice president 1941-1945, was the furthest left of the top New Dealers, sometimes to the point of dreaminess, sometimes to meanness. In the 1940 campaign, he had said that "you can be sure that every Nazi, every Hitlerite and every appeaser is a Republican." The Democratic bosses, seeing that Roosevelt would not live out a fourth term, dumped Wallace in 1944 for the more reliable and electable Harry Truman. Wallace was the 1948 nominee of the Progressive Party, which championed friendship with Stalin's Russia.

[2] Wendell Willkie, 1892-1944, the Republican presidential nominee of 1940, had testified in favor of Lend-Lease in 1941, though only 24 G.O.P. congressmen voted for it. In August 1942, Roosevelt asked Willkie to go on a world trip as his personal envoy. Willkie met Stalin and Chiang Kai-shek, circumventing the globe in a 4-engine Liberator. *One World* was his account of the trip and his argument for an internationalist foreign policy. It topped *The New York Times* bestseller list for five months. On the strength of it, Willkie tried for the 1944 G.O.P. nomination, lost heavily in the primaries, had a heart attack and died.

[3] Both were agreements for Germany to pay war reparations to Britain and France, but not the United States. The Dawes plan came after the German hyperinflation of 1923 had wiped out the mark. Germany fell behind in payments by 1929. Then came the Young plan, which set Germany's debt at $26 billion to be paid over 58 years. The Young plan was adopted in 1930 and came crashing down in 1931. Germany paid no more.

[4] George Canning, 1770-1827, the British foreign secretary who had proposed the deal with President Monroe.

[5] Owen J. Roberts, 1875-1955, Supreme Court justice 1930-1945. Roberts was one of two centrist justices who switched sides in 1937, ending the court's opposition to the New Deal.

[6] Welles served under Secretary of State Cordell Hull, and was a more skilled diplomat than Hull. In 1943 the Welles-Hull rivalry became public, and Hull told Roosevelt either he or Welles would have to go. Roosevelt had more use for Welles, but Welles was a closet homosexual who had gotten drunk and propositioned two black porters on a funeral train. Welles had to go. "Blue-Print for Peace" was published in 1943 in a book called Preface to Peace, which included essays from Wendell Willkie, Herbert Hoover and Henry Wallace.

Sources

Garrett's letters to Rose Wilder Lane and Herbert Hoover are on file at the Herbert Hoover Presidential Library in West Branch, Iowa. His letters to Bernard Baruch, Baruch's replies and Garrett's letter to Donald Nelson are from Box 121, Bernard M. Baruch Papers, Seeley G. Mudd Manuscript Library, Princeton University Library. Some details of Garrett's wartime life are from the Garet Garrett Papers, Houghton Library, Harvard University.

Index

INDEX

Caxton Press

312 Main Street
Caldwell, Idaho 83605

www.caxtonpress.com